WITHDRAWN

HARVARD LIBRARY

WITHDRAWN

Bert Musschenga (ed.)

DOES RELIGION MATTER MORALLY?

A Critical Reappraisal of the Thesis of Morality's Independence from Religion

MORALITY & THE MEANING OF LIFE

Pharos

Does Religion Matter Morally?

MORALITY AND THE MEANING OF LIFE

Edited by:
Professor Albert W. Musschenga (Amsterdam)
Professor Paul J.M. van Tongeren (Nijmegen)

Advisory Board:
Professor Frans De Wachter (Louvain)
Professor Diethmar Mieth (Tübingen)
Professor Kai E. Nielsen (Calgary)
Professor Dewi Z. Phillips (Swansea)

In this series the following titles have been published:

1 Michael Moxter
  Güterbegriff und Handlungstheorie:
  eine Studie zur Ethik F. Schleiermachers
  ISBN 90 390 0042 5

Does Religion Matter Morally?

The Critical Reappraisal of the Thesis of Morality's Independence from Religion

Albert W. Musschenga (ed.)

KOK PHAROS PUBLISHING HOUSE
KAMPEN - THE NETHERLANDS
1995

CIP-GEGEVENS KONINKLIJKE BIBLIOTHEEK DEN HAAG

Does

Does religion matter morally? : the critical reappraisal of the thesis of morality's independence from religion / Albert W. Musschenga (ed.). - Kampen : Kok Pharos. - (Morality and the meaning of life, ISSN 0928-2742 ; 2)
Result of a symposium on belief, worldview, and morality, organized by the Interdisciplinary Centre for the Study of Science, Society, and Religion ('Bezinningscentrum') of the Vrije Universiteit Amsterdam.
ISBN 90-390-0404-8
NUGI 619/635
Trefw.: christendom en ethiek.

© 1995, Kok Pharos Publishing House
P.O.Box 5016, 8260 GA Kampen, The Netherlands
Cover design by Rob Lucas
Lay-out by PIKAAR TEKSTEN, Rotterdam
ISBN 90 390 0404 8
NUGI 619/635

All rights reserved. No part of this publication may be reproduced, stored in a retrieval system, or transmitted, in any form or by any means, electronic, mechanical, photocopying, recording or otherwise, without the prior permission of the publisher.

Foreword

This book is the result of a symposium on Belief, Worldview, and Morality, organized by the Interdisciplinary Centre for the Study of Science, Society, and Religion ('Bezinningscentrum') of the Vrije Universiteit in Amsterdam. Participants were theologians and ethicists from The Netherlands and Belgium. They discussed first drafts of the contributions which are now published in this book.

I wish to thank the participants of the conference for their contribution to the discussion.

The editor

Table of Contents

Introduction   1
Albert W. Musschenga

1 From 'Group Morality' to 'World Ethos':
  The Universality of Morality in the Perspective of Moral Theology   9
  Karl-Wilhelm Merks
  Comments   28
  Arnold Burms

2 God, Morality, and the Transformation of Human Beings   31
  Antonie van den Beld
  Comments   54
  Karl-Wilhelm Merks

3 Sexual Morality, Worldview, and Social Change   59
  Gerrit Manenschijn
  Comments   89
  Albert W. Musschenga

4 Moral Taboos and the Narrow Conception of Morality   95
  Arnold Burms
  Comments   108
  Hans S. Reinders

5	Radical Transcendence and the Unity of Morality and Conception of Life	115
	Paul J.M. van Tongeren	
	Comments	136
	Gerrit Manenschijn	
6	The Meaning of Sanctification Stanley Hauerwas on Christian Identity and Moral Judgment	141
	Hans S. Reinders	
	Comments	168
	Antonie van den Beld	
7	Narrative Theology and Narrative Ethics	173
	Albert W. Musschenga	
	Comments	205
	Paul J.M. van Tongeren	
Contributors		211

Introduction

Albert W. Musschenga

'If morality is dependent on religion, then we cannot hope to solve our problems, or resolve our differences of opinion about them, unless and in so far as we can achieve agreement and certainty in religion (not a lively hope); but, if it is not entirely dependent on religion, then we can expect to solve at least some of them by the use of empirical and historical enquiries of a publicly available and testable kind (inquiries that are improving in quality and scope).' These were the words of William K. Frankena in 1973 (Frankena 1973, 295). To him, the thesis that morality is dependent on religion was of crucial importance: It is often asserted, assumed, or clung to; but it is rarely - if ever - carefully formulated by those who believe in it (295, 296). In his article, Frankena concentrated on the claim that morality is logically dependent on religion. He argued that religious or theological premises are not *necessary* to justify logically some or all ethical principles. On the question whether they are *sufficient* for justifying ethical principles, he answers: 'In fact, I believe, we would not and should not think that our ethical beliefs were justified by being shown to rest on and follow from certain religious or theological beliefs, unless we thought that these were themselves in some way rationally justifiable' (313). Frankena does not believe that the essential beliefs of theism can be justified in a rationally conclusive way, but he concedes that the outcome of that debate is uncertain. If I understand him well, he does not deny that the thesis that religious or theological beliefs are sufficient for justifying ethical principles is defendable. But he is very clear on his motives for not defending that claim: 'But then one is impelled to wonder as if there is anything to be gained by insisting that all ethical beliefs are or must be logically grounded on religious beliefs. For to insist on this is to introduce into the foundations of any morality whatsoever all of the difficulties in the adjudication of religious controversies, and to do so is hardly to encourage hope that mankind can reach, by peaceful and rational means, some desirable kind of agreement on moral and political principles' (313).

It is important to underline what Frankena did not contend: 'I have not contended that morality is in no way dependent on religion for dynamics, motivation, inspiration, or vision. Nor have I contended that religion adds nothing to morality - it may add motivation, an additional obligation to do what is right, new duties, a new spirit in which to do them, a new dimension to already existing duties, or a sense of sin' (314). Neither does he deny that religious considerations are among those capable of determining the intellect to give assent to a certain ethical principle. 'It seems to me plausible to claim that religious beliefs and experiences do *suffice* to justify this (the "law of love", awm), and perhaps other, ethical principles in this wider sense of the word "justify", at least for those who have them. It does not follow, however, that they are *necessary* to justify those ethical principles even in this larger sense, for it may be that certain nonreligious considerations are also capable of determining the intellect to give assent to them' (316).

The purposes of these extensive quotations from Frankena's authoritative article are to draw attention, first, to the fine nuances of his position and his own insight in the limitations of rejecting the thesis of the logical dependence of morality on religion, and second, to Frankena's motives, assumptions and hopes. His hope was that an agreement on moral and political principles could be reached by peaceful and rational means. His assumption was that such an agreement could indeed be established by rational means. He believes that rational men who take the same point of view will agree on normative matters if they are fully informed, clear-headed etc. (1976, 123).

One might wonder whether such an assumption is realistic in the light of the wide-spread intra- and intercultural moral diversity. Frankena believes, however, that many moral disagreements are diverse interpretations and applications of the same basic principles. The differences in moral beliefs are differences in derivative, not in basic moral beliefs. These differences in derivative beliefs can be explained by referring to differences in nonmoral background beliefs. He holds that there are universally valid principles; moralities of different times and places may differ in the implementation of these principles (Frankena 1963, 92). Absolutism as such is compatible with the acknowledgement of moral diversity. Not every 'morality', however, needs to be a legitimate interpretation and application of universally valid moral principles. Some 'moralities' might, in the light of these principles, have to be rejected as immoral.

Frankena connects his rejection of the claims concerning the logical dependence of morality on religion with his belief in the need for - and the possibility of - a universal, rational morality. It is, however, imperative to point out that there is no necessary connection between those two convictions. The thesis of the logical independence of morality does not imply the thesis of the autonomy of morality. One might be convinced that morality is logically not dependent on religion, without believing in the idea of a universal morality. A specific morality might be compatible with diverse sets of metaphysical assumptions, and, reversely, the same metaphysical assumptions might be used in justifying diverse ethical principles. In those cases, it would be impossible to end moral disagreements by means of rational moral argumentation. There are, luckily, other peaceful means to end moral disagreements, such as bargaining or compromising. Rescher points to yet another way out: One could just learn to acquiesce to such disagreements (Rescher 1993, 163 ff.).

Many authors nowadays do not believe in the idea of a universal, rational morality. An interesting question is, whether they also reject that morality is not logical dependent on religion. One does, however, not need to be a relativist to doubt that ideally rational and well-informed people can, or will come to an agreement about the solution of moral conflicts. According to absolutists only those moral conflicts that involve cognitive moral disagreements might be solved by rational argumentation, on the condition that the partners are ideally rational and well-informed. Many conflicts, however, do not involve cognitive moral disagreements, and in many cases conflicting parties are not ideally rational and well-informed. It is one thing to argue for the universal validity of basic moral principles such as human rights, to have them universally accepted is another.

The framework of Frankena's theory lends itself very well to classify the contemporary students of the relation between religion and morality, and thereby the contributors to this volume into four groups.

The *first group* of students accepts or even defends morality's independence and universality. *Karl-Wilhelm Merks* defends, in his contribution, the universality of morality from the perspective of catholic moral theology. In his view, the claim of universal validity for one's moral beliefs might be reduced to a justification for imposing one's own morality upon others. It might also work in the reverse direction and relativize one's own position. He claims that the latter has actually been the case in catholic moral theology.

The *second group* accepts the thesis of logical independence, but not the idea of a universal morality. The members of this group believe that morality is always dependent on a worldview, whether it is a religious or a non-religious worldview. *Antonie van den Beld* argues that morality is always dependent on worldview. People can only be said to share a morality, if their fundamental thoughts about life and the world agree. Therefore, a change in a person's worldview cannot but have moral consequences for him. He exemplifies the dependence of ethical theory on worldview by his treatment of the topic of the moral transformation of human beings by God. *Gerrit Manenschijn* argues that all sexual moralities, including the sexual morality of political liberalism, are connected with a particular worldview.

The *third group* directly attacks the idea of a universal morality, which for them lies at the base of the thesis of morality's logical independence of religion. The members follow MacIntyre in his criticism on the idea of a universal morality. Universal morality is, according to MacIntyre, a harmful illusion. Why an illusion? No theory of universal morality has been able to gain general adherence. The Enlightenment philosophers promised a universal morality, based on rationality as a universal human feature, that could end conflicts between conventional moral traditions. Conflicts between traditions were, however, succeeded by conflicts between diverse proposals for a universal morality. To be able to explain why for MacIntyre the idea of a universal morality based on universal rationality is harmful, I have to clarify his notion of rationality. Central in his argument is the thesis that different conceptions of morality - he concentrates on justice - are connected with different conceptions of practical rationality. Not only are there diverse conceptions of justice, but also diverse conceptions of what counts as a good reason in moral debate. Moral traditions not only differ in their content, in what they regard as values, virtues and justified principles, but also in the nature of their practical reasoning. For MacIntyre, rational enquiry is only possible within the context of a tradition; it is, in his words, a tradition-constituted and tradition-constitutive enterprise. The Enlightenment, with its ideal of universal rationality, robbed us of the conception of tradition-constitutive and -constituted enquiry. That is why fundamental moral disagreements became irresolvable. In MacIntyre's view that is the harm done by the Enlightenment's project of universal rationality and universal morality.

Arnold Burms joins the critics on the idea of a universal morality. He accepts the concept of a narrow, minimalistic morality, but denies that it has no necessary connections with traditional, culturally determined conceptions of the good life. He argues that moral taboos are a necessary element of a narrow morality. If morality in a narrow sense cannot be divorced from moral taboos, it cannot be universal. Moral taboos have a categorical character; their content, however, is culturally determined. The categorical character of moral taboos cannot be seen as an expression of universal rationality. Moral taboos can only be articulated and defended within the framework of a religion that reminds us of what exceeds our powers of prediction and control. *Paul van Tongeren*, in his contribution on the relation between conception of life and morality, also rejects what he calls 'neutral universalism'. Morality and conception of life are joined on a deeper level, that of transcendence. Both constitute forms of a relation of human life to the transcendence. In this sense, morals and conceptions of life - however contingent and particular - are expressions of what is essential for human life. Wherever morality or religion distort that relationship to the transcendent by reducing everything to immanence, they alienate themselves from the transcendence that characterizes human existence and makes it possible. There are different ways in which such an immanentization can occur. The fundamentalism that identifies the particular with the universal exhibits one way. A neutral universalism which supposes that every particularity can be surmounted forms another. Neither can pass the test of transcendence.

Critics of the idea of a universal morality not only reject a rationalistic foundationalism, they also criticize the mode of moral reasoning, which is dominant in foundationalist circles, and takes its starting point in general and universally valid principles. David Burrell & Stanley Hauerwas call this dominant mode the 'standard account of moral rationality'; an account that distorts the nature of the moral life by placing an unwarranted emphasis on particular decisions or quandaries (1), by failing to account for the significance of moral notions and how they work to provide us the skills of perception (2) and by separating the agent from his interests (3) (Burrell & Hauerwas 1976). Following MacIntyre, they propose a narrative ethics.

Hans Reinders analyzes Hauerwas' views. The independence thesis assumes that religious sentences are descriptive statements of (metaphysical) fact, while moral sentences are not concerned with description, but with evaluation. According to Hauerwas' account of the matter this assumption is false, because the 'gap' between the two modalities - description and evaluation - does not exist. Christian convictions shape the way in which Christians describe the world, and this description entails a 'morality'. Christian ethics should not be considered as reflection on moral actions to be performed by Christians, but as the description of a way of being. The notion of character is central to this description. Christians have their character formed according to the story of God's reconciliation with the world. Consequently, Christian identity governs the moral judgments by Christians, mediated not by moral principle but by character. Christian character is formed by learning to accept God's forgiveness and to act accordingly. Thus, there is a strong connection between 'truth' and 'truthfulness' in Hauerwas' theory. The transformation of the self that is characteristic of Christian existence is a precondition of knowing Christian convictions to be true.

Albert W. Musschenga criticizes what he calls 'the strong version of narrative ethics'. Adherents of this narrative ethics, such as Burrell & Hauerwas, argue that moral rationality and the justifications of moral decisions are narrative in their structure. In their view, the central ethical question people should ask themselves when taking decisions is not whether a particular decision is right, but whether it can be shown to fit into their life story. Musschenga argues that this narrative explanation is indispensable for justifying choices between incommensurable options. Narrative explanation, however, does have limits. In a modern pluralistic society no moral tradition has a monopoly. Each moral tradition is just one among many others. An ethics which takes the problems of plurality seriously, cannot confine itself to the question 'Who am I/who do I want to be?' (or: 'Who are we/do we want to be?') Another ethical question must be added: 'Who am I/do I want to be among/together with others who think and act differently?' It goes without saying that the willingness to live together with people who think differently should become part of one's own identity. And in this sense, the theme of identity comes up time and again. Nevertheless, a Christian who lives in a pluralistic society cannot be the same as one who lives in a homogeneously Christian world. The identity of the first is more layered, as he is both a member of the Christian community and a subject of a democratic society. This insight does not follow naturally from any narrative ethics, however.

The students who belong to the *fourth group* are not interested in logical and epistemological questions. They study the historical, causal or psychological relations between specific moral convictions and specific religious convictions. A good example of such research is found in the new discipline of 'comparative religious ethics'. David Little & Sumner B. Twiss study the structure of practical justification in the ethics of religious traditions (Little & Twiss 1978). In this volume, this approach is represented by *Gerrit Manenschijn*, who argues that changes in moral convictions are preceded by, or go along with social and economic changes. Other members of this group are not interested in the relation between religion and morality as such. They want to know which moral convictions fit into, i.e. are compatible with their own religious belief (and - more importantly - which are not).

REFERENCES

Burrell, D. & S. Hauerwas, From System to Story: An Alternative Pattern for Rationality in Ethics. In: D. Callahan (ed.), *The Roots of Ethics*, New York/London 1976, 75-119.

Frankena, W.K., *Ethics*, Englewood Cliffs 1963.

Frankena, W.K., On Saying the Ethical Thing [1966]. Reprinted in: K.E. Goodpaster, *Perspectives on Morality*, Notre Dame/London 1976, 107-125.

Frankena, W.K., Is Morality Logically Dependent on Religion? In: G. Outka & J.P. Reeder Jr. (eds.), *Religion and Morality*, Garden City, NY 1973, 295-318.

Little, D. & S.B. Twiss, *Comparative Religious Ethics*. A New Method, New York etc. 1978.

Rescher, N., *Pluralism. Against the Demands for Consensus*, Oxford 1993.

1

From 'Group Morality' towards 'World Ethos': The Universality of Morality in the Perspective of Moral Theology

Karl-Wilhelm Merks

My article deals with the question whether, and to which extent morality is dependent on religion. I will approach that question from the point of view of moral theology. According to many contemporary philosophers and theologians morality is not dependent on religion. Their main argument is that morality is universal and rational, while religion is not. However, what is meant by (in)dependence, what by universality? Does universality mean *universal acceptance*, or *universal validity* (Schüller 1982)? Is *the whole* of morality supposed to be universal (in one of the two senses) or only parts of it? Does independence mean *logical independence* or *de facto independence*? Because of the ambiguity of the meaning of both the concepts of (in)dependence and universality, a discussion about the relation between independence and universality of morality becomes complicated. Even when moral beliefs are not dependent on religion, they need not be universally accepted. The reverse is also true: even when certain moral beliefs are universally accepted, they still may be closely connected with certain religious convictions. Some moral convictions are regarded not to be dependent on religion, while they are also not universal, as for example is demonstrated in our culture by the common opinions on certain social rights and duties, such as certain welfare rights. The Israelite ethos, for example, is very closely connected with the JHWH-faith, but nevertheless it contains a number of ethical notions which are most certainly nonparticular, not specifically Israelite.

The thesis that morality is not dependent on religion because it is rational, is also disputable. It is not at all clear that rationality is a universal, culture-independent concept.

1.1 CONCEPTUAL CONSIDERATIONS

In view of the complicated nature of our subject, it seems appropriate to me to explicitate some presuppositions which form the background of the present essay. They may be considered as a kind of insert, to keep ready at hand for a better understanding of the intended scope and the presented argumentation. I will summarize these presuppositions in a number of theses.

Whenever I speak of universality:
1. Universality of morality does not mean universal acceptance, but universal validity. In my view this universal validity has to be founded on a conception of what is worthy of a human being. Universal moral rules, such as the prohibition on killing human beings, are valid, whether or not they are universally accepted;
2. Even if a religion is not logically, necessarily, but only contingently connected with morality, it might be possible that it contains specific, idiosyncratic reasons that justify morality: religious and 'rational' argumentation are neither mutually exclusive, nor identical.
3. In the thesis of the rationality of morality, rationality is not identical with the Enlightenment's ideal of rationality, let alone the technical-scientific rationality: what is meant is, in general, a procedure through which morality can develop on the basis of experiences which can be communicated and 'verified': it concerns the coherence between experience of meaning and the reflection on meaningfulness on the one hand, and normative obligation on the other. Normative convictions (also those of religious morality), have to 'prove' their meaningfulness. ('Good' and 'evil' are directly related with value-experience, i.e. they can be put to the test by 'reality', in other words by their effects);
4. Of course, these experiences of meaningfulness and commitment always have a particular cultural setting. However, it is possible that one discovers universal, in the sense or intercultural similarities in the experiences of meaningfulness and obligation. This involves a reflective process that is focused on discovering what is commonly human, and not a deductive process starting from what is already known to be commonly human;
5. As a matter of result, universality of morality, in the sense of universal acceptance of what is universally valid, is not an a priori fact, but a goal to be pursued and elaborated; it is realized in the historically growing insight in what is 'human'.

6 The epistemological and logical independence of morality on religion means that no religion can claim to be the unique source of moral knowledge and that moral convictions have to be justified by moral arguments.[1]

Summarizing, the project of a universal morality aims at general communicability of the experiences of meaningfulness and obligation. Therefore in my view, universality of morals implies the acknowledgement that the experiences of human beings and the resulting moral obligations, show, or at least can show certain similarities, and rightly so.[2]

As I said, I will discuss the universality of morality from the point of view of moral theology. I will show that the universality of morality can, at least in Christian theology, be defended within a theological framework. This argument is not a sophisticated way to impose one's allegedly universal religious convictions on others. In the following sections, I will show to what extent the claim of universality can also work in the reverse direction, to what extent it can relativize one's own position (section 2), and after that I will argue that this has actually been the case in the recent development of catholic moral theology (section 3).

1.2 UNIVERSALITY OF MORALITY - A PROBLEM OF EXISTENTIAL SIGNIFICANCE

The question of the universality of morality not only confronts moral theology with a methodological problem. Much more, it is a problem which concerns its identity. This problem can be described as follows. On the one hand, precisely in the Jewish and Christian tradition faith and morality are very closely related. Biblical morality as well as the morality of the Christian tradition are moralities of faith: in fact they are entirely permeated by convictions that - to limit the problem to Christian ethics - result from the Christian faith. In this sense, such a morality is specific and particularistic.

---

1 I prefer to describe the issue in this way; the usual discussions on the relation religion-morality sometimes do not sufficiently separate the various levels of the question.
2 Such a definition does not satisfy the simpleness of one-dimensional definitions, but takes into account the complexity of the issue of universality in morals.

But on the other hand, this same tradition is determined by its missionary character, and as such by the belief in the universal relevance of its moral convictions. Time and again, the Christian tradition has tried to elaborate the relevance of its morality also in a theoretical way. Moral theologians systematically go beyond the borders of their own community of believers.

Doing so, they are forced to conclude that their morality is obviously not exclusively connected with the Christian faith. Notwithstanding the connection already mentioned, a certain independence of the ethical seems plausible. Believers and nonbelievers can, at least partially, share the same morality without having the rest of their fundamental convictions in common.

From a theological perspective, the demand for a universal morality that has become stronger and stronger during the course of history, also concerns the identity of Christian, in sofar as it was seen originally as an indivisible whole of cognitive and normative convictions. The claim that Christian moral beliefs are not only valid for Christians, but universally valid implies the rejection of exclusivist conceptions of the identity of the Christian faith. History shows examples of Christians and Christian groups who claimed a monopoly for their moral convictions. For the sake of honesty we should add that it was not only Christianity that has been guilty of this.

The criticism of this approach seems justified to me. It is precisely from the perspective of their faith that Christians should be among the first to resist such absolutist claims of authority for their moral convictions. A fundamentalist will not agree with this, yet it seems to me that fundamentalism in ethics is not defendable, for theological as well as ethical reasons. From a theological point of view: a believer cannot continue to disregard the main difference between the knowledge of God at the one side and his own, human knowledge with the questions which arise from this at the other side. From an ethical point of view: on the basis of the demonstrably individual nature of moral convictions (which concern 'good' and 'evil' in the narrow sense), the purely authoritative argument is intellectually not defendable, although it is used very often (Merks 1994). However, the risk of abuse does not justify the total rejection of each attempt to have one's moral beliefs universally accepted, not even when this is undertaken from the perspective of faith. What is important, is the way in which one tries to establish this universality. Does one want to impose one's absolutely true and valid beliefs on others or does one try to convince them by rational argumentation?

Moral theologians defended a rational conception of morality, long before the Enlightenment. Each claim of universal rationality for a morality, is an explosive device for those who utter it. Such a claim does not only relativize the point of view of others who don't live up to the demands of this morality, it also relativizes the uniqueness of one's own position. It implies that one's moral convictions are not exclusively connected with one's religious faith. As a consequence, conceptions of faith that presuppose such exclusiveness, have to be reinterpreted.

By claiming universal rationality for one's own ethical point of view, the archaic position of an exclusive, special 'group morality' is fundamentally abandoned in this tradition and, consequently, the way is opened towards an ethical universality that is no longer based on a specific faith.

It will be clear that from this position, the question of a universal morality is really an existential problem for the Christian faith. It does not only concern the concept of morality, but also the self-understanding of faith itself. It leads to relativizing the exclusiveness of the relation between one's faith and morality. Christian faith as such may be unique, not the morality with which it is connected. Such a relativizing is not self-evident: sociologically, it has to be conquered and defended against the tendency towards self-preservation and the spontaneous mechanism to delimit one's own group. However, the universality of morality has been an important question throughout the history of theology. That might indicate that it is a type of question that is forced upon us by reality itself. The phenomenon of morality, as a reality sui generis, the ethical search for 'the good', offers resistance to even religiously motivated forms of moral separatism.

1.3 THE ABANDONMENT OF A MISTAKEN IDEAL OF UNIVERSALITY IN MORALITY

Ultimately, the idea of a universal morality is not the confirmation of the powerful position of faith and its institutionalization in religious bodies of authority. Rather, it helps to unmask the unjust power of religion and faith and exposes the intertwining relationship of faith and power. The claim of a universal morality can therefore be interpreted as part of the struggle for liberation, because it opens the possibility to criticize religiously justified moral oppression. The idea of a universal morality is a protection against religious moral positivism and against any other type of moral positivism. However, the problem of moral universality is often not primarily seen as a possibility to liberate humans from unjustified coercion. In a certain context, the very idea of universality carries itself the taste of suppression. The problem that I am hinting at here is actually present in the so-called post-modernist reflection. The question is, to which extent the pretended universality of moral concepts is - just like other claims on universality - no more than an extrapolation of our own dominant culture that we declare to be universally human.[3]

These issues lift the problem of universality of morality so to say to another level: a more important question comes up concerning the characteristics of the concept of universality itself. And as far as this concept is based on our ideas of rationality, this question also concerns the characteristics and the range of our models of rationality.

At face value, this question seems to be utterly embarrassing and irritating for an ethicist, who just thought to have unmasked by the greatest possible methodological strictness all forms of particularity which presented themselves unjustly as universal. And although the post-modernists may often express their criticism of universality all too quickly, it does make sense to question the alleged universality of our morality which we regard too easily as self-evident.

Post-modern criticism aims first of all at the ideals of universality of the Enlightenment which are developed until today. It is seems to be curious, at least for Catholic ethics, that this happens on the very moment it has begun to try to incorporate essential elements of the Enlightenment, after a long period of defence and denial. However, to me this seems not tragic. Elsewhere, I have tried to demonstrate that moral theology on the basis of its own history is well prepared to take account of the post-modern criticism of rationality and universality (Merks 1990). In this historical process of learning, moral theology has learned to deal with overstated ideals of universality.

---

[3] According to me, it seems appropriate to add a remark about the relationship between the particular and the universal. These concepts are not completely opposites: in principle, something which is discovered and experienced particularly can be generally valid. It goes without discussion that each and every universalisation takes place from a particular tradition, i.e. one's own. Yet, this does not say anything about its justifiability. There is no knowledge among mankind which has not emerged from a particular tradition.

In this way moral theology learned to approach the idea of universality critically.[4] The impulse for this came essentially 'from outside', from the methodological reflection, the substantive questions and results of modern philosophy and modern sciences, i.e. the human and the social sciences (biology, sociology, psychology, ethnology, psycho-analysis, etc.). Under this influence 'from outside', moral theology was forced to change its paradigm, its model of moral thinking: from (a specific form of) natural law ethics towards an ethics of responsibility. An essential element in this change of paradigm has been the liberation from an illusion of wrongly conceived universality in which moral theology had become trapped, namely the idea that it was possible to develop a universally valid ethics based on the metaphysical essence of man. In this type of ethics, insights from history and cultural anthropology are only of marginal, if any, significance.

However, it would be wrong - as is demonstrated by learning process of moral theology - to interpret the rejection of essentialistic ethics as a rejection of the very idea of a universal morality. On the contrary, the rejection of an essentialistic conception of universal morality clarifies the real meaning of the idea of a universal morality.

There are some structural similarities between an ethics based on a metaphysics of essence and the Enlightenment conception of universal morality, although the essentialistic ethics is infused by the spirit of rejection of modernity and the Enlightenment. This especially applies to the rationalistic attitude of both, their feeling of superiority and even the presumed monopoly of the truth of their convictions. The central difference lies in the fact that in modern thought this attitude is linked to a dynamic-expansive ideal of progress, while essentialistic ethics was fundamentally oriented towards retrospection and restoration. Here, the universality of the future is opposed to the universality of the origin.

Therefore, post-modern criticism of the Enlightenment's concept of universality shows clear congeniality with moral theology's criticism of the essentialistic ethics of essence when it blames this concept for universalizing a very outdated image of man (with its culturally determined ideals) into the ideal image of all of mankind. In the remaining part of this essay, I will not

---

4 I want to restrict this remark in first instance to moral theology as a discipline; in how far the magisterium of the church has been influenced by the critical reflection on the universality of morals, is another question. See my article at the occasion of the appearance of the recent encyclical *Veritatis splendor* (Merks 1993).

further comment on this - rather one-sided - post-modern criticism, but restrict myself to the internal moral theological developments.

The critical discussion regarding the ethics of essence has resulted in a purification of the idea of universality and in some insights which can also be of value for nontheological ethics.

Catholic moral theology has a long tradition in considering a possible universality of morality; once it was liberated from its nineteenth-century narrowness, it displayed an abundance of reflection on this question that we can use in the actual discussion on the possibilities and limits of this universality. I don't want to give the impression to merely recapture this tradition, however. Ethics as it existed before the Enlightenment cannot simply be transplanted to the era after the Enlightenment. Too much happened in the meantime which touches upon the question of a universal morality and added new dimensions to it. I only need to mention some keywords such as emancipation, individualisation, secularisation, autonomy, pluralism.

Now, it is not my intention to trace the where's and abouts of this tradition historically. I will try to bring some elements from this tradition together in a systematical way, in order to formulate a viewpoint on the question of universality of morality which is acceptable today. With regard to tradition, this does not mean a simple repetition but a process of rereading in which congeniality and analogy between traditional ideas and actual experiences are incorporated.

I will successively deal with the process of differentiation as the principle of and structural condition for an acceptable idea of universality (section 4); the concept of an autonomous morality as a reflective framework for a universal morality (section 5); the elaboration of a universal morality in the concept of human rights (section 6); and the new appreciation of particularity as a condition for real universality (section 7). I will conclude by dealing with the question what all this means for the identity of Christian ethics.

1.4 DIFFERENTIATION AS STRUCTURAL CONDITION FOR AN ACCEPTABLE IDEA OF UNIVERSALITY

One might think that the leading principle and criterion of universality of morality consists in striving for the greatest possible unity of the various moralities. Yet, the history of ethics sufficiently demonstrates that not a single principle of unity, but the dual principle of unity-in-differentiation forms the basis of a universal morality. This means that universality of morality has not to be sought in the uniformity of moral rules. In reality, such an ideal is permanently contradicted by the omnipresent diversity of moralities, synchronically as well as diachronically. Also from a theoretical point of view, such a uniformity does not seem worth pursuing as a moral ideal.

Internal coherence of a morality, and unity between morality as far as the principles are concerned, do not exclude diversity in actual concretization. A classic example is the enormous variation in the way cultures show respect to, and take care for the elderly, ranging from special nurture to killing. This example indicates that attempts to reach a universal consensus should to solely be directed at the level of principles, while the level of the concretization of these principles is disregarded. In fact, from the moment they meet one another, cultures do engage in discussions on a lot of concrete moral questions! The theoretical elaboration of the distinction between fundamental and concrete moralities operates with a layered model of generality of norms, e.g. in the form of principle-conclusion-determination, or of primary and secondary norms of natural law, or of natural law and positive law, just to name some conceptualisations in the lex-treaty of Thomas Aquinas.

The idea of such a layered concept of normativity constitutes a central moment in the Jewish-Christian history of ethics, because the image of the morality of the Old Testament and, in connection to it, of the New Testament - always considered to be an indivisible whole - is itself changing. Biblical morality shows the image of a process of growth, while 'rationalising' tendencies are present to formulate and warrant the unity of morality in unifying principles rather than in positivistic similarity of concrete norms. Such principles are for example the summaries of the multitude of prescriptions in norms and principles considered more fundamental, e.g. the decalogue or the love of God and one's neighbour, or the demand of justice (Merks 1989). These summaries also function as a test, a criterion, by which concrete norms and acts can be judged on their degree of justice. They establish identity between differences and within processes of change, not by straightening out differences, but by summarising them under a common denominator.

Next to the distinction between the fundamental and the concrete, another form of differentiation is present in the Scriptures, in a more concealed way but worked out theoretically later in the history of theology. This differentiation is about differences in urgency and obligatoriness of prescriptions; e.g.

the Sabbath rule can be suspended in order to defend oneself against an enemy, to heal a human being and even to rescue an ox from the well. Christian theology will continue to reflect on this later. Confronted with the fact that the rules of the Old Testament are after all the law of God, theologians came to the differentiation between *praecepta moralia*, *praecepta caeremonialia* and *praecepta iudicialia* (moral, ceremonial and legal precepts), in which the claim on universality only holds for the first category, again seen in the light of principle vs. application. A modern version of this differentiation is e.g. the one between ethics and positive law.

I will summarize these indications. In the light of the biblically founded moral theological tradition, differentiation between various kinds of norms and differentiation between principle and application, between depth and surface, forms the structure for dealing with the problem of universality in a meaningful way.

1.5 AUTONOMOUS MORALITY AS A REFLECTIVE FRAMEWORK FOR A UNIVERSAL MORALITY

The Catholic moral tradition has elaborated the idea of a universal morality into the model of natural law morality. This model has a rich history and there are various versions. They have in common the intention to found morality on universally valid principles that make a universal acceptance possible. Because of its ambiguity - we already mentioned the aberrations of an essentialistic morality - natural law is currently not held in high esteem. Also, the concept of nature does not seem fit to grant the modern reflection on morality conceptual unity.

Therefore, many Catholic moral theologians have changed over to develop a different model of morality, the 'autonomous morality'. This model also has various forms which I will not go into here. The word 'autonomous' easily suggests that it is a morality in which moral decisions are regarded as subjective. Should that be the case, it would affect that morality's claim on universality negatively. In Catholic ethics autonomous morality is not subjective. It means a purified and balanced concept of rational morality, which, on the contrary, can promote the idea of possible universality.

I will briefly present what I consider to be the central moments of this concept of autonomous morality in order to show where the place for a universal morality is to be found in it (Merks 1992; Auer 1984[2]; Böckle 1977).

Autonomous morality in a theological context means nothing else than thinking about morality in terms of the freedom and the responsibility of human beings. The ethical defines itself not by quantities extrinsic to the human (nature, authority, Scripture, church, tradition, society) but by man itself and in reference to him/her. In the realization of their responsible freedom, human beings discover their moral duty. Autonomous morality is characterized by the modern turn towards the human: anthropocentrism. True morality does not consist in living as good as possible according to the normative order with its commands and laws. True morality means taking one's own responsibility and acting according to it. Autonomous morality is a morality of the reasonable insight and as such a continuation of natural law morality as, for example, was formulated by Thomas Aquinas in the form of an morality of practical reason. Judging by the discussion about it, autonomous morality seems to be very complicated matter. However, autonomous morality eventually boils down to a couple of simple principles:

1 Morality is autonomous in the sense that the commitment of man to the good as the good can only really take place on the basis of a self-commitment of human freedom which accepts its responsibility.
2 Morality is also autonomous in the sense that such a self-commitment is inescapably tied to one's own insight in the goodness of that which is presented as good.
3 Ethics (as reflection on morality) is autonomous insofar as the good to be done has to result from a specific way of reflection and cannot be deduced from other forms of knowledge.

Thus, human freedom is the basis of morality, formally as well as substantially. The measure for what has to be done is also gained from a self-interpretation of man as a being with freedom. Nowadays, ethics as the science of the good life in its fullest sense can only understand this good life if the central meaning of freedom with its various dimensions for this good life is taken seriously. Of course, these implications of freedom are not merely an objective fact. Humans always have to explain the meaning of their freedom themselves. Freedom is only a reality in a concrete historical, social and cultural situation. Still, freedom has its objective and even universally demonstrable structures which can be made visible despite the great variety of particular and cultural concretizations. The concept of human rights is the best example. Not surprisingly, human rights take a central place in the material-concrete normative elaboration of autonomous morality.

1.6 UNIVERSAL MORALITY TODAY - HUMAN RIGHTS AS THE 'MEETING POINT' BETWEEN AN MORALITY OF FAITH AND SECULAR MORALITY

It is inherent to human rights that they want to be understood as universal moral principles. I will deal with the question in as far, and under which conditions this can be the case, more extensively in the next section. In this section I would like to draw attention to an interesting development recently taking place in the reflection on the relation between 'morality of faith' (Glaubensethik) and 'secular morality'.

This is the convergence which takes place because in concepts of secular morality as well as in theological morality, human rights become more and more important as moral principles. On the theological side, this does not only apply to the more advanced moral theology; the social teaching of the popes pays more and more attention to human rights as well. This is interesting because a nonreligious moral concept thus became a 'meeting point' between various moralities. It seems that new forms of moral universality are being developed here which are acceptable despite differences in worldview.

Of course, human rights show affinity with for example the decalogue or with other moral convictions from theological traditions. Nevertheless, it remains striking that they developed into a new conceptual frame for a universal morality which does not remain purely formal, but can be elaborated into concrete and substantial principles.

I am convinced that in our present culture, human rights offer the framework in which a universal morality can be formulated in a meaningful way. Still, there are indications that things aren't quite as simple as they seem. Even something as fundamental as human rights, which are supposed to be globally human since they start from respect for each and every human being, is not safeguarded from particularism. Are they as universal as they are supposed to be, or do they, after all, bear the mark of their Western descendence? This is the question I would like to dwell upon now. It is my intention to show that respect for diversity leads towards a substantial conception of true universality.

1.7 A NEW APPRECIATION OF PARTICULARITY AS CONDITION FOR TRUE UNIVERSALITY

The subject I want to deal with here is the relation between universality and relativity of human rights. In itself, with regard to its intention, the idea of human rights claims universal validity and strives for universal acceptance. It does not concern the rights of Dutchmen, Germans, Indians or Vatican citizens, but the rights of human beings as such.

However, man as such does not exist. There are women, men, Indians and Vatican citizens. There are whites and blacks, lords and servants, homosexuals and heterosexuals, rich and poor people. Those who have everything and those who have nothing, not even rights. Obviously, the human rights are not rights *all* human beings actually enjoy. This is, unfortunately, a fact which many human beings know by experience. This can be an indication for us that talking about universality of human rights is often but naive or cynical rhetoric. Human rights are selectively granted and selectively practised. The universal element of human rights seems to exist first and most in the universality of their selective application, this means in the permanent violation of their true universality.

This inconsistence, though not easy to abolish practically, can be easily pointed out theoretically as non tenable. Such a selectivity is an attack on the basic principles of morality itself. Such a 'relativity' of human rights is not worth a discussion, it can only be fought against.

The fragility of a universal recognition of human rights, however, can also be attributed to a different cause, namely when it does not follow from the refusal of ethical impartiality (to be blamed as immoral), but when it is caused by a (morally founded) doubt about the pretended universality. Taken at close range, such a doubt usually concerns concrete human right claims. The universal willingness to respect human rights in a nonselective way, leaves open the question what exactly has to be respected as human rights. When it comes to human rights, it turns out to be difficult for us to apply the self-evident distinction between form and content, between principle and application of a normative duty, as present in the logic of morality. Too easily we equate the *idea* of human rights with substantial conceptions of human right. The idea of rights and the corresponding duties that obviously apply to all humans are, as it were, automatically identified with the idea of what these rights are. The concept or idea of human rights obligation is immediately identified with specific interpretations and elaborations in substantial conceptions of human rights. Yet, these substantial conceptions of human rights are the result of our Western history of culture. If this is true, can they be universalised as such? The human rights we want to respect might be rights that not all of those people to which they apply, have asked for; perhaps they have different priorities. Despite our good will, we forgot to ask one question: who actually determinates which demands are rightly claimed to be unconditional human rights? The answer to this question is more complicated than might appear at face value. Apparently, the ideas on the content of the human rights that should be generally recognized widely diverge, depending on the cultural context.

The idea of a possible plurality in the interpretation of human rights is rather recent. It is indeed a strange thought that not everybody would spontaneously appreciate the ethos of human rights with its humane intentions, especially where he or she is the beneficiary of such a respect. If the universality of human rights is thus contested, the next step seems not to be far away. Could not then the idea of the obligation of human rights, and thus of human rights in themselves, also be interpreted as a product of Western cultural history and therefore as particular - contingent? Does this not mean that not only our idea about the concrete content of prevailing human rights, but also the idea of human rights in itself becomes questionable? However, if one does not want to go through this last step - and according to me there is no reason for it - what could be the meaning of a concept of human rights if it is not connected with some ideas of universal content? This question can also be formulated as follows: how can one save the universality of human rights, and at the same time formulate their content in such a way that the original eurocentrism is relativized?

According to contemporary insights, an answer to this question can hardly be given by replacing the eurocentrism by a worldwide monism. The answer to this question has to be found in searching for grounds for and limits of a legitimate plurality within the human rights ethos itself. What is being claimed here, in this central chapter of a modern morality and modern law, is nothing more or less than a new balance between universality and plural particularity. The idea of a possible plurality within human rights presupposes a high level of experience and reflection. Its presupposition is an acknowledgement of the value of cultural independence and the inherent otherness of the other. We have only just begun to develop such an understanding of foreign cultures.

True enough, the recognition of the value of foreign cultures and, consequently, a relativizing of the own culture, has already been for some time a partial aspect of our occidental reflection. As I said before, this recognition does not have to lead to questioning the idea of a universal morality. It leads to an awareness of the limits of concrete cultural legal and moral rules and convictions, rather then to questioning the universality of the idea of human rights. The positive significance of the autonomy of cultures and nations for the elaboration of the contents of human rights has not been under discussion for a long time. It is not necessary, either to deny the universal character of human rights or, eventually, the dignity of the particular culturally determined sense of value. We will have to develop a new understanding of the relation between universality and particularity in the concept of human rights itself.

I mention several issues that have to play a role in this. Normally, the right[5] to have one's own concrete interpretation of the idea of human rights is discussed today in connection with the diversity of cultures. This is indeed an important aspect. The human rights ethos should not lead to the suppression of one culture by another, dominant one. But besides the problem of the relation between various cultures, there is the one of the relation between individuals and the social order of his/her own culture. It is precisely the point of human rights to create legal rules and institutions for the defence of the individual, if necessary against his/her own culture. Concerning the question of the universality or the cultural relativity of human rights, it thus seems that a double issue is at stake: the demarcation of the unconditional and inviolable rights of the individual against his own culture on the one hand, and the diverse interpretation of concrete human rights by the various cultures on the other hand.

Another element that I want to mention is the distinction between obligations which determine that no harm may be caused to a human, and obligations to ameliorate the conditions of living of all human beings, a distinction that is expressed in the differentiation of freedom rights on the one hand, and social and participation rights on the other. Traditionally, there is also a difference in degree of obligatoriness, i.e. the distinction between negative

---

5 I mean by 'right' not: arbitrary, positivist legal right, but the right to participate on an equal basis in the discourse on the interpretation of human rights. It is therefore the expression of the self-responsibility of every human being.

and positive prescriptions, of which the first hold 'semper et pro semper' (always and in every situation) and the second 'semper sed non pro semper' (always, but not in every situation). It is more easy to prove what is harmful and what is necessary to avoid harm, then what contributes to the improvement of the conditions of living for everybody. An answer to this last question will be less compelling. Discussions on the improvement of living conditions will have the character of a much more flexible communication of value-insights. Here, universality is dependent on a very difficult intra- and intercultural process of communication.

The central question is, what should be the foundation for a generally relevant doctrine of goods? If one starts from the classic ideas of freedom in their political-civil connotation, mainly rights of protection forbidding serious infringements of freedom will be established. According to me, however, the starting point should not be man as a being with a right to freedom in the form of a number of liberties, but the interconnectedness of the dignity of man and his freedom. Therefore, human rights should flow from the idea of man as a being with dignity and the right to freedom founded on it. Such an approach is much more far reaching than the minimum of freedom rights which is evidently not further founded. After all, dignity not only needs to be defended, it also needs to be realized and cherished. Above all, such an approach means that it is impossible to state a priori to which man has a right. This can only be done by involving the judgment of human beings themselves. Every human being must be able to bring in his own interpretation of human dignity. The content and the meaning of human dignity cannot be derived from a pre-given nature neither from a pre-given culture. Human dignity can only be conceived in a process of human self-interpretation.

The true core of the universality of the demands of human rights is therefore human dignity, and freedom as one's own responsibility. This is the common essence of each and every human being. If this is considered to be the common foundation, it is clear that it needs further elaboration and differentiation. Still, in the recognition of the common dignity and freedom, there is at the same time a criterion which imposes limits to this diversity. Precisely this shows that universality of human rights is not a given fact, but a programme; a programme in which the common right of all people to live according to their dignity, i.e. to live in freedom, according to their conscience, must be realised. Yet, this means that universality cannot be reached by eliminating the differences as much as possible, but exactly by integrating them. The real doubt regarding the universality of human rights therefore results from the fact that the conception of human rights is often not sufficiently universal. They do not really integrate all the acceptable and defensible points of view.[6] Such a dominant conception of human rights does no justice, neither to the individual voices of those who are suffering, poor and marginal, nor to the voices of entire cultures that are suppressed.

The question is how such an ideal of a true universality can be fulfilled. I think that this depends on the sympathy with which we are able to make the point of view of the other our own by understanding its legitimacy. This means that we have to develop respect for the particular experiences of value in the different cultures.[7] But above all, it is the assignment to engage in a common culture integrating the different cultures where one and the same universal standard reigns: the concrete human being with its dignity. The point of departure for a universality of human rights must be the unequivocal concentration on its core: a life in dignity for all humans.

We may ask ourselves whether these are typical European convictions. The answer is that the demand to make human society more humane, is a kind of culture-transcendent norm. This transcendence is only warranted when one keeps distinguishing between this general demand as such, and the always imperfect, partial and provisional realizations. So far, with a view to the question of universality, the concrete contents of human rights are, even if not arbitrary, of secondary nature. Insofar as they are connected in a nonarbitrary way with the project of making human society more humane, they are more or less universal. The more we realize the arbitrariness of our presuppositions and relativize our own position, the more we feel ourselves free to engage in a discussion with people from other cultures. This does not at all mean that we have to give up our moral convictions, but it does mean that we have to be prepared to open up our group morality towards a 'world ethos'. Therefore, the answer to the cultural differences lies not in refraining from attempting to establish universal agreement on universal human rights, but in a further differentiation of universality.

---

6   'Defensible' is, of course, an open concept. In any case, the measure is what has been called above the core of human rights: human dignity and freedom as one's own responsibility; further realization of this cannot be formulated in abstract terms, separated from the historical context and the standards of consensus on human rights.

7   This entails more than only respect for the subjects of those experiences; as far as they are experiences of value, in the formal sense of imposing themselves urgently upon human beings, they deserve respectful attention as such.

1.8 CONCLUSION: THE IDENTITY OF (A) CHRISTIAN MORALITY

The conclusion can be short. We have seen that universal acceptance of a morality becomes only then possible when we allow for differences on the concrete level. Further, we saw that this even applies to the human rights that we regard as the paradigm of universal morality.[8] Does this conclusion have consequences for the identity of Christian morality itself? According to me, we need to reflect on this question seriously.

I said that the human rights ethos is gaining more and more plausibility, also theologically, especially if we make a careful distinction between the fundamental aspects of this human rights ethos and its concrete culturally determined forms. The question I want to raise at the end of this article is, whether the same model of universality can be applied to Christian morality. This is a much more challenging question than the question whether Christians have the same moral convictions as non-Christians (Merks 1986).

Yet, our own biblical tradition (cfr. the question of the first, 'apostolic' council) explains to us that even in questions considered to be fundamental, a plurality of legitimate solutions can be possible on the basis of a common ground; therefore, in important questions plurality is based on a more fundamental unity. Nevertheless, this model has to be conquered time and again on our spontaneous group bound instincts of dominance; not even the Christian communities of faith are free from this.

Translated by dr. Jan Jans

REFERENCES

Auer, A., *Autonome Moral und christlicher Glaube*, Düsseldorf 1984².
Böckle, F., *Fundamentalmoral*, Düsseldorf 1977.
Merks, K.-W., Spezifisch christlich im Plural. In: G.-W. Hunold & W. Korff (Hg.), *Die Welt für morgen. Ethische Herausforderungen im Anspruch der Zukunft*, München 1986, 367-378.
Merks, K.-W., De universele ethiek - een illusie? Een ideaal van het moderne denken in

---

[8] It makes little sense here to fix a priori the scope and the limits of legitimate plurality in abstract formulas; this has to take place every time in a concrete discussion. To me, it seems more important to accept the model as such in total honesty, against our quasi-instinctive reservations.

postmodern licht. In: I.N. Bulhof & J.M.M. de Valk (red.), *Postmodernisme als uitdaging*, Baarn 1990, 70-97.

Merks, K.-W., Autonomie. In: J.-P. Wils & D. Mieth, *Grundbegriffe der christlichen Ethik*, Paderborn 1992, 254-281.

Merks, K.-W., ' "Veritatis splendor" is beginpunt, niet het einde van het gesprek', *Een-twee-een* 21(1993), 645-648.

Merks, K.-W., De boom der kennis van goed en kwaad in eigen tuin. Fundamentalistische argumentaties in de katholieke moraaltheologie. In: H.L. Beck & K.-W. Merks (red.), *Fundamentalisme. Ethisch fundamentalisme in wereldgodsdiensten*, Baarn 1994, 42-59.

Schüller, B., Das Proprium einer christlichen Ethik in der Diskussion. In: *Der menschliche Mensch. Aufsätze zur Metaethik und zur Sprache der Moral*, Düsseldorf 1982, 3-27.

Weren, W., De Tien Woorden in het Nieuwe Testament en in de rabbijnse literatuur. In: K.-W. Merks, N. Poulssen & W. *Weren, Weg of wet? Over de Tien Woorden*, Boxtel/Brugge 1989, 33-69.

Comments

Arnold Burms

In his attempt to represent human rights as the basis of a universal morality ('World Ethos') Merks formulates a number of remarks which indirectly reveal some limitations and weaknesses of the program he wishes to defend.

The ideal of human rights is sometimes criticized for not being sufficiently universal. It is thought that human rights, as commonly understood, do not take into account all the points of view they ought to take into account. Merks mentions this objection and tries to deal with it. But he does not seem to see any difficulties in accepting an assumption he shares with his opponent: he apparently assumes that one's respect for other human beings is identical with one's willingness to take there point of view into account. This assumption is enormously popular nowadays, but I think that it is a disastrous mistake. Our respect for other human beings should include a respect for infants and for those who are mentally handicapped or insane. But what sense could be given to the injunction that we have to take their point of view into account? Either they have no point of view at all about what their real interests are or their point of view is hopelessly confused and not to be taken seriously. Also in many other, nonmarginal cases it would be wrong to take it for granted that what is really good for a person is the same as what that person considers as good for him. Taking the point of others into account is only one way to respecting them. Why is this simple fact so often ignored or denied? An answer to this question will have to refer to the privileged position the ideal of individual autonomy occupies in the actual hierarchy of moral values. And an interpretation of why the ideal of individual autonomy has its high status, would, I think, have to be related to a kind of narcissist temptation which makes people believe that their self-image is absolutely correct.

Another objection mentioned by Merks says that the ideal of human rights tends to neglect cultural diversity. Merks' reply is that the ideal of human rights has a universal character, but that it will have to be realised in many different forms; the many concrete embodiments of the universal ideal should presumably mirror the diversity of cultures. This reply is not only vague, it also seems wrong. When we speak about human rights, we primarily think of strict constraints limiting what a society can require from its members or what a government can impose on its citizens. The central aim of the ideal of human rights is a kind of damage control: the point is to protect individuals against unlicensed acts of force or violence, performed by the police or military of some regime. Human rights primarily function as checks on the tendencies specific cultures may have to threaten the security of individual persons. They cannot fulfill this important role unless they can be formulated in terms of strict, culture-independent constraints. Therefore it does not make much sense, as far as I can see, to claim that the program of human rights should adapt itself to specific cultural traditions; such concessions or adaptations would destroy the main point of the program.

In Merks' view a respect for individual persons can be harmoniously combined with a respect for cultural diversity. He seems to think that a defense of human rights is really analogous to a defense of particular cultural traditions. This strikes me as a somewhat amazing assumption. For at first sight there is much more reason for seeing here conflict rather than harmony. The ideal of human rights has a liberal, individualist inspiration and liberalism itself has been powerfully challenged in recent years by communautarianism. The least one should say is that there is a tension between talk of human rights and talk of attachments to local communities of specific cultures.

If it is true (as I think it is) that human rights are primarily projective and aim at some kind of damage control, than it is also true that human rights are to be connected with the narrow conception of morality. It would then be wrong to expect that the idea of human rights might be developed into a substantial theory of human happiness or well-being. Merks admits that it is easier to establish what is really harmful for human beings than to establish what is ultimately satisfying for them.

He nevertheless seems to believe that a theory of human rights should also be a substantial theory about the good life. I think that this is a mistake. On the one hand it is very dubious whether images of an ideal life could be universal and whether human flourishing could be described in culture independent terms. On the other hand (and perhaps more importantly) the ambitions of those who want to turn the ideal of human rights into a theory about the good life, might well hinder that ideal from fulfilling its vital, protective function.

2

God, Morality, and the Transformation of Human Beings

Antonie van den Beld

2.1 INTRODUCTION

What I intend to do in this contribution is, first, to give a succinct exposition of how, according to me, the relation of worldview, morality and ethical theory (or ethics) should be conceived. I shall argue that both morality and ethical theory are dependent on worldview. The dependency of ethical theory on worldview will then be exemplified by my treatment of the topic of the moral transformation of human beings. Regarding this, my basic theses are, first, that such a transformation is generally necessary; and, second, that belief in God makes a difference precisely at the point of how to account for its possibility. The truth of the first thesis is more or less assumed, since I have argued for it elsewhere. The greater part of this essay will therefore be devoted to the clarification and elaboration of the second thesis.

2.2 ON THE RELATIONSHIP BETWEEN WORLDVIEW, MORALITY AND ETHICS

Is one's morality (logically) dependent on one's worldview - or view of life?[1] It is often asserted that the answer to this question must be in the negative. An argument for this so called independence thesis is that a change

---

1 The words 'worldview' and 'view of life' are used interchangeably for a set of beliefs which are central to the way a person looks upon herself, her life and the world; for example, beliefs concerning the existence or nonexistence of God, and the origin and destiny of human life.

in a person's view of life is not necessarily coupled with a change in his morals: '... if Jones is today an atheist, and tomorrow becomes a theist, his knowledge of what is right and good will not have changed, except possibly with regard to duties of worshipping God' (Cunningham 1970, 31). A second argument is that you do not have to be a christian or a humanist in order not to lie, not to steal, not to kill innocent people, to keep your promises, to be honest with your tax declaration, or to give to charity. In other words, it appears to be possible that people with different worldviews share a morality. So, at first sight, the independence thesis looks plausible.

But let us go somewhat deeper into the question of what it means to say that people share a morality. If John and Peter have the same morality, we may expect that they will perform the same - morally relevant - actions when situated in similar circumstances. Now the question is crucial of how we must interpret 'same actions'. When do two people perform the same actions? Suppose John and Peter are driving lorryloads of food from Kenya to a refugee camp in Southern Sudan. Both are hired by the same relief organization. John is a rather cynical adventurer and a confirmed atheist. He would just as well transport arms - as he had done in the past. Peter has taken a year's leave from a well paid United Nations' desk job in Nairobi in order to devote himself to the care of the thousands of starving African refugees. He looks upon his new assignment as a personal calling from Christ. Now, are John and Peter doing the same thing? Are they performing the same actions?

That John is driving an old Mercedes and Peter a Ford of a more recent date does not detract from the similarity of their actions. Neither does the fact that they are going along different routes. Things change, however, as soon as we take into consideration the widely divergent intentions with which they drive: John primarily for the kick he gets out of the dangerous adventure and with an eye on the promised premium. Peter, on the other hand, in order to execute a divine mission and bring food to the hungry. John, quite unlike Peter, would not consider the expedition to have failed had the goods been seized upon delivery by a military gang. If only he had got his money. As far as their publicly observable behaviour is concerned, John and Peter are performing the same, i.e. similar, actions. But when their intentions have been taken into account, things look different. They both drive a lorry loaded with food to the same refugee camp. But their actions are expressive of diverse intentions. Even if John and Peter had had the same primary intention in driving their lorries, namely bringing food to the refugee camp, their more fundamental intentions would have been different. And that is the point. The basic wants on which they act are not the same. Peter's action, unlike John's, can be described as 'doing the will of God'. Moreover, Peter's desire to do God's will presupposes belief in the existence of God (and a network of related beliefs), while John's cynicism could hardly have been compatible with such a belief.

So, the conclusion seems to be that John and Peter can only be said to do the same (morally relevant) actions if we focus on their publicly observable behaviour and leave out the fundamental thought - the wants and beliefs - which direct their actions. As soon as we include in the analysis the intentions with which they act, they can no longer be taken to perform the same actions. The former - behaviourist - stance should be rejected as being superficial. (Judas betrayed Jesus by kissing him. Did he perform the same action as the nameless woman in Luke 7 (vs. 38) who kissed Jesus out of affection?) A corollary of this view is that a necessary condition for two people sharing a morality is that there is agreement in their fundamental thought about life and the world; in other words, in their respective worldviews.[2] We shall shortly see from a somewhat different perspective that a change in a person's worldview cannot but have moral consequences for him or her.

In addition to morality, ethical theory (or ethics) depends also, at least partly, on a view of life. Elsewhere (Van den Beld 1992, 22-38), I have tried to demonstrate that it is difficult, if not impossible, to give within an atheistic context a theoretical account of an adequate morality. Such a morality, so I argued, has to meet at least two conditions. First, it must recognize obligations which involve the possibility of suffering considerable costs or losses on the part of the human subject. This condition is entailed by the metaethical view that the point of morality is to contribute to the betterment, or nondeterioration, of the human predicament. The institution of morality should do so by counteracting man's strong tendency to egoism. In the second place it must be psychologically possible that human beings fulfil their moral obligations. Or, in other words, ought implies can. I could show that naturalistic ethical theories in the Humean, subjectivist tradition are

---

[2] The quintessence of the foregoing argument against the independence thesis is derived from Sutherland (1982). Elsewhere I have discussed the argument more extensively, see chapter 12 (on 'worldview and morality') of Van Willigenburg (1993).

generally capable of meeting the second condition, but fail the first. Whilst the opposite is the case as far as objectivist and Kantian theories are concerned. At the end of the essay it was suggested that a theistic ethics might succeed not only in founding costly moral obligations, but also in giving an explanation of why people would be willing to fulfil those obligations. What I had in mind with regard to the latter suggestion was the idea of God bringing about a moral transformation in man. Now, what I want to do in the rest of this paper is to elaborate this idea. Does God really change people - and if so, how does he do it?

2.3 SUBJECT, OBJECT AND DIRECTION OF CHANGE

Let me begin with some clarifications in order to bring our topic into focus. From the introduction of the leading questions it can already be gathered that I am not so much interested in human change in general, but in change for the better. Is it possible that a human being turns from a strongly selfish and self- or group-centered individual into a person open to God who cares for the well-being of his or her fellow human beings? From the point of view of systematic theology, we here touch upon the doctrine of sanctification. However, I do not want to go deeply into that. In dealing with our central problem we can ignore distinctions, within the so called 'ordo salutis', such as between vocation, regeneration and conversion.[3] Of minor importance too, at least for the moment, is the issue whether one should understand the transformation of a human being as an event or a process.

More important is the question of what exactly is subject to change. We should not think immediately of publicly observable behaviour. Most people exhibit usually socially acceptable, some even praiseworthy behaviour. In the latter case it may even seem to be costly for the agent concerned. Nevertheless, this kind of behaviour is not as such indicative of the source from which it originates. It does not reveal unambiguously the human 'heart'. It may have been inspired by rational self-interest or expediency. Social conformism may even be enforced by the threat of sanctions. The action pattern shown is then inherently unstable. It will change as soon as it is

---

[3] For the concept of 'ordo salutis', originating from the old-protestant orthodoxy, see Marquardt (1990, 29-53).

perceived by the agent to be against self-interest. On the other hand, decent and praiseworthy social behaviour can also be the product of altruism in its diverse forms; and thus have a relatively stable basis. The question of what it is that changes under divine influence should therefore be answered primarily in terms of motivational structure. At stake is man's practical identity. This identity is a complex whole, constituted not only by deeply rooted desires and traits, but also by fundamental beliefs of a factual and normative nature.[4]

Now that some light has been shed on the direction and object of change, we turn next to the subject - or agency - of change, that is God. God's relationship with the world can be conceived in, at least, two different ways. Let us call them theological realism and theological nonrealism respectively. First, one could assume that a believer who talks with and about God refers to a reality which is ultimately independent of her and the world in which she lives. To be sure, God is related to the world, as its creator and redeemer, for instance; but he is not reducible to it. Talk about God cannot be interpreted merely as a way of talking about life in the world. For example, the assertion that God has created heaven and earth does not only express a certain attitude to the world, but it also contains a factual claim concerning the origin of world and (human) life. Likewise, the assertion that God transforms human beings is to be taken as expressing a factual claim. In statements such as these God is referred to as an existing entity, a real agent. This is in rough outline the position of a theological realist.[5]

Is it, then, possible to look upon God as a nonreal agent? The answer to this question is yes. It brings us to the alternative way in which the relationship of God and the world can be conceived. The position of the theological nonrealist has already been foreshadowed in the denials by which the theological realist's view was characterized. The meaning of the word 'God' is bound up with the religious - in our case: christian - context in which it is used. Its natural environment is eucharist and prayer, preaching and exhorta-

---

4 Cp. Wong (1988, 330): '... practical identity just is the set of attributes of the self that provides an individual with a practical orientation. This orientation is a kind of constant frame that fixes the parameters of practical deliberation. It is the set of motivational factors - firmest normative beliefs, primary desires, goals and traits - that we hold constant in the course of practical deliberation ...'
5 To prevent misunderstanding, there are varying forms of theological realism ranging from naive to subtle. For a subtle form, see Soskice (1985, esp. ch. 7 and 8).

tion. Practices such as these deeply influence the way in which the christian, both as subject and object of these practices, understands his or her life in the world. When talking about God, the believer does not claim ontological status for God, either implicitly or explicitly. The word 'God' does not refer to a being which exists independently of the human world. God is the main character in the continuing story which has been told in the christian Church since the coming of Jesus of Nazareth. God does not exist outside this story. He does not evoke the story by making himself present in the world. On the contrary, it is the story which evokes him and makes him present in the world. So, when it is said of God that he transforms human beings, the statement should not be understood as if he - as a real, independent agent - brings about a change in them. Rather it is the story about God which influences people. The change is effected by the story, not by a God who exists independently of the story.

Initially we ignore this latter way of conceiving the relationship of God and the world. In what now follows, the basic position of the theological realist is presupposed.

2.4 DOES GOD EFFECT NO REAL CHANGE FOR THE GOOD?

Before entering upon our main question, we have to face the possibility that a divine transformation of human beings is denied. We shall pass over the atheist's position. We can easily agree with him that God cannot bring about a change in us if he does not exist. The more interesting question, however, is what his influence on people is if he does exist. The atheist, by the way, does not have to deny that a human being can be changed for the good; and that this transformation is sincerely ascribed to God by the person in question. But sincerity, he would rightly maintain, is no guarantee of truth.

Now there are people who believe in God and yet defend the thesis that God does not effect a real change for the good in any human being. It may come as a surprise that this stance is taken by some classical theists (and theological realists). The theological reasoning behind it is, however, not without cogency. It is to be found particularly in the Lutheran tradition.[6]

---

[6] For Luther, see Deuser (1987, 37-39), the section on the problem of 'iustitia aliena'. As to the Lutheran tradition in general, one could first of all think of Matthias Flacius

The heart of the matter is that God does not bring about a change in a human being, but a change for him or her. In other words, God does not make people righteous, but rather declares them to be righteous. People in the state of grace remain sinners. God, however, regards them as being in Christ. He identifies them with Christ. Christ's righteousness, his goodness is imputed to them. In this way, men and women are looked upon by God as righteous, as good. It is not a question of their being good. The righteousness which is imputed to them remains a iustitia aliena, that is, literally, another's righteousness, namely Christ's. In this life, goodness never becomes a property of a human being.

How is this theological position to be assessed? In support of it one could adduce biblical material especially from the Pauline letters. But apart from that, it takes the edge off a traditional sceptical argument against the christian faith: believers do not live up to their claim of being redeemed people.[7] The reply is that believers are not morally better people than nonbelievers. Rather they are in a better condition vis à vis God - they are better off - than their nonbelieving fellow-human beings, because they look better in God's eye. God sees them as being sanctified in Christ. It is a classical theme which can be heard in many an orthodox-protestant sermon up to the present day. From a pastoral point of view, an important consideration is that this position preserves a believer from despair or resignation. For the gospel does not morally demand the psychologically impossible from a human being. Moreover, it prevents a christian from falling too easily prey to false pretensions and self-deception.[8]

Nevertheless, however interesting this view of the relationship of God and man in the state of grace might be, and however positive its effects, there are telling arguments against it. In the first place there is strong scriptural testimony in favour of the transformation thesis. Because its opponent can also appeal to the Bible, I will not insist on the point. Another and stronger

---

(1520-1575) and the so called Gnesiolutherans.

[7] 'Christians should look more like people who have been redeemed.' The aphorism which, going by my memory, I ascribed to Nietzsche could not be traced in his works, neither by me nor by some Nietzsche experts whom I consulted. However, they could confirm its essential authenticity.

[8] For striking examples of false pretensions and self-deception, see Passmore (1970, 140-143).

argument is the following. As a rule, the theologian who rejects the idea of man being really changed for the good by God, asserts that God does not impute Christ's righteousness to all human beings, but only to those who have faith. Man, however, does not become a believer by his or her own efforts. Faith is God's gift. As John Calvin says (1960, 541), 'faith is the principal work of [God] the Holy Spirit'. In this saying Calvin is representative of the whole christian tradition, Catholics and Lutherans included. So it seems that our theologian can deny God's transforming work in man only on pain of inconsistency. He might attempt to remove the apparent inconsistency by making a distinction between a human being's faith and his or her actions in the world. The former would be effected by God. At this point our theologian would wholeheartedly side with the tradition. But, according to him, it is out of the question that God would bring about a change in the way man acts in the world.

In this manner, however, the relation between thought and action is misconceived. Man's practical identity which was earlier regarded as the primary object of divinely inspired change is moulded, among other things, by his fundamental thought about himself and the world in which he lives. When this thought is subject to change, other elements of the person's practical identity are changing with it. Ultimately the inner transformation will reveal itself in the way he or she acts. Ceteris paribus, someone who has come to believe that the world, and her life in it, is being guided by a God who is just and merciful, gracious and powerful in his love, will be more inclined not to lie to fellow human beings, not to deceive or otherwise harm them than somebody who looks upon the world as a jungle and upon life as a struggle for survival. Even if, in the former case, the person's publicly observable behaviour would not change after coming to faith - she did not lie, deceive etc. then, as she does not do now - this does not mean that she acts in the same way before and after her conversion. On a more fundamental level her actions could be described differently. While, before her conversion, her actions could be characterized as forms of prudence, now, after her coming to faith, they are expressive of her love of God and neighbour and of her new sense of justice.[9] For that matter, the publicans and

---

[9] The argument which was developed in section one to the effect that people showing the same behaviour do not necessarily perform the same actions, now appears to be valid just as well when the same behaviour over time of only a single person is concerned.

whores who met Jesus make perfectly clear that even publicly observable behaviour might change as a result of faith and conversion.

So, within the context of theological realism, there does not seem to be sufficient ground for the denial of the idea that God effects a real change for the good in human beings. On the contrary, the weight of the arguments points in the opposite direction. Let us therefore return to our main question. How can we best account for the way God brings about that change?

2.5 GOD AND HUMAN TRANSFORMATION: THE FIAT MODEL

My thinking about this problem has been much stimulated by William Alston's (1989, 223-252) essay on 'The Indwelling of the Holy Spirit'. In it the American philosopher introduces three models for the analysis of the work of the Holy Spirit within human beings: the fiat model, the interpersonal model and the sharing model. According to the fiat model, there is an analogy between God's action in creating the world and his action in the sanctification of man. As God created the world ex nihilo, just by willing that there be light - fiat lux - a firmament and the rest, so he creates in man a new heart or, in other words, a new motivational structure. While the person concerned first led a self centered life turned away from God and her neighbour, God now brings about a new beginning - a new life - within her, for her, but also without her. This particular human being is 'born again', and a 'new creation'. The formulations used indicate already that this model finds support in biblical testimony. For Alston, this is reason enough not to reject it out of hand.

Another argument in favour of the fiat model is that it is confirmed by dramatic conversion histories in the christian (literary) tradition. Besides, there is no ground for the assumption that God could not change (part of) the practical identity of a human being in such a manner. Anyway, he is able to do it; and 'at least sometimes' he might in fact do it (Alston 1989, 231-233). However, it is hardly conceivable that this is God's usual way of dealing with people. So, what then is, according to Alston, objectionable to the fiat model? First of all there is the consideration that God has created man to be a person with all the characteristics belonging to that status. The capacity for free choice is among the most important of these. As persons, human beings co-determine the way their inner and outer life develops. The 'co' in 'co-determine' matters much to Alston. Because a person's motivational structure and, more broadly, the course of her life are determined by a great many other factors besides her own free actions. Even apart from an intervening God, man is anything but a self creating agent. Alston is, therefore, not willing to discard the fiat model for the sole reason that it encroaches upon human freedom. God's unilateral action by which a human being's practical identity is (partly) changed does indeed limit his freedom of action, but it does not destroy it. Alston acknowledges that the restriction of human freedom which is involved in the fiat model might be held against it. But the objection is, in itself, not prohibitive.[10]

Another objection is this. When God changes a human being, it unmistakably takes him in most cases a lot of time. Now thinking from the fiat model it remains in the dark why the transformation is extended over such a long period. Why does God usually do such an incomplete job? (Alston 1989, 239). The third objection is connected with the divine-human relationship as portrayed in Scripture and Tradition. God's purpose in the creation of human beings is the establishment of a personal relationship with them. God is seeking communion with man. God's gift to man, the Spirit, 'is not a spirit of slavery ... but a Spirit that makes us sons, enabling us to cry Abba! Father!', so cites Alston the apostle Paul. The problem is that if God is after a personal relationship with us, the fiat model is not the most appropriate model to clarify the way in which God transforms us. It is hardly conceivable that God will not take our freedom very seriously if he is so much interested in the establishment of a personal relationship with us. And it is precisely this freedom which is endangered in the fiat model. Without expressing himself so strongly, Alston (1989, 234) does see the point. Hence his introduction of the interpersonal model.

2.6 THE INTERPERSONAL MODEL

This model implies that God proceeds in his work of man's sanctification in the way a human being tries to influence a fellow human being with whom he or she stands in a particular relation. Thus God can call somebody to repentance, obedience and a new life of love, for example by means of a

---

[10] The foregoing is a reconstruction of Alston's argument from different parts of his essay, see Alston (1989, 228-230, 234-235).

sermon or some other personal or impersonal medium. While in cases such as these God is identified as the caller, he can also exert influence in a more hidden way on man's practical identity. Thus, he could bring it about that someone comes to see his present life as shallow and empty, and a life of love and devotion to God and neighbour as attractive. Or God could provide a role model in the person of Christ which inspires to a life of imitation. To mention still another of the many possibilities which Alston envisages within the boundaries of this model, God 'could make new resources available for the individual, new resources of strength of will, of energy for perseverance in the face of discouragement' (Alston 1989, 235, 236).[11]

Characteristic of this model is that God is not pictured - as was the case in the fiat model - as directly bringing about a positive change in a human being, for the person concerned but also without her. Rather, God is trying to affect people. He attempts to exert a positive influence on them, again for them but this time not without them. The model, therefore, at first sight accords better with human freedom and integrity than the fiat model. Still it is, as presented by Alston, not without problems. In the first place, it seems that God is a kind of manipulator and the question is whether there is logical space in an interpersonal model for manipulation of one of the partners by the other. Surely, things, and by no means persons, are object of manipulation? Secondly, if it is granted that there is logical space for manipulation in the model, then the question is whether the model is not falling apart when used to clarify the relationship of God and man - and almighty God is the manipulator. Alston's answer to the first question can be reconstructed in the light of what has been said in the context of his criticism of the fiat model. It is a matter of fact that people influence each other, people standing in a personal relationship not excluded. They try mutually to evoke reactions with each other; reactions of a cognitive, conative and emotional kind which might or might not be under control of the person being affected. If there is no control, then manipulation occurs. So there is no reason to think that a personal relationship should be seen as protected from manipulation. I think that Alston reasoning along these lines is in fact right. But he seems to

---

11 The work of the British theologian G.W.H. Lampe (Lampe 1977) is mentioned by Alston as a 'live example of this [interpersonal] way of approaching the matter'. Is not Augustine an even better - i.e. more direct (personal testimony) and more classical - example? Think of his Confessions in which all the ways of divine influence mentioned by Alston are impressively described.

overlook an important thing. Within the interpersonal model the moral space available for manipulation varies between the diverse relations. For example, it is smaller in a love relationship between adults than in a parent-child relationship. Human freedom should be respected more in the first case than in the latter. But in virtually each personal relationship there are moral limits to manipulation.[12]

As to the question whether the interpersonal model can be squared with a manipulating omnipotent God, this problem is ignored by Alston. His only remark is that as a person God has 'infinitely greater resources for the task', i.e. of transforming people (Alston 1989, 236). But this exactly is the crux. It is linked directly with the criticism which was mentioned first in connection with the fiat model and then in the context of Alston's interpretation of the interpersonal model: human freedom seems to be in serious danger. So the crucial question is how human freedom can be preserved when almighty God is transforming human beings. I shall deal with this question presently.

2.7 THE SHARING MODEL

The reason why Alston turns to a third model for the clarification of God's sanctifying work in man is not the drastic limitation of human freedom in the fiat and - presumably - the interpersonal models. Rather, it is the failure of the latter models to show that God acts within human beings in transforming them. In both the fiat and the interpersonal model, God is external to them. He works at a distance, separated from the people he wants to change. Why does Alston hold this as an objection against these models? The criteria which he uses to test the adequacy of the various models are, first, Scripture (New Testament) and Tradition (Church) and, second, the religious experience of christians in past and present. Both suggest often a much more

---

[12] Can God be thought as respecting moral limits in his dealings with human beings? The answer is a straightforward yes. God's goodness implies his moral perfection. The more interesting questions are (1) whether these limits are internal or external to his will (I would say internal); and (2) whether God's actions are bound by these limits or, rather, are always done, as a matter of fact, within these limits. For the latter option, see Morris (1987, 107-121). These remarks should not be understood as implying a doctrine of special revelation concerning the knowledge of those moral limits.

internal or intimate relationship between God and man than either the fiat or the interpersonal model allows for. (Think of biblical expressions like the 'indwelling of the Holy Spirit', the Spirit 'being poured out' into us, and people coming 'to share in the very being of God'.) That is why Alston proposes the sharing model. It accords better with the particular data (Alston 1989, 239-244).[13]

The question now is how the transformation of human beings should be understood along the lines of this model. To begin with, the divine nature, or the divine life, is the object in which a person shares when being sanctified. This sharing, however, is not like having, to a certain extent, some of the same properties as God. For example, I love to some extent as God loves; I am merciful partly as God is merciful. Such an interpretation would make the present model vulnerable to the same criticism that was levelled at the other: God remains external to man. There is a partial correspondence between divine and human properties. But no life is shared. We should rather think of a mutual interpenetration. Alston's leading idea is that of two people whose brains have been connected up. As a result the thoughts, feelings and attitudes of either of them is directly accessible to the other. On the other hand, the model does not imply that the human person is taken up in God. A wholesale identification is out of the question. Otherwise we should fall back into a taking over model which was rejected by Alston from the start. If a human being would merge into God - a thought which might be provoked by Paul's saying: '...it is no longer I who live, but Christ who lives in me' (Gal. 2:20) - he or she would lose personal identity. And, as is clear from the context, this could not have been Paul's intention. Moreover, a relationship of love between God and man would be impossible. God would be without a partner who can love him and by whom he can be loved. A third argument against the taking over model is that the phenomenon of sin, which does not disappear from the life of a believer, is inexplainable. There would be no place for it in a believer's life if that life had been taken over by Christ (or the Spirit). From this latter objection against the taking over model a further specification of Alston's sharing model can be derived. It

---

[13] As for the data of religious experience, Alston argues elsewhere in a subtle and lucid way for the possibility that people have direct experience of God in their lives, see Alston (1983, 103-134); see also his more recent magnum opus in epistemology (Alston 1991).

must be consistent with the idea that the divine transformation of man has a gradual and partial character (Alston 1989, 228, 244-246).

What else can be said about the manner God brings about a change for the good in a person's life according to the present model? How can God change people's practical identities by letting them share in his nature, his life? Suppose someone has a rather loveless and callous character. How can God transform these traits into their opposite? Alston offers two options. First, God wills that the person in question shares in his loving and merciful nature and as a result the full change occurs. Sharing these divine traits is sufficient for having them. This interpretation comes close to the fiat model. The important difference, however, is that God does not remain external to the person being transformed. The result of the other option is that the person's sharing of divine love and mercy amounts to something less than fully possessing these traits, while at the same time amounting to something that can be a push or a tendency in that direction. This can be achieved by God letting the person be aware of his loving and merciful tendencies in the same direct way that she is aware of her own. This is the more cognitive approach. But God could also directly introduce into her conative system initially weak and isolated tendencies of his love and mercy. Thus God would have 'a foot in the conative as well as in the cognitive door; it would be ... a beachhead from which the progressive conquest of the individual's motivational system could get a start' (Alston 1989, 248-251).

2.8   EVALUATION AND CRITICISM

As we have seen, Alston had a reason for introducing the sharing model. Neither the fiat nor the interpersonal model could give a satisfying account of God's work of sanctification as it is presented in Scripture and Tradition. God remains too external, too much at a distance from man.

My question is whether this externality detracts from the value of the divine human relationship. If this is not the case, are we then forced by the biblical (and other) data to embrace the sharing model? Notice that Alston did not deny that Scripture can be called upon in support of the taking over model.[14] Yet, he did not hesitate to reject it for systematic reasons. Likewise, I have my doubts about the sharing model in spite of the fact that it does not lack biblical support. On systematic grounds the interpersonal model is to be preferred above the sharing model. The former model allows better for, and gives a better account of, the relationship of love and friendship which God wants to establish with the human individual. Human lovers and friends are not capable of literally sharing a life. There might be profound mutual knowledge, intimacy and even a far-reaching mutual identification. Also fundamental unanimity and like-mindedness belong to the possibilities. Not, however, a literal merging of lives. Does this impossibility detract from the value of their relationship of love and friendship? On the contrary, it seems to be a necessary condition for such a personal relationship; and the more so when God and man are the partners. Since God and man are that much unequal, especially unequal in power, the possibility of seeing their relationship as one of love becomes doubtful indeed, if God would literally share in the life of the human partner.

The power difference between God and man brings the discussion round to another point of criticism. It applies to all three models of human transformation as presented by Alston. A love relationship is inconceivable without the mutual freedom of the partners involved. Freedom is a necessary condition, constitutive of a relationship of love or friendship between human beings. I can offer my love or friendship to another person, but it is up to the other to answer it. In this encounter coercion and (most forms of) manipulation are out of the question. They would destroy the relationship from its very beginning. On the other hand, it is not possible for the other to answer my love if I have not first offered it to him. Thus, there is both mutual freedom and mutual dependence in a love relationship. Now, the same is true of a love relationship between God and man. It too is characterized by mutual freedom and mutual dependence. It goes without saying that this relationship is not entirely symmetrical. God created the possibility and he has taken the initiative. Human beings owe their existence as free persons to God who has shown his love for us 'in that while we were yet sinners Christ died for us' (Rom. 5:8). Another point of asymmetry is that God, unlike

---

14 Not only Scripture, I would add, but also data from the - often heterodox - tradition. See Passmore (1970, 135-136, 142-143).

man, is immutably faithful in his love: 'if we are faithless, he remains faithful - for he cannot deny himself' (2 Tim. 2:13).[15]

On the assumption that this is true, God will be very reluctant in the use of his power while transforming human beings. If he does not want the intended love relationship with them to degenerate into a purely manipulative relationship, he will have to limit his power in his proceedings with them. It is then hardly thinkable that God will effect psychological changes within human beings in a manner as suggested by the fiat model. In order to avoid this conclusion one could play down the divine intention of establishing a love relationship with human beings. Instead of emphasizing that particular intention one could argue that God's primary intention as regards human beings is the effectuation of their goodness, or even their sanctity and perfection. And to this end God deploys his power. He brings about unilaterally changes in their motivational structure in accordance with the fiat model. However, not only the love relationship between God and man is greatly endangered in this line of thought. Even more is at stake: human freedom. I have already hinted at its problematic status in the fiat model when dealing with Alston's presentation of the model. Granted that Alston is right in arguing that human freedom is not annihilated in the fiat model, the freedom which is left is extremely restricted, if not empty. It is a freedom of choice in circumstances such that both the action opportunities for the human agent outside him, and the action tendencies - his dispositions to act - inside him are determined by God. And if not strictly determined, at least controlled by him. Because when God does not intervene in the motivational structure of a human agent (or in his or her action opportunities), this too happens according to his fiat. The fiat model calls up almost of itself the ghost of theological - or better: divine - determinism.[16]

---

15 It has been assumed in this paragraph and before that the love relationship between God and man should be understood primarily in terms of friendship (Greek: philia) and not in terms of passion. For more about this, see Van den Beld (1989, 530-534). Further, to avoid a possible misunderstanding, I do not think that the divine human relationship can only be described by means of the friendship metaphor. In some respects, e.g. when the establishment or the repairment of the relationship is concerned, other metaphors are more adequate, for example that of parent and child, and that of the beggar. See for the latter, Van den Brink (1993, 236-240).

16 In the sense that God has not only power, as Nelson Pike (1983, 20) puts it, 'to determine the occurrence or nonoccurrence of any possible event but ... does in fact determine whatever it is in the universe that actually happens.' Pike refers, to my

The interpersonal model accords at first sight better with the love relationship between God and man, as set forth above. But even here, at least in Alston's interpretation of the model, the danger is not entirely absent that the personal relation of God and man degenerates into a manipulative one. The danger is less obvious than in the fiat model, but it is no less real. For God, using his tremendous power, is able to expose people to all kinds of influences which they are incapable of controlling. In that case God might not be said to directly effect changes in human beings, all the same he is manipulating them. Now I could agree earlier with Alston that personal relations must not in all cases be exempt from manipulation or the exertion of influence by one of the partners on the other. Even a relationship of love and friendship does not exclude all forms of manipulation. But if there is ever a cause for respecting mutually the freedom of persons then it is so when persons enter into, or stand in, a relationship of love and friendship. And this is no less true when God and man are the partners concerned. The freedom to be respected should be conceived more strongly than as a mere freedom of choice such that both the situation in which the human agent acts, and his motivational system leading up to his choice, are completely out of his - and entirely within God's - control. Of course, no human being is the sole creator of his or her motivational structure (or, more broadly, practical identity), as he or she is not the unique creator of the circumstances in which must be acted, either. But, on the other hand, it cannot be the case that the person in question has not freely contributed anything to his motivational structure, nor to the situation in which he finds himself. Thus a necessary condition for the acceptability of the interpersonal model is a concept of God in which he has greatly limited his power in his dealings with human beings.[17]

After the foregoing I can be short in my comment on the sharing model. Apart from the problem of how to conceive a literal sharing in the divine life or nature by a human being, it too suffers from a lack of freedom for man in his relation with God. This is especially so in the fiat version of the model. The 'bridgehead' (or 'beachhead') version is not that drastic in its infringe-

---

knowledge correctly, to Calvin for this view of determinism.

17 For an argument to the effect that the concept of divine omnipotence does not exclude a limitation of power willed by God himself, see Anglin (1990, 64-69). For historical references to such a concept, and for an argument in favour of understanding God's limitation of his omnipotence in terms of a divine self-restraint of his power, see Sarot (1992, 172-185).

ment of human freedom, but it does imply an unacceptable form of manipulation. Because, though what is implanted by God in a human being is not a complete trait indeed, yet it is a part of his divine nature. And though it is done for that particular person, all the same it happens without him or her. And that is a bridge too far.

A final qualifying remark at the end of this section. The objections raised against divine interventions in, and manipulations of, the practical identity of a human being would be met considerably if they would follow upon that person's free prayer to God for change.[18]

2.9 THEOLOGICAL NONREALISM AND HUMAN TRANSFORMATION

I do not want to end this contribution without saying something about the possibility of a divine transformation of human beings as seen from the position of theological nonrealism. In spite of the differences between representatives of this position, there is a characteristic point which is common to all.

When God is changing people for the good, he should not be looked upon as an external agent who somehow acts upon them from the outside. The divine human relationship in which God transforms man must be understood as an internal relationship. What is meant by this 'internal relationship'? Alston, being a theological realist, also criticized God's externality over against man in both the fiat and interpersonal models. And did not he prefer the sharing model because, in line with that model, God is seen as working on man's transformation from within? That is surely correct. However, in Alston's view of the matter God does not lose the character of a real agent with his own nature and life. God is willing to share part of his life and nature with human beings; to become internal to them. But he remains a unique, independent being. The nonrealist, on the other hand, denies the ontological independence and primacy of God, or, at least, has serious reservations about it.

---

18 Eleonore Stump (1988, 395-420) argues along this line in a subtle way for the possibility that God intervenes in the formation of the human will without encroaching upon that will's freedom.

According to him, God exists in the life world of human beings. The God of the Bible is present in the practices of Jewish and Christian communities. His existence is bound up with those communities. His real presence is to be sought there. Because it is in those communities that, from one generation to the other, stories are told and rites are performed in which God is the main character. Every time the stories are told and the rites are performed, in the old or in a new way, people might be 'affected' by them. If this happens in the right way, people are influenced by God - in a manner of speaking. They are being changed into a 'new being'.[19] They become better people or are prevented under life's pressures from moral backsliding. Dewi Phillips (1992, 155) has clarified the internal relationship of God and man as intended by the theological nonrealist with an example. It also sheds light on how the nonrealist understands God's moral influence on man: '... when I say that my father watches over me, I ... [am not thinking] of anything akin to a policeman in the sky. What I am referring to first, is a life worthy of contemplation. Second I think of myself as answerable to him for my conduct in ways which did not end with his death. Thus, thirdly, I believe that if I behave in certain ways, I shall be unworthy in his sight.' The existence of God need not be ontologically more real than the existence of a dead person who was very much loved and respected during his lifetime. But that does not mean that God is not able to change the life of a human being for the good.

Other nonrealists do not go as far as the British philosopher in their reduction of God's ontological status. The American theologian Gordon Kaufman is reluctant on epistemological grounds in ascribing ontological status to God. According to him, we cannot know whether the word 'God' refers to a real being; whether there is reality behind the conceptual constructions which we connect with 'God'. In one of his earlier publications he states that belief in God is not so much a matter of knowledge. Rather it is voluntary devotion to God and to the community which speaks about him, and it is hope of 'increasing reorientation of the self'. Understood in this way, that is as 'expression more of a life-policy than possession of an esoteric item of information, the phrase "I believe in God", may still be affirmed' (Kaufman 1972, 250). Later he is no less sceptical of the possibility to refer with the word 'God' to anything at all, and of the human capacity to acquire knowledge of the object referred to. God might still be described

---

19 Cp. Paul Tillich's (1955, 15-24) sermon on 'The new Being'.

as 'that ultimate mystery in which both our being and our fulfilment are grounded'. But on the other hand he states that God is 'beyond our knowledge and understanding'. This scepticism, however, does not prevent him from stressing the significance which God-talk has for human transformation (Kaufman 1989, 43-44).[20] In Sally McFague's metaphorical theology the referential meaning and descriptive content of the images and models of God are reduced to almost nothing. We do not know if and how our God metaphor refers to somebody or something. The assumption that it refers to a power 'which is on the side of life and its fulfilment' is a gamble: 'At the most one wagers it does [refer] and lives as if it does' (McFague 1987, 195-196).

The nonrealist conception of a divine transformation of human beings is, of course, not only to be found in the English speaking world. To give but one example from another context, the contemporary German theologian Hermann Deuser (1987, 54) states that 'God's action [in the sanctification and redemption of man and the world] should not be thought of as a supernatural intervention of some superior power. On the contrary, God's action should be conceived of as present, in a hidden way, in our experience of life, in the religious subjectivity of feeling as well as in our daily life's experiences of contrast'.[21] In other words, God and his actions are part of (religious) man's experience of life and the world. This should not be understood exclusively or primarily as an epistemological point, that is as an answer to the question of how we know about God's actions in our life. But more as an ontological point: God and his actions are part of man's interpreted experience.

For theological nonrealists the emphasis is on the nonreferential and nondescriptive meanings of the language with which people speak about and to God. People express in their religious and theological language something of themselves and of their relation to each other and to the world in which they live. They commit themselves to a certain attitude to the world and their fellow human beings, and to a certain way of life. And they call upon others to share this attitude and this way of life with them. Thus nonrealists do not

---

20 See also Kaufman (1981).
21 'Gottes Handeln ... ist nicht als übernaturliches Eingreifen einer wie immer vorgestellten höheren Macht zu denken, sondern als verborgen anwesend in unserer Existenzerfahrung, in der religiösen Subjektivität des Nachempfindens ... ebenso wie in den Differenzerfahrungen unserer Existenz.'

have to deny that God changes people for the good. However, the subject which transforms them is not the divine being which exists independently of us and our world. Rather, it is the tradition, the stories, the preaching and the rites in which God is one of the dramatis personae, which exert the positive influence. In the context of theological realism it is God himself who brings about the human transformation either directly or indirectly by all kinds of means. Whereas in nonrealism it is those means which are the virtual agent of transformation.

2.10 EVALUATION

Theological nonrealism is an answer to the intellectual challenge which was put to the christian faith by western culture stamped as it is by modern science and learning. The classical idea of an almighty and all-good God is, at first sight, hardly compatible with the knowledge and experience of educated modern people. To some it looks like as if, in Gustafson's (1981, 190) words, 'we have a Ptolemaic religion in a Copernican universe.' It seems to them to be necessary that the coherence between theology and modern, intellectual culture be restored. This could be done by a radical reinterpretation of christian thought about God in his relation with man and the world. The nonrealist has felt the need and filled it. The result of the operation is, however, a loss of substance and relevance of the christian faith. We have already dealt with the loss of substance. The christian who thinks along the lines of nonrealism is more or less deprived of God as a real being, as really existing. As to the loss of relevance, the following can be said (of course, within the limits of the present topic). A theological non-realist does not have to reject out of hand the classical christian belief in a divine transformation of human beings. He or she is able to give a new, coherent interpretation of it. However, as soon as this new interpretation is dawning upon an involved member of the christian community, the loss of meaning and relevance is discovered. I am praying for moral change: 'Create in me a clean hart, o God, and put a new and right spirit within me' (Psalm 51:10). I realize suddenly that I am not asking God to change me. What I am actually doing is expressing the wish to be a different, better person. The words do have their impact on me having been raised in a profoundly christian community. The community itself and its biblical tradition which has been handed down from one generation to the other do not fail to have their influence on me either. But God himself cannot have any effect on me. Thus loss of substance is coupled with loss of relevance. Is it inevitable that those losses are suffered?

REFERENCES

Alston, W.P., Christian Experience and Christian Belief. In: A. Plantinga, N. Wolterstorff (eds.), *Faith and Rationality. Reason and Belief in God*, Notre Dame 1983, 103-134.

Alston, W.P., The Indwelling of the Holy Spirit. In: Alston, *Divine Nature and Human Language. Essays in Philosophical Theology*, Ithaca 1989, 223-252.

Alston, W.P., *Perceiving God. The Epistemology of Religious Experience*, Ithaca 1991.

Anglin, W.S., *Free Will and the Christian Faith*, Oxford 1990.

Beld, A. van den, Does an Adequate Morality Need a Theistic Context? In: G. van den Brink a.o. (eds.), *Christian Faith and Philosophical Theology. Essays in Honour of Vincent Brümmer*, Kampen 1992, 22-38.

Beld, A. van den, Non Posse Peccare: On the Inability to Sin in Eternal Life. *Religious Studies* 25(1989), 521-535.

Brink, G. van den, *Almighty God. A Study of Divine Omnipotence*, Kampen 1993.

Calvin, J., *Institutes of the Christian Religion*. Edited by John T. McNeill. (Volumes XX and XXI of the Library of Christian Classics), Philadelphia 1960.

Cunningham, R.L. (ed.), *Situationism and the New Morality*, New York, 1970.

Deuser, H., Gottes Handeln - Rechtfertigung, Versöhnung und Erlösung. In: W. Härle, R. Preul (Hrsg.), *Marburger Jahrbuch Theologie I*, Marburg 1987, 33-55.

Gustafson, J.M., *Ethics from a Theocentric Perspective*, Volume I, Chicago 1981.

Kaufman, G.D., *God the Problem*, Harvard University Press 1972.

Kaufman, G.D., *The Theological Imagination. Constructing the Concept of God*, Philadelphia 1981.

Kaufman, G.D., 'Evidentialism': A Theologian's Response. *Faith and Philosophy* 6(1989), 35-46.

Lampe, G.W.H., *God as Spirit*, Oxford 1977.

Marquardt, M., Die Vorstellungen des 'Ordo Salutis' in ihrer Funktion für die Lebensführung des Glaubenden. In: W. Härle, R. Preul (Hrsg.), *Marburger Jahrbuch Theologie* III - Lebensführung, Marburg 1990, 29-53.

McFague, S. *Models of God. Theology for an Ecological, Nuclear Age*, London 1987.

Morris, Th.V., Duty and Divine Goodness. In: Th.V. Morris (ed.), *The Concept of God*, Oxford 1987, 107-122.

Passmore, P. *The Perfectibility of Man*, New York 1970.

Phillips, D.Z., Between Faith and Metaphysics. In: Van den Brink e.a. (eds.), *Christian Faith and Philosophical Theology*, 146-158.

Pike, N., Over-Power and God's Responsibility for Sin. In: A.J. Freddoso (ed.), *The Existence and Nature of God*, Notre Dame 1983, 11-35.

ANDOVER-HARVARD
THEOLOGICAL LIBRARY

PURCHASED FROM THE INCOME
OF THE BEQUEST OF

MRS. LOUISA J. HALL
Widow of Edward Brooks Hall, M.D.,
Divinity School, Class of 1824
Mother of Edward H. Hall
Divinity School, Class of 1851

n den Brink e.a. (eds.), *Christian Faith*

, and Frankfurt's Concept of Free Will.

B. Hebblethwaite, S. Sutherland (eds.),
ology, Cambridge 1982, 153-167.

eeger, M. Verweij, *Ethiek in Praktijk*,

ntity. In: P.A. French e.a. (eds.), *Ethical
es in Philosophy*, Vol. XIII, Notre Dame

Comments

Karl-Wilhelm Merks

When one looks at a painting through coloured spectacles, certain details will be more prominent than without such an alienating instrument. In the following comment, I will look at Van den Beld's argument through spectacles that are coloured by the Catholic tradition. From the point of view of someone who has been educated in this tradition, I will make some remarks on his article.

1 It is evident that Van den Beld does not try to argue that theological realism could be proved to have a more solid basis than theological non-realism regarding God's relationship to the world. For that matter we refer to what F. Böckle (1977, 70 ff.) said about the compatibility of belief in God and moral autonomy: although they fit together, and although in his view moral autonomy would have an even better foundation if God is postulated as the cause of human freedom, this compatibility can never be used as a kind of modern proof of the existence of God. When is understood that there is no necessary disjunction between God and the modern idea of human autonomy, a lot has been gained already. Given the tragic history of the relationship between faith and the modern ideal of freedom, I consider it important indeed to reflect on the relation between faith and human freedom, and, subsequently, on the relation between faith and morality.

   However, this reflection does not and should not automatically mean that the religious justifiability of our modern anthropocentric attitude to life is questioned, as one is apt to do these days. On the contrary: such a questioning more often than not undermines the traditional image of God and sometimes even God Himself. The direction of thought should be rather the inverse. Our reflections should be led by the question why we somehow do not seem to be able yet to combine our image of God - and not the least the theological-realistic conception of it - with the inevitable anthropocentrism we experience in daily life. Human freedom and power, which display themselves in the ever growing influence of man on the world, do not necessarily exclude the idea of a God as the bearing ground for everything that is. Modern thought is tainted with the sad inheritance of the competition model; in this conception, God's power and freedom is understood as irreconcilable with human power and freedom. God and man are wrongly considered to be of the same order. Where one is, the other cannot be, what belongs to one, cannot belong to the other.

In scholastic thought, which teaches that the Creator as causa prima instigates beings (causae secundae) to develop themselves in an active way, the problem of the relation between God and man is approached in a totally different manner. God is the principle of life of everything that exists as His creation, and He gives it the possibility to develop itself, if I may say so. It follows then, that any doctrine of creation should provide an answer to the question of freedom, as freedom belongs to human nature, but alongside and thanks to God's omnipotence. This problem brought Thomas Aquinas to some almost paradoxical statements, such as the remark that God's all-ruling providence is beyond doubt, but that this providence signifies precisely that He gave man 'in manu consilii sui' (Sir 15, 14), that is, he gave man his own judgement (Merks 1983, 161-179). Man must organize his own life and be his own governor. Divine rule means that God governs man 'libere' (freely), as suits his nature ('prout competit suae naturae' STH I-II, 4 ad1). Karl Rahner, speaking more generally about the image of God, formulated this as follows: 'Gott wirkt die Welt, nicht aber eigentlich wirkt er in der Welt' - 'God brings about the world, but properly speaking he does not act in the world' (1976, 94).

From this perspective, one should seriously rethink the reconcilability of theological realism and non-realism, positions that Van den Beld seems to understand as more or less opposed. One should especially discuss the question whether revelation is from a totally different order than the 'natural' processes of (created) reality, or whether it is rather something that pervades these processes. If the latter is true, everything that happens on a 'natural' level, can always at the same time be the epiphany of the

Divine. I won't discuss this problem in general terms, however, but concretize it with respect to its ethical implications.

2   I consider it of vital importance that morality cannot be understood properly when only the idea of freedom of decision is taken into account. Morality also has an objectum: the content of that which moral freedom of decision is - morally - guided by. In the tradition, this is called 'the good'; something that can be conceived as having a certain 'objective' quality. Of course, morality has to do with freedom, with defining one's own position. But it is also true that this position is determined by a certain standard that presents itself; this standard is the good, which attracts us and at the same time forces itself upon us.

Modern moral theology, in sofar as it tries to give the idea of autonomy a theological foundation, follows the best of its own tradition when it considers the good to be autonomous. That is to say, the good does not depend on the identity of some authority, not even the will of God. The good is that which fits in with and contributes to a truly happy human existence. From the ethical point of view, the good is that which is good for humans. This should not be misunderstood as narrow-minded anthropocentrism, in which only the interests of humans count; it should be understood as that which contributes to the realization of a perfect human existence, to the full development of man's abilities, including the sense of responsibility to respect everything that is entrusted to his stewardship.

This conception of the good always involves an experience of the 'convenit', 'it is fitting'. However, such an experience cannot be forced: the good presents itself as the inevitable. It can only be denied, on pain of the loss of one's deepest identity. In fact, it seems typical of this human identity that experiences of meaningfulness can never be turned into experiences of senselessness without self-deception and loss of one's self. This means in the last resort that experiences of commitment, experiences of being attracted and experiences of meaningfulness go hand in hand. In other words: the experience of commitment is necessarily connected with the experience of being in harmony with the meaning of one's own existence.

3   This outcome, if true, has certain consequences for the ethical question whether God changes people. From an ethical point of view, the answer

can only be positive in the sense that He does so by letting man (also) change himself. Man has to give his own answers, guided by his own sense of what is good and evil. The good presents itself *as such*, i.e. it must be understood in the inner self, and is never given as a pure authority. How and when God interferes in this process cannot be demonstrated; it is, so to speak, an act of faith in itself.

4 Although moral change may be ascribed to inner human processes, we cannot conclude that God, as a result, can never be the cause of this change. 'Gott wirkt die Welt, nicht aber eigentlich wirkt er in der Welt'.

5 Considering that it does make sense to postulate that God changes people for the better, Van den Beld distinguishes between publicly observable behaviour (actions) on the one hand, and intentions on the other. To me, this distinction seems indeed necessary. As I see it, in the discussion about the impact of faith on moral convictions, it is never questioned that there may be differences between people on the level of intentions, depending on whether they believe in God or not, and that therefore on this level people can actually change as a result of their religious faith (or: can change through God). The question is, however, whether this change on the level of intentions leads to a change of actions.

I shall not answer this question here. But I do want to point out that the actions as described by Van den Beld are, of course, not the same as what we traditionally call 'moral behaviour'. Moral behaviour is not observable, physical action; just because it is *moral*, moral behaviour has an (intentional) 'soul'. It is always determined by a number of different factors (fontes moralitatis, i.e. sources of morality: objectum, circumstantiae, intentio). That means that from a moral viewpoint, an adventurous car drive and a rescue are by definition not the same. They may seem identical at first sight, that is to say at the starting point of a moral analysis; though physically similar, they are morally - i.e. considered as moral facts - of a completely different nature. Of course it is thinkable that faith (and God) might be the cause of a moral change on the level of actions. But departing from the conception of an autonomous morality, it should be stressed that no religious process of change for the better can take place without the experience of goodness as such; just an experience of God without an experience of moral goodness is not sufficient here. If

God changes man (morally), He does so through man's own moral insight.

6 We may conclude that the answer to the question whether belief in God - or God himself - could change man for the better, cannot be found in the opposition between non-religious, selfish behaviour, determined by well-conceived self-interest on the one hand, and a presumed, religiously inspired altruism on the other. It seems to make more sense to distinguish and compare two modes of altruism: an unselfish attitude that is based on belief in God, and one - indeed possible - that is not. Wherever belief in God brings about altruism, this means of course, as such, a change for the better. But isn't it also possible that a nonreligious morality is unselfish? Shouldn't such a morality be unselfish, to deserve to be called 'morality'? Thus, the question whether God changes people for the better, and if so: how, had to be posed again in those cases where moral behaviour - without the presence of religious faith - meets the two requirements Van den Beld mentions in his introduction, namely 'preciousness' and performableness.

Translated by Birgit Kooijman

REFERENCES

Böckle, F., *Fundamentalmoral*, München 1977.
Merks, K.-W., '...et reliquit illum in manu consilii sui' (Sir 15, 14). In: *Reflecties op Schrift, opstellen voor Prof. dr. G. Bouwman*, Averbode/Apeldoorn 1983, 161-179.
Rahner, K., *Grundkurs des Glaubens*, Freiburg-Basel-Wien 1976.

3

Sexual Morality, Worldview, and Social Change

Gerrit Manenschijn

3.1 INTRODUCTION

3.1.1 A Plurality of Sexual Moralities

Saturday evening January 16, 1993. On the Dutch television the weekly talk show is being presented. This time it's about different sexual lifestyles. A neatly dressed woman introduces the female condom Femidorm. She explains how it must be put in place and how it works. The important aspect appears to be that by using this condom it will be possible for women to keep the sexual situation under complete control. Several samples are distributed to people who are willing to try them out at home and to report on that the next time. Especially men show up, which does not exactly seem to be the idea. After all, it's a female condom!

The second item is the making acquaintance with a number of men and women who have taken a course at the Academy for Eroticism and Intimacy. It quickly becomes obvious that the course dealt with being freed from any shackles to accept one's own body and that of others. In order to attain that, one was regularly invited to undress in front of the others. Making love was not part of the program, but the opportunity for it was available, and it certainly was not passed up. The instructor explained that she encouraged no one to have sex, but merely 'provided the structures wherein people could perform explorations in the bodily sphere, so that they would become familiar with the care toward themselves'.

Finally a roundtable was held in the show with a group of traditional Catholics, old as well as young, who had made the official Catholic point of view concerning sexual morality completely their own. Out of inner conviction they rejected intercourse before marriage and outside of it, as well as the use of birth control, abortion, and divorce. Their argument for this was that sexuality needs to be imbedded in a loving, lasting relationship, that birth control is not permitted, but it is possible to make use of the infertile time of the woman, as there is also no objection whatsoever to having sexual intercourse at an age where the possibility of pregnancy is definitely past. According to their conviction sexuality is not only for propagation, but also to convey love and faithfulness to each other. This can only achieve its purpose within the monogam marriage.

What intrigues me is that within one program two groups of people were represented whose opinions about sex were completely opposite. A modern libertine view stood over against a traditional Catholic one. This was, as it were, a reflection of our modern, pluralistic society: within one society there exists a plurality of moral opinions and therefore also concerning sexual morality, opinions that often are incompatible. It is possible, however, for them to exist alongside each other thanks to the widely shared idea of tolerance, according to which sexuality should be considered as a strictly private matter, and that we must respect each opinion on it. I shall call this the liberal point of view. In order to clarify exactly what I mean, I shall make a clear distinction between a libertine sexual morality and a liberal view concerning equal rights for various sexual moralities.

3.1.2 Libertine Sexual Morality and Liberal Ethics

By a libertine sexual morality I understand an opinion as advocated by the Academy for Eroticism and Intimacy: sexuality is a basic human need and it is not essential how and with whom one experiences sexuality, provided that force and violence are excluded. A libertine sexual morality excludes the option of abstinence, since without a free experience of sexuality one cannot achieve the necessary self-realization.

By a liberal view on equal rights for sexual moralities (in short form: liberal sexual ethics) I understand a view which places individual freedom of choice at the center and does not have a special preference for any specific sexual moral code or for the type of relationship within which sex is experienced. According to Maris (1992, 279-314) people should have the freedom to choose in which way and with whom they want to experience sexuality, provided force and violence are out of the question, namely because that is in conflict with freedom of choice.

Particular sexual moralities as such are closely connected with particular views on the good life. In what follows I shall make this clear, using three sexual moralities as examples: the Thomistic, the Puritan, and the libertine sexual moral view. All three moralities take sexuality to be fundamental for our humanness, which fact one cannot ignore without doing harm to oneself.

What is the difference between these moralities and liberal sexual ethics? Liberal sexual ethics is part of a narrow, liberal political morality. The other three moralities are part of more comprehensive moralities. Liberal political morality consists of preferences of the second order: preferences regarding the satisfaction of first-order preferences for a certain life-style, including sexuality.

In this paper I will develop three arguments concerning the relation between Thomistic, Puritan, and libertine sexual moralities at the one hand, and liberal sexual ethics (as a part of liberal political morality) at the other. First, not only the Thomistic, Puritan, and libertine morality are connected with a particular worldview and conception of the good for man, but also liberal sexual ethics. The liberal preference for individual freedom of choice is founded on the view that a person cannot optimize his humanness without autonomy. In other words: in that view autonomy is a necessary component of the good life. Second, all these moralities, including liberal sexual ethics, are connected with a certain view on the good society and the desirable social order. Regarding liberal sexual ethics I will argue that its philosophical presuppositions are for a great deal the same as those of the modern idea of the market society. Third, changes in social and economic conditions in one way or another trigger changes in moral beliefs. Changes in moral convictions do not come out of the blue.

3.1.3 Some Conceptual Presuppositions

I interpret 'conception of life' broadly, as containing the religious as well as the nonreligious conception of lives. (Thus I interpret worldview as belief.) The minimal that shall be required is that they contain cognitive claims that could be considered directive for moral behavior. I interpret 'morality' as the sum of moral action guides that claim suprapersonal validity. As for Thomistic and Puritan sexual morality, I am faced with the difficulty that we know a considerable amount about the morality prescribed by the church and worldly authorities, but very little about the moral convictions of ordinary people. So I shall have to limit myself to sexual morals as they were prescribed by the authorities.

3.1.4 Why Focus on Sexual Morality?

Why then do I focus my investigation on sexual morality? If there is one sphere of life where morality appears to have become completely independent of religious worldviews, it is sexuality. Sexological researches since the Kinsey reports (Kinsey 1948, 1953; Masters & Johnson 1966; Hunt 1974), have demonstrated that all kinds of forms of sexuality are being applied, usually regardless of religion or conception of life of those involved.[1]

During the last thirty or forty years opinions about sex have very much become private, a matter of free choice. At the same time there has been an increase of public interest for diversity of sexual practices. Most sexual taboos seem to have disappeared. What used to be called 'taboos' are now regarded as individual preferences with which others should not interfere. Few Roman Catholic believers heed their church's prohibition of anticonception and premarital and extramarital sexual intercourse. If one sticks to the regulation of the church concerning sexuality, it is because of one's own conviction and not because the church decrees something or forbids it. This appears to provide the evidence that sexual morality has indeed become a private affair.

3.2 THOMISTIC SEXUAL MORALITY

3.2.1 Augustine and Thomas Aquinas

In the development of Christian sexual morality (which has actually always been a marriage morality) until the time of Thomas Aquinas, all kinds of opinion of Christian as well as non-Christian origin played a major role (Murstein 1974; De Knijff 1987). Seen historically the influence of those views are of the greatest importance, but for my purpose (demonstrating the

---

[1] Francis Bennion (1991, xi) offers his sexual ethics as designed for a society 'where morals do not depend on religion' and in which 'sex is seen as a human right and glory'.

mutality between faith, sexual morality and social presuppositions in the views of Thomas Aquinas) not of such import that I need describe those views and their influence. Concerning the predecessors of Thomas I can limit myself to Augustine.[2] As far as Augustine was concerned, marriage had but one reason for existence: procreation.[3] For that view he appeals to 1 Timothy 5:14: 'For that reason it is my wish that young widows should marry again, have children, and manage a household; then they will give the enemy no occasion for scandal.'[4] Sexual intercourse is sinful (it is a 'malum concupiscentiae'), unless the intention to conceive children is present. The good of conceiving children compensates for the evil of lust.[5] According to the view that marriage exists for the purpose of providing descendents, Augustine stood in an old tradition, which said that it is according to nature that the sexual genital organs are exclusively for the service of procreation, and that in this respect people are no different than plants and animals. Augustine's following of this view resulted in a dualism. To achieve procreation in a similar manner as animals, marriage is not necessary and sexual intercourse is not wrong; however, according to Augustine sex is still an indulgence to the 'malum concupiscentiae' and only tolerable on two grounds: within marriage and in service of procreation.[6] Procreation is not only a function of marriage, it also has a social function, namely, the first realization of the social nature of man.[7]

---

2 Here I am following Beemer (1983) and Jansens (1966).
3 Concerning abstinence within marriage, seen as ideal by the Manicheans, Augustine judges as follows: 'filios autem inviti suscipiunt, propter quod solum coniugia copulanda sunt'. Contra Faustum, XV, c.7. (Janssens, 517).
4 De bono coniugali, c.24, n.32: 'Generationis itaque causa fieri nuptias, Apostolus ita testis est: 'Volo, inquit, iuniores nubere'. Et quasi ei diceretur: Utquid? continuo subiicit 'filios procreare, matresfamilias esse'. (Janssens, 518).
5 De coniugiis adulterinis, II, c.12, n.12: 'Filiorum quidem propagine compensatur quod incontinentiae nubendo ceditur'; De bono coniugali, II, c.12, n.12: 'Habent etiam id bonum coniugali, quod carnalis vel iuvenilis incontinentia, etiamsi vitiosa est, ad propagandae prolis redigitur honestatum, ut ex malo libidinis aliquid boni faciat copulatio coniugalis'. (Janssens, 552).
6 Augustine is then also against a 'copula cum contractu', (De coniugiis adulterinis, II, c.12, n.12; Janssens, 528).
7 'Potest igitur christianus cum coniuge concorditer vivere, sive indigentiam carnalem cum ea supplens, quod secundum veniam, non secundum imperium dicit apostolus, sive filiorum propagationem, quod iam nonnullo gradu potest esse laudabile, sive fraternam societatem, sine ulla corporum commixtione, habens uxorem tanquam non habens, quod est in coniugo Christianorum excellentissimum atque sublime: ut tamen

Besides the procreative and social function marriage also has a sacramental function: marriage is an image of the unity of Christ and the church. Thereby the indissolubility of marriage is given.

3.2.2 Thomas Aquinas

Although Thomas Aquinas concurs with Augustine in several ways, he has a much less pessimistic tendency than his great predecessor. Thomas puts great stress on the naturalness of sexual intercourse. He does that by placing procreation in the larger context of preservation of the human race. It is entirely according to nature that man strives for the preservation of his own life; that is the first level of human instinct for survival, which he has in common with all living creatures.[8] On the second level it is according to nature that humanity procreates itself; this level man also shares with plants and animals.[9] It is only on the third level where the law of nature functions that mankind manifest itself in its typical human characteristics which distinguish us from animals. This is the level at which we try to learn to know the truth concerning God and natural life. The level, therefore, of rationality.[10]

Marriage plays a role on the second and third level of natural law. In the area of procreation Thomas distinguishes a general level, which man and animals have in common, and a specific human level, where man tries to know and practice the true characteristics of social life. On the general level procreation is entirely a matter of nature; for Thomas this is a matter of biological reality. Put differently: here nature differs from ratio (or: on the general level natural law is not the same as on the human level).[11] On the human level it is not natural law that is determinative, but rather reason.

---

    oderit in ea nomen temporalis necessitatis et diligat spem sempiternae beatitudinis'. (De sermone Domini in monte, I, c.15, n.42; Janssens, 525-526).

8 Thomas Aquinas, Summa Theologiae, (ST) II-II, q.64, art.5.

9 'Secundo inest homini inclinatio ad aliqua magis specialia, secundum naturam in qua communicat cum ceteris animalibus. Et secundum hoc, dicuntur ea esse de lege naturali quae natura omnia animalia docuit, ut est coniunctio maris et feminae, et educatio liberorum, et similia'. (ST, I-II, q.94, art.2).

10 Et talis participatio legis aeterna in rationali creatura lex naturalis dicitur. (ST, I-II, q.94, art.2).

11 'Et quia natura contra rationem dividitur a qua homo est homo...'. (ST, Suppl., q.65, art.1 ad 4).

Both ways of relating to 'nature' are entrusted to mankind by God, since the biologically determined order of nature as well as our reasoning nature comes from God, whereby the natural order comes first, and only after that our rationality.[12] On the general level, sexual intercourse is a natural action in which there is no wrong. In this people differ from animals only in so far as people can see through the end purpose of nature, and so can know what purpose sexuality serves. They know that they were given genitals for the purpose of procreation (Jansens 1966, 534).[13]

In summary: Thomas strongly pulls to the fore the natural purpose of sexuality. The first goal (finis principalis) of sexuality is the preservation of the human race. The theological argument for this is that God has created human nature in such a way that sexual activity has the goal of conceiving descendents. Humanity shares this characteristic with all living beings. The second goal (finis secundarius) exists in mutual loyalty between the spouses; this is the social dimension of sexuality. And finally, the third goal (finis tertius) is the sacramental status of marriage. Here one can speak of an increasing appreciation. The social is more than the biological and the sacramental is more than the social.

Within the view that procreation is the first goal of sexuality, there is differentiated between natural (secundum naturam) and counternatural (contra naturam) sexual behavior, depending on whether the end purpose is respected or thwarted (Janssens 1966, 535; Beemer 1983, 16-18).[14] Belonging to the first group of sexual sins, in progressive order of seriousness, we find: sexual intercourse between two unmarried people (fornicatio simplex), then adultery (aldulterium), sexual assault (stuprum), rape (raptus) and the most serious, incest (incestus). No matter how serious these offenses are, they remain sins according to nature, since the possibility of fertilization is not purposely excluded. Sexual sins against nature do exclude that possibility. Thomas considered as the least evil masturbation (mollities, pollutio, immunditia),

---

12 'Ordo naturae humanae inditus est prior et stabilior quam quilibet ordo superadditus'. (ST, II-II, q.154, art.12).

13 Here Thomas also makes the statement that the male sperm is already in essence a human being: 'Et ideo inordinatio circa emissionem seminis est circa vitam hominis in potentia proxima'. (De Malo, q.15, art.2.).

14 'Sed vitium contra naturam consistit circa actus ex quibus non potest generatio sequi.' (ST, II-II, q.154. art.11).

then the prevention of conception (coitus interruptus), next homosexuality (sodomia)[15] and as the worst stiality (bestialitas). Bestiality was extra sinful because people believed that contact with animals could result in hideous hybrids between man and animal. Janssens (1966, 535) concludes that for Thomas the least evil of the unnatural sins (masturbation) is more serious than the most evil of the natural sins (incest), and that because coitus between man and woman is in harmony with what is natural on the most general level. By means of voluntary pollution you distort that order.

According to contemporary viewpoints concerning sexuality in which a high value is normally contributed to sexual pleasure, the Thomistic sexual morality is usually typified as hostile towards sexual pleasure and therefore condemned. That is too simple. We must judge according to the presuppositions in those times. Lust is not wrong (Thomas differs from Augustine in this), but must be kept under control. Chastity (castitas) becomes a key concept, also later in the Reformation.[16] Besides, we must consider that at that time people had no exact idea about how conception took place. They knew that there was a causal connection between genital intercourse of a man with a woman, on the one hand, and procreation, on the other. That they called this relationship 'natural', speaks for itself, certainly if procreation is seen as the first goal. That this 'naturalness' received a decisive moral meaning, was something quite different, but it did constitute the core of sexual morality. It is also understandable, because to purposely prevent pregnancy goes against the intention of creation according to Middle Age views. The infertile period of a woman, however, was also a natural given and people probably knew how to make use of that. In any case, it is anachronistic to judge Thomistic sexual morality according to insights that were not yet known then. Furthermore, one should keep in mind that the chance of survival of mankind was quite a bit less then than today. Van

---

15 It is actually an anachronism to call sex with the same gender 'homosexuality' in that time. For that, homosexuality is too modern a concept. In ecclesiastical morality the main concern was behavior, not disposition. The term 'sodomy' also points to that, for this is not synonymous with homosexuality, but with anal sexual intercourse. Men could also do this with women.
16 See for example the Heidelberg Catechism, Lord's Day 41, question and answer 108: What does the seventh commandment teach us? That all unchastity is accursed by God; and that we must, therefore, detest it from the heart, live a chaste and continent life both within and outside of holy marriage.

Eupen (1982, 29) points out that around the year 1000 an end finally came to the century in which Europe was ravaged by the plundering of the Vikings, by pestilence and famine, and by a real decline of the population figure. Under such circumstances it is not surprising that sexuality orientated to procreation was seen as a first requirement. To draw a social parallel: population growth then had the same social naturalness as economic growth today. (Until that too will be considered outdated.)

3.2.3 An Encompassing Ontological Framework

A following point of consideration is the encompassing Thomistic ontological framework in which sexual morality was perceived. That ontological framework is a theological worldview in which total reality is seen as a universum which is regulated according to the divine creation will. (De Clercq, 1988, 74-78). For Thomas 'order' is a key concept, not in the first place as a political concept, but as a theological and metaphysical one. This meant that in spite of all the plurality, unity must be kept in focus, and the appropriate spot for that was the ontological level. The 'eternal law' (lex aeterna) has the highest status: the ratio of divine wisdom which is the guidance and direction of all activity and movement.[17] The eternal law is God's wisdom by which He directs and guides creation. Beemer (1983, 33) calls attention to the given that in the eternal law God does not let Himself be known as the Maker of all things, but as the Lord of history, who guides it to the ultimate goal: His Kingdom.[18] In the time between creation and completion there is room for change and development, and therefore also room for growth in knowledge and insight for people - who, after all, live in that time. With this Beemer wants to demonstrate that ecclesiastical moral teaching should be linked not so much to an unchangeable order of being (stoic ontology), but to God's actions in history (biblical view). Thomas offers the possibility for that.

'Natural law' (lex naturalis) has a lower status than eternal law. Man participates in divine providence by means of natural law. Natural law is the

---

[17] 'ita ratio divina sapientiae moventis omnia ad debitum finem'. (ST I-II, q.93, art.1).

[18] Beemer appeals to ST I-II, q.93, art.1, where Thomas distinguishes between ars and artificiata, on the one hand, and on the other hand between lex and opera justa, whereby the first pair of concepts relate to the creation and the second pair to the maintenance.

rational insight of man into the principles and laws of the order God has willed. Natural law does not coincide with eternal law, but it involves man in God's ruling: '...the light of natural reason whereby we discern what is good and what is evil, which is the function of the natural law, is nothing else than an imprint on us of the Divine Light. It is therefore evident that the natural law is nothing else than the rational creature's participation in the eternal law'.[19] De Clercq (1988, 75) says that through thinking man becomes his own source of providence (sibi ipsi providens) and the providence of everything else. In the same spirit Beemer (1983, 34) calls the natural law a theological construction about 'the moral rules which human intelligence constantly discovers on the basis of the inclinationes naturalis of man, to be inserted within the all-embracing concept of God's rule, the eternal law'. Finally, there is still 'human law' (lex humana), meant to apply the principles of natural law in human society and to establish concrete jurisprudence. This, then, has no divine status, but it is exactly the opposite: jurisprudence may not be in conflict with natural law, and natural law does not have the status of eternal law. Concrete jurisprudence, therefore, can be brought under criticism by means of the natural law.

The meaning of the eternal law is that the ontological order must not be conceived statically but teleologically: God has created the world in such a way that it is goal-directed to God's Kingdom. A completion is waiting. Within this teleological order the reproductive goal-directedness of marriage and sexuality is entirely logical. Ontological presuppositions cover a morality that has propagation as a primary goal.

Further, it needs to be considered that the ontic order is not isolated from the social order. Just as human law fits into the larger whole of natural law, individual people fit into the larger whole of society. Individuals are subordinate to the political community. 'Moreover, since every part is ordained to the whole, as imperfect to perfect, and since one man is part of the perfect community, the law must needs regard properly the relationship to universal happiness', and therefore the good of one human cannot be an ultimate goal, but rather it is placed under the communal good: 'And therefore as the good

---

[19] 'Quasi lumen rationis naturalis, quo discernimus quid sit bonum et malum, quod pertinet ad naturalem legem, nihil aliud sit quam impressio divini luminis in nobis. Unde patet quod lex naturalis nihil aliud est quam participatio legis aeternae in rationali creatura'. (ST, I-II, q.91, art.2).

of one man is not the last end, but is ordained to the common good, so too the good of one household is ordained to the good of a single state, which is a perfect community'.[20] From this point of view it is entirely logical to disapprove of extramarital sexual activity. The good of the community was seen in both the maintaining of the level of the population as well as in the stability of social relations, whereby the family occupied a central position. With this the social aspect of (hetero)sexuality is guaranteed in a lasting relationship: marriage, and that by means of the communal good (bonum commune). However, that is not an ontological justification (by means of an unchangeable ontological order), as Beemer (1983, 36-37) correctly argues. He points out that Thomas rejects nonmarital sex between a man and woman (fornicatio simplex) not on essentialistic but on practical grounds: such an unregulated coitus poses a threat for the child that eventually is born out of it. Beemer then also reproaches ecclesiastical doctrinal authority that since the end of the nineteenth century it has 'metaphysically exalted' natural law, as becomes apparent from the equalization of natural law with eternal law, whereby natural law also is interpreted as static. The leeway that Thomas offers is taken away entirely.

Finally, one must bear in mind that with Thomas the individual person is not subordinated to the community in such a way that he would not be a goal in himself and that totalitarian authority would be justified. That certainly is not the case. Man is an end in himself and his completeness is not realized in the polis, but in salvation through beatification (De Clercq 1988, 76).[21] Man is not attuned totally nor in everything to the community, but in everything he must be orientated toward God. Not only does the church then receive its independence overagainst the state, but also the third aspect of marriage (its sacramentalness) is brought in harmony with the divine wisdom by which God rules the world.

---

20 'Rursus, cum omnis pars ordinetur ad totum sicut inperfectum ad perfectum; unus autem homo est pars communitatis perfectae: necesse est quod lex proprie respiciat ordinem ad felicitatem communem'; ST I-II, q.90, art.3 ad 3: 'Sicut homo est pars domus, ita domus est pars civitatis: civitas autem est communitas perfecta... Et ideo sicut bonum unius hominis non est ultimis finis, sed ordinatur ad commune bonum; ita etiam et bonum unius domus ordinatur ad bonum unius civitatis, quae est communitas perfecta'. (ST I-II, q.90, art.2). The English is taken from the translation of the Fathers of the English Dominium Province, published by Christian Classics, Westminster (Maryland) 1981.

21 'Est autem ultimus finis humanae vitae felicitas vel beatitudo'. (ST, I-II, q.90, art.2).

We can conclude that there is a logical connection between Thomistic sexual morality and Thomistic ontological order; as well as the existing political order. The end purpose of the ontological order of being justifies the end purpose of sexuality, first of all in the area of reproduction, then concerning the exclusiveness of the marriage relationship (social aspect), and finally in regard to the sanctification of marriage (sacramentalness).

3.3 SOCIAL CHANGE AND CHANGE IN WORLDVIEW

The metaphysical framing of Thomist sexual morality within an order of being cannot be viewed separately from concrete political and ecclesiastical interests: the family, besides being a reproductive and social community, was also an economic unity which was presupposed to contribute to the stability of society. The so much desired preservation of the population through procreation must also first find its place within the family. That prevented fathers (or rather: begetters) from withdrawing themselves from their care-responsibilities without punishment. Otherwise society would end up paying for it. The church also had a distinct interest in this situation, because via morality she could channel sexual behavior in such a manner as she desired, so that she could safeguard her own authority, also in this respect over-against the political power.

In the seventeenth century, important social changes took place, which shifted the social weight from the collective to the individual. That shifting may be typified with Berki (1977, 115-119) as follows. The general context is the decay of the Corpus Christianum and the emergence of civic society. People no longer have an appointed place in the social whole and no longer are their needs determined by that position, but the opposite is the case: their legal relationship to the state is primary and the self-definition of their needs follows naturally. People are seen as citizens gifted with natural privileges and the state is seen as a voluntary association of citizens, formed to guarantee their safety and to promote their interests. The class society of the Middle Ages is radically broken through (at least in theory; in practice even until today there are bits of the feudal system present): In principle everyone is equal and all have equal rights to strive for happiness and prosperity. The most important shifting, which is the ideological foundation for all other shifting, is the acceptance that the fundamental cornerstone of society is not a certain social tie (the family or a group), but the individual. Thomas

Hobbes, for example, the founder of civic philosophy, sees the individual as the last no longer dividable element of society, as a kind of 'social atom' (Manenschijn 1979, 13-15). This goes together with a mechanistic view of reality and therefore with a description of events in terms of cause and effect (Dijksterhuis 1950). Socially this means that the individual (and not the community) is the self-evident bearer of privileges and interests, that his existence reveals itself to be determined by all kinds of powers and that society is considered as an arena in which all types of social powers fight each other for precedence. The role of self-interest in social reality is compared to the function of the point of gravity in science. Self-interest is the motor of social development (Hirschmann 1977).

During the Reformation individual responsibility had received much more weight than was customary in the Middle Ages, but the family was still seen as the untouchable cornerstone of society, socially as well as morally and economically. The traditional views concerning sexual morality were maintained as usual. Nevertheless tension developed between morality as determined by the community, on the one hand, and on the other hand the individually determined privileges overagainst the community. As long as those privileges and interests demanded a strict sexual morality, such a morality remained in place; as soon as they made this morality superfluous, it began to disappear. Social factors which determined the dynamic of society initially supported traditional sexual morality and then proceeded to undermine it. The Puritans, as I will show, tried to keep sexual morality within the family, but at the same time the dynamic of society drove economy in the direction of the individual, who as a laborer outside of family ties and in service of an economically defined production-unit, had to see that he earned his keep. This went together with the transition from an agrarian society to an industrial one. Opposing forces exercised their power on the family; economical powers drove it apart, moral powers tried to keep the pieces together. As long as society was mainly agrarian, with the main goal as providing the vital necessities of life for the community itself, traditional sexual morality was not damaged. That only happened when the family could not maintain itself as an economic unity.

3.4 PURITAN SEXUAL MORALITY

3.4.1 Puritans in North America

My second example is the sexual morality of the Puritans in North America in the seventeenth century. The reasons for this choice are threefold. First, it is a period in which the puritan morality was most pregnantly present. Second, in the seventeenth century important social and economic changes take place. That is why the morality of the Puritans in North America is such a good example to illustrate the influence of social and economic factors on worldview and sexual morality. Third, I have at my disposal a richly documented source about this period (D'Emilio & Freedman 1989).

3.4.2 The Family as a Central Unit

In each American colony the family was the central economic and procreative unit: 'Reproduction and production went hand in hand, for family survival in an agricultural economy depended on the labor of children, both in the fields and in the households' (D'Emilio & Freedman 1989, 16). Young people learned sexual morals through observation in the family and through moral teaching by the parents and the church. The first is normal in an agrarian society: 'Procreation was everywhere, in the barnyard as well as in the house', noted the seventeenth century chronicler Laurel Thatcher Ulrich concerning farmlife in northern New England (17). Colonial laws against bestiality and widespread prosecution of sodomy with animals, point to the fact that people on the farm also gained knowledge of which the practical application evoked a deep repulsion and was punished extremely severely, also because people feared that bestiality could cause deformities. This is why not only the person found guilty of bestiality was punished, but also the animal. As far as 'normal sexuality' is concerned, children at home could observe this and how their parents had intercourse, because often they slept in the same room, and sometimes even in the same bed. The moral teaching included as a matter of course that sex was for adults who were married to each other. And so in New England fornication, rape, sodomy, adultery, and sometimes incest, were against the law.[22] Often there was a death sentence for sodomy and rape, but in the case of rape this was very often not executed. It was often difficult to prove, for seldom were there witnesses. Since a wife and children were considered possessions of the man, rape was considered an offense against the 'possession' of the man. In practice that resulted in applying the death sentence for rape only in the case of the woman who was unmarried, engaged, or younger than ten years old (31).

A few Puritan preachers considered sexuality itself as unpure (18). Giving into feelings of lust would mean a danger for the body and the soul. Marriage was a remedy against this danger, but also within marriage moderation had to be exercised.[23] Along with this, it was expected that men, gifted as they were with rationality, could control their passions better than women.

Overagainst this extreme view there was the custom that engaged couples had the opportunity to express their sexual feelings within the limits that were considered decent. There was even the custom that engaged persons were permitted to spend the night in one bed, keeping their clothes on, or placing a 'bundling board' between them. It was expected that they would

---

22 Adultery was defined as sexual relations between a man and a married woman, and fornication as sexual relations between a married man and a single woman, or between a single man and a woman (28). It is a mistake to see sodomy as equivalent to the modern concept of homosexuality, for it referred to nonprocreative sexual acts (mostly anal intercourse), which could be performed between two men, a man and an animal (called 'buggery' or 'bestiality'), or between a man and a woman (30).

23 This strongly recalls Calvin, Institutes, II, VII, 41-44, 'The seventh commandment', where, among other things, it is stated: Because God loves chastity and purity, the intention is that we withhold all impurity far from us. Thus the main content will be that we do not defile ourselves with any uncleanness or lustful excessiveness of the flesh. The positive command relates to this, namely that we must direct all parts of our life chastely and modestly. The Latin text says: 'Finis eius: quia pudicitiam et puritatem Deus amat, facessere a nobis omnem immunditiem oportere. Summa igitur erit, ut nequa spurcitia, aut libidinosa intemperie carnis inquinemur. Cui respondet affirmativum praeceptum, ut caste et continenter omnes vitae nostrae partes moderemur'. (Corpus Reformatorum, XXX, 295.) Calvin also states here that marriage has been ordained for those who cannot abstain, in order to avoid prostitution: 'Si ad domandam libidinem vires deficiant intelligat iam sibi coniugii necessitatem a Domino impositam. Hoc demonstrat apostolus, quum praecipit (1Cor. 7,2 and 9) ut ad fugiendam scortationem unusquisque uxorem suam habeat, et unaquaeque mulier virum' (op.cit., 298). According to Calvin, the Lord forbids lascivious ornamentation of the body, obscene gestures and dirty jokes: 'Ergo dum scortari prohibet, simul vetat et lascivo corporis ornatu, et obscoenis gesticulationibus, et impuris sermonibus alienae pudicitiae insidiari' (op.cit).

not have sex. If however, that did happen and had consequences, the couple would certainly marry. After a confession the child could be baptized and the married couple was taken up in the community with full rights (22-23).

Within marriage, sex was not only permitted but even compulsory. In one case it is known that a man was excommunicated because he refused his wife intercourse for two years (23). Women looked upon childbearing as a divine mandate. It was no wonder that the population doubled in one generation during the seventeenth century, this despite the high percentage of death among children, sometimes up to 30 or 40% of all those born (26). As far as the punishment of sexual transgressions was concerned, social status was a cause of class justice. Generally women were punished more severely than men, blacks more than whites, and 'lower class' people more than 'higher class' people (31). The most severe punishments fell to negroes who had attempted to have intercourse with white women. In New York a black man was burned alive because twice he had attempted to rape a white woman. In several colonies the punishment for these transgressions was castration.[24] There was an economical interest hidden behind all these views. 'Bastardy, like adultery, sodomy, and rape, threatened the centrality of marital, reproductive sexuality, but it also posed a particularly troubling economic problem for the colonists: who would provide for children born out of wedlock in a society in which the family was the central economic unit?' (32). Also for that reason marriage was considered the only institution in which sex was permitted, the main purpose being the conceiving of lawful descendents.

We can establish that sexual morality was maintained by the strong religious conviction that God himself had instituted marriage in order to guide sexual lusts in lawful paths and so provide lawful descendents. Along side of that, an economical interest was present for the preservation of sexual morality: So long as work on the farm demanded the dedication of many family members and so long as there was enough ground in the neighborhood to help sons get their own farm, procreation was a natural purpose of marriage and marriage was the only institution in which sex was permitted.

---

24 This didn't apply to white men in regard to black women. In the South, for example, planters had the right to have sex with negro women (36).

3.4.3 Changes in Patterns

After 1750 all that begins to change. The central place of the family was gradually undermined by economic, social and political changes (39). 'These economic developments undermined the patterns of stable community life which had largely regulated sexual morality... In farming areas, young couples increasingly established their homes in outlying areas where land was available, beyond the reach of family, church, and traditional community surveillance' (40). Furthermore, during the eighteenth century an increasing influence eminated from the new ethical and theological insights. In ethics the individual and his needs and desires more and more took the place of the community, instead of the family. The individual 'pursuit of happiness' became a new political ideal, which later was even laid down constitutionally. In theology sexuality no longer was associated with the fall into sin, but with 'nature'. Therefore it could be seen as permissible and desirable. Benjamin Franklin, for example, called sexual intercourse a 'virtuous action'. Not propagation, but love became the most important aspect of marriage (41).

It should be kept in mind, however, that these changes of opinion which were not so much enacted in Puritan thought, but rather in that of the Enlightenment, also didn't leave America unperturbed. Generally speaking, the Puritans kept to their traditional views. The change that took place was that Puritan views continually had less influence on new generations, also on the Puritans themselves. The transition to a more liberal sexual morality, which had the individual, rather than the family as point of reference, began to express itself more clearly.

3.5 THE SEXUAL REVOLUTION

3.5.1 The Transition to a Freer Sexual Morality

The transition from a strict sexual morality to a freer one has gradually taken place, but during the sexual revolution of the sixties and the seventies of the twentieth century it has gained momentum. The sexual revolution has shaken a lot of things loose; it is impossible to map it out in short here. That isn't necessary, either, since everyone is already familiar with it. I shall limit myself to mentioning the most important element, namely: the view that sexuality is the source of personal identity (D'Emilio & Freedman 1989, 327).

The perfect orgasm was celebrated as a personal climax-experience and there was abundantly experimented with that accomplishment. This made sexuality ripe for commercial exploitation, because those who were deprived of this climax-experience could enter into therapy or consult a sex manual. Following from this commercializing of sexuality - but sometimes also going against it - sexologists tried to free people from antisexual feelings and 'to give them a good feeling' as far as sexual relationship go and the conducting of sexual acts (329).

These were only symptoms, more important were the underlying structural changes. The discovery of the pill, legalization of abortion, and the application of trustworthy contraceptive methods permanently broke the tie between sexual intercourse and procreation. If that tie was maintained, however, then it was consciously wanted by those involved. Women could be sexually active without the fear of pregnancy. This led to a decline in the number of births and at the same time to an increase of pre- and extramarital intercourse, as well as raising the frequency of intercourse (331). The amount of divorces also increased in America, between 1960 and 1980 even up to 200%. After 1980 the amount of divorces decreased again, but statistically marriages of the late 1970s only have a one out of two chance of surviving. Common-law living also increased, and even if one does finally marry it is often not with the first partner with whom one lived together.

Clearly, marriage was no longer the only legitimate place for sexuality: the dominant thought was that sex belonged to the individual person and no longer exclusively to marriage (333). This also led to change in sexual practices. In the 1950s Kinsey (1948 and 1952) found that very few heterosexuals applied fellatio and cunnilingus; however, Morton Hunt (1974) discovered at the end of the 1970s that this practice had become normal among those in their twenties. 'Petting', once so important for gaining a first experience in sexuality, had by then become an archaic curiosity (D'Emilio & Freedman 1989, 335).[25]

Social acceptance of homosexuality belongs to the most important assets of the sexual revolution (338-340). This has caused much struggle and even today an American politician cannot permit himself a public homosexual

---

25 'Petting' is an intense form of love-making without arriving at penetration.

relationship. The official points of view are often liberal, but public opinion is still prudish and sometimes discriminating.

Also within marriage much has changed. Sexual gratification has come to be high on the agenda of a successful marriage, and very much is expected of it (336-337). But if the expectations are stretched too far, disappointment must follow. It became continually more difficult to resign oneself to a not totally gratifying sexual relationship and that, again, led to an increase of divorces and to a looking for a new relationship, in the often vain hope that one would find more satisfaction and understanding by a succeeding partner.

3.5.2 Contradictory Emotions

All in all, sex continually became more surrounded with contradictory emotions. High demands and expectations overagainst unsatisfactory gratification; the utopia of sexual gratification overagainst the reality of sexual violence, the marred portrayal of people in hard porno, the return of some sexual diseases (herpes for example) and the rise of a new disease: Aids (341-342). Sexual liberalism threatens to collapse. If, after all, sexuality is considered to be the most important contribution to human happiness, but people are not successful in having a gratifying sexual relationship, how then can they still be happy?

In the 1980s, then, the repercussion came. The Moral Majority arises and with a great show of power tries to restore traditional values (344-354). President Reagan finds himself obligated to put great emphasis on family values.[26] Activists as Anita Bryant try to push back the rights gained by homosexuals and the conservative John Birch Society systematically picks on sexual reformers. Fundamentalistic television preachers acquire a large following - and even more income - until some of them turn out not to practice what they preach and to look to prostitutes to get what they apparently can't get at home. The success of the 'new right' has therefore also remained limited. On the local level some could reverse the situation, but not on the national level (350).

---

26 This continued to the election debates between Bush and Clinton in 1992. 'Family values' was a republican issue, but Clinton could not permit himself to be inattentive to it. Thus, after it became known that he had earlier had extramarital escapades with a photo model, he had to publically demonstrate the strength of his marriage and family.

The outcome of two decades of sexual revolution and one decade of reaction cannot yet be estimated. However, the following portrays itself. The utopia of sexual liberation has been exchanged for a more down to earth, almost businesslike approach to limited human possibilities, as far as the expression of sexual identity goes. The night side of sexuality, which has become visible in hard porno, sexual violence and the misuse of women and girls in dependent relationships, is generally acknowledged nowadays. At the same time, people won't let the sexual freedom which they have obtained with much difficulty be taken away. Personal responsibility for your actions, especially also in your relationships, is strongly emphasized. Even more since the discovery of Aids, with its irrevocable deadly results. Sexual morality has entered calm waters since the turbulent sixties and seventies. 'Safe sex' has become the motto and many see a monogam relationship as the most successful and also the most gratifying form of 'safe sex'. One can also hear a few voices suggesting that foregoing sexual intercourse voluntarily could mean an enrichment of your spiritual life. But that is a strictly personal opinion, for the dominant idea is that everyone has a right to the sexual satisfaction which one prefers, in whatever type of relationship.

3.5.3 An Example of a Libertine Sexual Morality

I would like to give an example of a libertine sexual morality, without claiming that this is the sexual morality of this time. It is interesting, because it is approximately the opposite of the Puritan sexual morality, but it is just as much connected to a certain view of humanity and the world. I have in mind Francis Bennion (1991), who propagated the nonbelievers' guide to sexual conduct, meant for people who see sex as a human right and glory. There are three startingpoints: we should accept, respect and fulfil our sexual nature, and assist others to do the same (1).

The first startingpoint is called the 'Duty of Self-Acceptance' (15). That includes the acceptance of one's own sexual nature and that of others (35-50). Society may not be divided up into two types of people: sex-citizens, those who can show a passport of good behavior to the authorities, over-against sex-aliens who do not have such a passport. According to conservative values heterosexuals who experience their sexuality within marriage are reckoned to belong to the first group, and to the second group all those who do not, including especially homosexuals, lesbians, bisexuals, pederasts, transvestites, transsexuals, fetishists, sado-masochists and the like. Each sex-alien must be totally accepted. It is, after all, impossible for one to choose a different sexual nature (45).

The second startingpoint is called the 'Duty of Sex-Respect' (75). This implies that 'we should treat our own or another's sexual organs, functions and desires with respect'. By this he means that sex cannot be totally disassociated from procreation and from certain moral norms. And so voyeurism is not totally acceptable - the sexual privacy of others is violated (77-78) - and promiscuity is wrong when the other person is used solely for one's own lust gratification.

The third startingpoint is the most interesting, because this includes the 'Duty of Sex-fulfilment' which says that everyone has the duty to bring others and oneself to a gratifying sexual life (89-130). The basis for this duty is the 'need' that people have for a 'periodic sexual release' (89). This need is seen as a kind of biological determination for the man: 'The male on the other hand is programmed instantly to fecundate every woman within his grasp. From puberty onwards, his testicles produce nonstop the fluid called semen. His body is designed to void this fluid at frequent intervals. If it is not able to do so, mental pressures build up' (90). It all centers around orgasm (92-100). Besides a physiological necessity there also exists a psychological need, and that is even more important, because that determines the emotions and the fantasies with which orgasm is surrounded (97). People should be able to enjoy this freely, because it is harmful if orgasm is accompanied by feelings of guilt and shame (98). Furthermore, out of the need to be emotionally attached to someone it is better to experience orgasm with a partner, rather than alone. However, if that is impossible, 'solitary sex' is not wrong (99). For, frustration of sexual desires is disastrous; then one becomes a frightened and joyless being. 'Sexuality is indeed the key to human joy. But that joy is the birthright of every human being' (103). To fulfil that right sexual service must be available: education and training; assistance to reach orgasms through 'erotic Samaritans', and the like: 'Sex-therapy, sex-enhancing equipment, contact services, so-called prostitution, so-called pornography, provision for contraception, sterilization, and abortion, sex-information - all these and more are supplied somehow because the demand is irresistible' (114).

The ultimate goal for Bennion is that we people, who no longer have admission to what once was the Garden of Eden and who are threatened by all kinds of developments, gain free entry to the paradise of sexual happiness: 'One comfort available to us in facing future shock is true sexuality, which is, thankfully, independent of technology. All it asks is honesty to human nature. Men, women and children fortunate to dwell already in the Garden of Happy Emotions (and there are many of these) are not repressed or inhibited' (285). You become truly human through your sexuality.

It is quite clear that Bennion's sex code is a simple naturalistic morality, whereby a certain normativity is inferred from presupposed facts concerning humanity and the world. Everyone's sexual nature is determined and therefore everyone must gratify their own sexual needs according to that nature. In order to make that possible, society must, within certain limits, offer all forms of sexual gratification, so that clients have a large assortment from which to choose. Sexual individualism connects seamlessly to the presuppositions of the market society: the preferences of the sexual subjects count as a given and the market exists in order to provide that. Bennion, then, has nothing against the commercialization of sexuality. It is just the core of his naturalistic sexual morality.

3.6 LIBERAL SEXUAL ETHICS

3.6.1 Sexual Individualism

In modern society the previously described naturalistic morality of sexual fulfilment certainly exists, but there is much more. In fact, there are a great many variations of sexual morality and sexual behavior: from puritan to libertine moralities, from maximalizing of sexual enjoyment to voluntary abstinence, from promiscuity to monogamy, and everything inbetween. It is not true that sexual individualism is an exact version of economic liberalism. It is possible that someone accepts economic liberalism, but rejects sexual individualism, or the other way around: there have often been sex experiments arising precisely out of socialistic views. To give a picture of what is possible in the Netherlands concerning types of relationships, in a number of communities homosexuals can let themselves be registered at the city hall in a relationship similar to that of marriage; they imitate, as it were, the monogam marriage. Other homosexuals, on the contrary, consider promiscuity as an essential expression of their disposition[27], while there is an increasing number of homosexuals who prefer a LAT-relation to a permanent one, and who combine that, or not, with sexual freedom and therefore with promiscuity if the opportunity appears. Or also: Even if in the economy the individual has replaced the family as the production unit and the bread-winner principle is subject to the wear and tear of social legislation, that does not mean that the same changes occur in sexual morality. A strictly economic orientation toward the individual can go together very well with an as strict sexual orientation toward marriage and family. Modern society, directed to individual preferences, has evoked not only one type of sexuality, but many. Individualism has promoted plurality, particularly because there are so many diverse individual opinions. However, it now appears that liberal sexual ethics can cover all that, because it puts the human freedom of choice and human responsibility central. This is apparant in the manner in which Cees Maris describes sexual ethics. Maris (1992, 293-294) places liberal sexual ethics in the middle of the scale which runs from traditional sexuality, on the one side, to Marcuse's freedom utopia, on the other side. Traditional sexual morality ties sex to the social utility of propagation. On top of that, Christian and Kantian versions of this morality tie propagationally-directed sex to monogamy. Marcuse's sexual utopia is the direct opposite; it consists of the idea that all perversions are free, except the sadistical. The thought behind this is that free sex can free people from capitalistic repression.

3.6.2 The Basic Principle of Liberal Sexual Ethics

The basic principle of liberal sexual ethics is generally derived from John Stuart Mill: freedom, provided that no harm is done to others. However, the problem is that freedom and harm can be understood in different ways, also within liberalism itself. Maris (1992, 296) demonstrates that most liberals think that the government should leave the people freedom to live according to their own convictions; also, the government should consider certain

---

27 Research in America has shown that lesbians are mainly monogam oriented - only 28% does not have a monogam relationship and that is hardly different than the 25% of married men and the 21% of married women - while for homosexual men promiscuity is a 'way of life' (D'Emilio & Freedman, 339).

convictions immoral.[28] All the same, liberals reject the total freedom of anarchism. That doesn't have to be inconsequent. For total freedom turns into total submissiveness. (Hegel's much quoted dialectic on freedom.) Maris demonstrates that quite nicely using the example of De Sade's sexual-freedom utopia, which prescribes that everyone must have the freedom to have others at their disposal in order to give reign to one's passions, and in order to make that possible it is necessary that others subject themselves entirely to them. The only restriction is the principle of reciprocity: one who subjects now will be subjected, and the other way around. That is, however, no relativizing of total subjection, but a confirmation that total subjection is logically the reverse side of total freedom (282-284).

As stated before, anarchism is rejected, and that means that liberalism has a filled-in concept of freedom, but in which manner? Maris mentions two views. The first says that freedom has a humanity-forming meaning: it makes you human. Freedom is an ethical ideal according to which all people should live. Rawls would characterize that view as philosophical liberalism.[29] Liberal sexual ethics is, as I said before, part of liberal political morality, according to which people are free to form their own conception of the good life, including the sexual life. Liberal political morality presupposes a social structure that puts people in a position to live according to their own convictions, and which offers the government the possibility to solve conflicts between adherents of diverse conceptions of the good impartially (297). With regard to sexuality that impartial solution means that everyone will have the opportunity to follow their own sexual preference: heterosex or homosex, monogamy or promiscuity, love or paid sex, and whatever alternatives one can think of. These preferences could not be combined with each other if they were ascribed. That leaves only one solution: leave everyone free to follow her or his own sexual preference. This concept of freedom of the second order is no longer internally connected to morality, but only external-

---

28 This seems challengeable to me. The ruling administration may have certain moral objections, but according to the neutrality thesis the government cannot as government have a *private* moral opinion. If in her function as government she would have a moral opinion, that is per definition a *public* moral opinion, which would have to be expressed politically.

29 According to Rawls political liberalism applies the principle of toleration to philosophy (and religion) itself, whereas philosophical liberalism is a comprehensive worldview in the same way as a religious worldview is (Rawls 1993, xiii-xxxiv; 3-46).

ly. It is an option for the public square of politics in order to make it possible that people will not be forced to live according to a sexual morality which is not their's. Thus far the parallel with economic freedom is perfect: sexual preferences of the individual are considered as a given, and the government need only provide that nothing stands in the way of the realization of those preferences (311).

3.6.3 A 'Thin Liberal View on the Nature of Humans and Society'

Rawls claims that his concept of liberal political morality (called 'political liberalism') is compatible with diverse worldviews (Rawls 1993, 150), but that seems to me questionable. After all, he says that the neutrality of the state is a neutrality in aim, not in value or effect.[30] In that sense his political liberalism has already an impact on the advancement of liberal values. To quote Rawls himself: '... it is surely impossible for the basic structure of a just constitutional regime not to have important effects and influences as to which comprehensive doctrines endure and gain adherents over time;... ' (Rawls 1993, 193). In consequence, traditional Thomist and puritan sexual moralities will, without a supporting social structure and social environment, more and more lose their adherents. So the outcome of the practicing of Rawls' political liberalism is more compatible with a liberal worldview than with a traditional christian one. But there is something more to say. I wonder how it is possible to state that political liberalism takes a freestanding view from a wider background, as Rawls does (Rawls 1993, 12). Of course, political liberalism is not a comprehensive worldview, but that does not mean that it is not, in some way or another, dependent on a worldview. In fact, the philosophical presuppositions of Rawls' political liberalism are: citizens are free and equal persons, society is a system of uncoerced cooperation, and tolerance is the main virtue for persons as citizens. It strikes me that Rawls sometimes speaks of free and equal citizens and the other time of

---

30 John Rawls distinguishes between neutrality of procedure, of aim and of effect. A liberal state cannot be neutral of procedure (for being neutral in procedure implies the value of impartiality), nor can the state be neutral in effect (for the value of impartiality will have an effect on the citizens' values). The liberal state can only be neutral in aim, which means that the state is not to do anything that makes it more likely that individuals accept any particular conception of the good life rather than another (Rawls 1993, 190-195).

free and equal persons (Rawls 1993, for instance, 15-22, 29-34), but in such a way that 'citizens' and 'persons' seem to be interchangeable. However, the concept of 'free and equal citizens' is a political category, implying nothing more than the right to equal treatment in political affairs, whereas the concept of 'free and equal persons' is a metaphysical one, derived from a certain view on human nature. The interchangeability of these two concepts suggests that Rawls' political liberalism depends more on metaphysical views than he says, as already is shown by William A. Galston and Jean Hampton respectively (Galston 1989, 711-726; Hampton 1989, 791-814). However, the connection between Rawls' political liberalism and the liberal worldview is rather loose. The interference from the liberal view on the nature of humans and society to the concept of political liberalism is a matter of simple evidence, but not the other way around. It is possible to accept the concept of political liberalism, without accepting the liberal worldview. We should distinguish between fundamental and pragmatic reasons to accept political liberalism. People who can combine their own worldview with political liberalism, will have fundamental reasons; people who cannot, will have pragmatic reasons. It is not irrational for fundamentalistic Christians to accept the concept of free and equal citizens, and at the same time to reject the concept of free and equal persons. In that case they have pragmatic or even self-interested reasons, but why should that be wrong? In any case, I conclude that the philosophical presuppositions of political liberalism consist in what could be called a 'thin liberal view on the nature of humans and society'. In as much as the liberal sexual ethics depends on such a 'thin liberal view' - and surely it does -, it is more in favour of a modern sexual morality than of a traditional one, regardless of the freedom to be as traditional as possible.

3.6.4 A Limiting Principle: Harm

There is, however, one limitation: the 'harm principle'.[31] De Sade's idea of society (and similar ideals) drops out. That also appears to apply to the

---

31 According to Joel Feinberg (1984, 26) the harm principle says the following: 'It is always a good reason in support of penal legislation that it would probably be effective in preventing (diminating, reducing) harm to persons other than the actor (the one prohibited from acting) and there is probably no other means that is equally effective at no greater cost to other values'.

heterosexual morality of propagation, because it limits the freedom to live differently from what it itself prescribes (297-298). On the other hand, for diverging reasons followers of De Sade or of Thomas Aquinas will open the liberal harm principle for discussion: De Sade would totally reject it, Thomas would find it too lenient. The harm principle can only be applied against the background of some ideas about, a 'thin theory of' (Rawls), the human good.[32]

How can it be explained that the harm principle is so generally accepted? Because for the majority it is an acceptable compromise. It makes people take into account other views than their own and to respect other people. The values underlying liberal political morality and its thin theory of the good are, within a democratic society, integrated into many diverse worldviews. However, it is not necessary to accept the harm principle for moral reasons; it is sufficient to have pragmatic reasons.

3.6.5 The Social Structure of the Free Market

The social structure which makes this possible is the model of the free market. The supply is large, the choice free, no one is forced.[33] In how far psychological mechanisms and ideological forces hamper the individual freedom of choice, is important for the person in question, but not for the accurateness of the parallel, because in economic actions these mechanisms also hamper the freedom of choice. What is of more importance is the moral limitation to freedom of sexual choice. As we have seen, in liberal sexual ethics this is the 'harm principle'. However, we also saw that the harm principle is not neutral, but is dependent on certain moral values for its concretization. The harm principle is concretized according to a social compromise that is drawn by applying democratic rules. But however it is done, the harm principle is always a moral limit to absolute sexual freedom.

---

32 Harm can be defined in totally different ways. I mention at random: direct harm, inflicted to a to-be-identified victim; indirect harm, inflicted to society (for example, the annoyance of prostitution); physical harm; spiritual harm; material harm; moral harm and the like, while there can also be a difference of opinion about the extent of the harm inflicted.

33 In an article called 'The come-back of ethics in economy?', I have shown at full length the analogy between liberal ethics and the market economy (Manenschijn 1993, 68-100). Since I take the liberal sexual ethics as a specimen of liberal ethics, the analogy between liberal sexual ethics and the market economy is quite clear to me.

That also produces a parallel with the market principle, because economic activities are also not entirely free according to the market model. They have freedom within the limits of decency, fairness and justice.

3.7   CONCLUSION

In this article I have argued, first, that sexual moralities are always embedded in a worldview, including a view on the social order, and second, that social and economic changes are usually followed by changes in (sexual) morality. The worldview of Thomistic and Puritan morality was determined especially on religious grounds.

In Puritan sexual morality we see demonstrated a transition from feudal society to a civic society: as the market economy slowly but surely pushes aside the subsistence economy, new opinions about sexuality arise which put the freedom of choice for the individual first and foremost. As we have seen, traditional sexual morality held out longer than traditional subsistence-economy.

The parallel to the market economy is finally pretty well perfect in the social presuppositions of liberal sexual ethics. In liberal political morality the freedom to live according to one's own opinions of freedom, is central. This strikingly coincides with what the ideology of a market economy says: the preferences of the people are taken for granted. Only here it does not concern the economic but the sexual preferences.

The development from an obligatory sexual morality to a freedom of choice to live according to one's own sexual preferences (which again are strongly determined by one's own sexual disposition and the special moral training which one has experienced) I consider to be irreversible. After all, it is the consequence of the civic emancipation process of individuals overagainst collective moral force, now not in the area of politics and economy, but in the that of sexual morality. People shall not want to miss that freedom any more.

Traditional worldviews wanted to bind people ideologically to a certain kind of view on humanity and the world. Liberal political morality only asks either agreement with its values, principles and thin theory of the good, or acceptance on pragmatic grounds. The structure of society should be such that people can live according to their own sexual disposition and/or their own conviction.

No one is forced to give up their traditional morality, as long as one leaves others the same freedom desired by oneself. The only thing which one must be able to withstand is the social pressure which uses all the methods of public opinion in order to force people into uniform thinking. But this public pressure is not an ecclesiastical or political force; to withstand it is a matter of character. Agreeing with liberal sexual ethics offers people the possibility to test their character, to make their own choices and to respect others in their choice for different sexual lifestyles.

Recognizing the irreversibleness of a development which strives for the liberation of individual men and women from collective moral pressure, does not mean that the church and theology must forfeit their own Christian view on the relationship between faith and sexual morality. Precisely not. It does mean that they no longer need to weigh down the development of their vision with the a-sexual obsessions from the church's past and that they don't need to begrudge believers their sexual freedom, trusting that mature believers have no less sense of responsibility than bishops and ecclesiastical assemblies.

Translated by Aria and Frank Sawyer

REFERENCES

Aquinas, Thomas, *Summa Theologiae* (ST). In: *Opera Omnia*, S.C. De Propaganda Fide, Rome, 1886, IV-X.

Beemer, Th., De fundering van de sexuele moraal in een door God ingestelde morele orde, In: *Het kerkelijke spreken over seksualiteit en huwelijk*, Publication of the Katholiek Studiecentrum, Nijmegen/Baarn 1983, 15-52.

Bennion, Francis, *The Sex Code. Morals for Moderns*, London 1991.

Berki, R.N., *The History of Political Thought*. A Short Introduction, London/Totowa 1977.

Calvin, Jean, *Institutio Christianae Religionis*, (1559), Corpus Reformatorum XXX, Apud Schwetschke et Filium, Brunswijk 1864.

Clercq, Bertrand J. de, *Macht en principe. Over rechtvaardiging van politieke macht*, Tielt 1988.

D'Emilio, John & Estelle B. Freedman, *Intimate Matters. A History of Sexuality in America*, New York 1989.

Dijksterhuis, E.J., *De mechanisering van het wereldbeeld*, Amsterdam 1950.

Eupen, Theo van, Een eigen kerkelijke sexuele moraal? In: Th. Beemer, et.al., *Liefde, Lust, Leven*, Kampen 1982, 23-40.

Feinberg, Joel, *The Moral Limits of the Criminal Law*, Volume I: Harm to Others, Oxford 1984.
Galston, William A., Pluralism and Social Unity, *Ethics* 99(1989), 711-726.
Hampton, Jean, Should Political Philosophy Be Done without Metaphysics?, *Ethics* 99(1989), 791-814.
Hirschman, A.O., *The Passions and the Interests. Political Arguments for Capitalism before Its Triumph*, Princeton, N.J. 1977.
Hunt, Morton, *Sexual Behavior in the 1970s*, New York 1974.
Jacobs, F.C.L.M., Inhoud en rechtvaardiging van de liberale moraal. In: Musschenga & Jacobs (ed.) 1992, 21-47.
Janssens, L., Chasteté conjugale selon l'encyclique Casti Connubi et suivant la constitution pastorale Gaudium et Spes, *Extrait des Ephemerides Theologicae Lovanienses*, t.XLII, fasc. III, 1966, Gembloux 1966, 513-554.
Jones, Gareth, God's Passionate Embrace: Notes for a Christian Understanding of Sexuality, *Studies in Christian Ethics* 5(1992), nr. 2, 32-45.
Kinsey, Alfred C., Sexual behaviour in the Human Male, Philadelphia 1948.
Kinsey, Alfred C., *Sexual Behaviour in the Human Female*, Philadelphia 1953.
Knijff, H.W. de, *Venus aan de leiband. Europa's erotische cultuur en de christelijke sexuele ethiek*, Kampen 1987.
Manenschijn, G., *Moraal en eigenbelang bij Thomas Hobbes en Adam Smith*, Amsterdam 1979.
Manenschijn, G., Terugkeer van de ethiek in de economie? In: Idem, *Mijn linkerhand is goed genoeg. Over medische ethiek, theologie, politiek en economie*, Baarn 1993, 68-100.
Maris, C.W., Dakini. Over erotiek en ethiek. In: Musschenga & Jacobs 1992, 279-314.
Masters, William H. & Virginia E. Johnson, *Human Sexual Response*, Boston 1966.
Murstein, B.I., *Love, Sex and Marriage through the Ages*, New York 1974.
Musschenga, A.W. & F.C.L.M. Jacobs (eds.), *De liberale moraal en haar grenzen. Recht, ethiek en politiek in een democratische samenleving*, Kampen 1992.
Pateman, Carole, *The Sexual Contract*, New York/Cambridge 1988.
Rawls, John, *Political Liberalism*, New York 1993.

Comments

Albert W. Musschenga

Manenschijn argues that morality is always connected with a religious or nonreligious worldview. One could think that changes in morality are the result of changes in worldview, but according to Manenschijn this is not the case, because morality as well as worldview, in their turn, greatly depend on social conditions. Changes in morality result from changes of the social and economical situation. The question in what way the social and economical situation influences morality, Manenschijn cannot go into.

The example Manenschijn takes to underline his argument is sexual morality, because this is, in his view, pre-eminently a domain which seems to have broken away completely from any religious worldview. Sexological research has proved that worldview is hardly distinctive when it comes to ideas about sex and sexual practices: sexual morality seems to be privatized. Private moralities are moralities connected with certain ideals of life which do not have a public character, but are part of a private view of life. Few people will regard their sexual morality as being universally binding; everybody is free to decide for him or herself how he or she wants to deal with sex. That is what liberal - political, public - morality says - a morality which is alleged to be ideologically neutral and universal. Manenschijn, however, wants to demonstrate that sexual morality is not privatized, and that liberal morality is not neutral, but connected with a particular anthropology and the social model of the market economy. Thus, the distinction between private and public morality is not value-free after all.

My objection to Manenschijn's reasoning, however, is that he makes several statements of which it is not entirely clear how they relate to each other. He wants to disprove that sexual morality is privatized, but the term 'privatization' can be interpreted in two ways. Firstly, it can be regarded as a limitation of scope. When sociologists of sociology speak of 'privatization of religion', they mean that religion is no longer relevant for social issues, but only for existential questions and issues within the private domain. Secondly, privatization could mean that sexual morality has become a matter of individual choice. From section 3.1.4 I understand that Manenschijn is mainly concerned with the latter meaning of the word. In this section, he associates the process of privatization with the seeming disappearance of the links between sexual morality and worldview. If I understand him rightly, Manenschijn argues that sexual morality, in the past as well as today, has always been connected with a certain worldview and a certain outlook on the social order. This leads him to the conclusion that sexual morality is not privatized.

I interpret this conclusion as follows. Sexual morality has never been a separate and isolated issue, but is connected with broader, more comprehensive outlooks on life and the social order. That was not only the case with Thomist and Puritan sexual morality, it also goes for modern libertine morality. If I understand Manenschijn well, he holds the view that the very existence of these connections are a refutation of the idea that sexual morality is privatized. This would imply, however, that the meaning of the idea 'privatization of sexual morality' has shifted and has become something like 'the gaining of independence of sexual morality'. Even if Manenschijn is right in saying that in *this* sense sexual morality is not 'privatized', this does not imply that sexual morality is not privatized in another sense, namely that it has become a matter of free choice.

Manenschijn also passes over an important development, namely the pluralization of sexual morality within religious groups. Among Christians, for instance, one may find traditional Catholic, Puritan and even libertine views. There is no longer a typically Christian sexual morality - nor a typically Catholic or Protestant one. In so far as Christians connect their sexual morality with their faith, they do so in very different ways, depending on the personal way they give meaning to their sexual views and behaviour within the framework of their faith. One Christian sees sexual assistance to the handicapped as a form of prostitution, whereas another will regard it as a service to one's neighbour. If Manenschijn is right in saying that sexual morality is always connected with a more general worldview, one is inclined to conclude that the Christian faith does no longer have a uniform worldview, and can apparently be combined with a variety of different worldviews.

According to Manenschijn, not only the first-order sexual moralities are connected with particular worldviews, but also the second-order, liberal political morality which says that everybody may follow his own preferences regarding sexuality. The worldview of what Manenschijn calls the liberal sexual ethics, is connected with the idea that it is good for human society and its members if everyone can live freely according to his own convictions. In other words: the liberal idea of autonomy is embedded in a certain conception of the good life and the good society, and therefore it is not ideologically neutral. Does Manenschijn actually mean to say that, contrary to what is argued by Rawls, there should not be made a distinction between a political, i.e. limited form of liberalism and an ideological, more comprehensive liberalism? Not a single contemporary liberal thinker, however, would claim that liberal morality is neutral, i.e. value-free, not founded on particular values, and free of ideological presuppositions. But the justification of liberal political morality does not depend on a specific comprehensive conception of the good life, because its presuppositions are limited to a 'thin theory of the good' (Rawls). It can be, and is indeed integrated in a wide variety of worldviews, each of which justifies it in its own way; in that sense, it can be connected with comprehensive worldviews. But that does not mean that it can be reconciled with, or coherently integrated in just any comprehensive worldview: neither the traditional Catholic, Thomist morality, nor the morality of theocratic, orthodox Protestants can be reconciled with the liberal political morality. But liberal morality does not demand that all citizens embrace and propagate its way of thinking - it is enough when citizens obey the rules of the game of democracy.

Liberal political morality allows for different sexual moralities to exist alongside each other by regarding sexual opinions and practices as preferences. Manenschijn remarks (on page 86) that on this point there is a parallel between the liberal idea of political freedom, and the economic idea of the free market. If I understand him correctly, Manenschijn means to say that from the point of view of liberal political morality, the choice between, for example, heterosexual monogamy and homosexual promiscuity may be compared with the choice between two brands of cars. In this way, moral convictions are reduced to private preferences, and deprived of their claim to suprapersonal validity. I do not deny that for some people sexual behaviour has indeed become merely a matter of preference, but I do not agree with Manenschijn when he suggests that it is typical of liberal political morality that it reduces - sexual - moral convictions to preferences. From the point of view of liberal political morality, no sexual morality is better or more valuable than any other. It abstracts from the claims to truth of the different competing moralities, and therefore treats them, in politics and policy-making, as if they were preferences. But that is not the same thing as liberal morality being essentially connected with moral subjectivism.

In section 3.6.3 Manenschijn concedes that liberal sexual ethics does not depend on a comprehensive conception of the good, but only on a - in Rawls' terminology - thin theory of the good. So far I agree with him. With Galston (1989) and Hampton (1989) he argues that the idea of 'free and equal persons' that is central in the 'thin theory of the good' is a metaphysical one, derived from a certain view on human nature. That might be true; I will not go into that. At the end of the section he concludes: 'In as much as the liberal sexual ethics depends on such a 'thin (i.e. metaphysical, awm) liberal view - and surely it does - it is more in favour of a modern sexual morality than of a traditional one, regardless of the freedom to be as traditional as possible' (p. 84). I presume he means by 'modern sexual morality' the libertine one. The implicit conviction here is that the metaphysical and anthropological ideas underpinning the libertine sexual morality, are essentially connected with the metaphysical beliefs that form the background of the idea of free and equal persons. He does, however, not offer any argument for that belief. Therefore, his conclusion is ill-founded.

Manenschijn is right, however, in saying that the typical liberal principle of defining boundaries, the 'harm principle', for its application depends on moral values, as 'harm' is not a value-free concept. For one person this means only physical or psychological harm, whereas someone else includes harm to the soul. Liberals will not deny, then, that one can argue about the application of the harm principle. But they shorten and simplify the political agenda by removing the question of what is good sexuality, and limiting the discussion to the question when a sexual practice causes unacceptable harm. It seems undeniable to me that it is much easier to come to an agreement about the latter question.

Translated by Birgit Kooijman

REFERENCES

Galston, W.A., Pluralism and Social Unity, *Ethics* 99(1989), 711-726.
Hampton, J., Should Political Philosophy Be Done without Metaphysics?, *Ethics* 99 (1989), 791-814.

4

Moral Taboos and the Narrow Conception of Morality[1]

Arnold Burms

4.1 INTRODUCTION

The distinction between a narrow and a broad conception of morality often serves as a starting point for the treatment of a couple of problems whose importance is not merely theoretical or academic. These problems can be formulated as follows: (i) can a universal, minimalistic morality exist which is no longer rooted in traditional, culturally determined conceptions of the good life? Can morality survive when it is disconnected from these traditional views? (ii) Can traditional pictures of the good life retain their inspirational power when they are relegated to the domain of private life?

When these questions are discussed, it is normally assumed that the distinction between a narrow and broad conception of morality is sufficiently clear. This presupposition, however, is mistaken. We do not really know the role of a morality in the narrow sense as long as we cannot precisely determine the meaning of the virtue - referred to by terms such as 'benevolence', 'beneficence' or 'altruism' - which lies at the core of this morality. What do we really care about when we care about others? I will attempt to show that one currently prevailing answer and prima facie evident answer to this question is wrong. A positive thesis will be added to this negative one, namely that the willingness to respect moral taboos is an essential part of our altruistic concern. If this positive thesis is correct, then morality in the

---

[1] I thank Albert W. Musschenga for his penetrating criticism of the first draft of this paper, Victor Kal for sending me an interesting letter about moral taboos, and Paul Moyaert for his inspiring, unpublished paper on charity.

narrow sense inevitably contains elements that do not fit in the liberal, humanistic framework in which this narrow conception is usually situated.

4.2 CARING ABOUT OTHERS

Morality in the narrow sense has to do with the ways in which the rights and interests of others can impinge on us. It requires that we should in some sense care about other people and be willing, if necessary, to put aside our selfish concerns.

The limitations of this kind of morality can be put in sharper relief by way of a double contrast. First, a morality in the narrow sense does not provide an answer to the question of what a good or meaningful life consists in, and therefore has no bearing on what Strawson calls 'pictures of ideal forms of life'. In the picture people have of a meaningful life, an altruistic concern will normally not be the only element, and may not even play a central role at all; people will perhaps give more importance to artistic creativity, the pursuit of scientific truth, or a lifestyle characterized by courage, lucidity, spontaneity, moderation or refined pleasure.

Secondly, a morality in the narrow sense must be distinguished from particularistic forms of altruistic concern. The attitude of those who are prepared to go to extremes in order to promote the well-being of their relatives and friends is not egoistic, but it does not belong to morality in the narrow sense because it is characterized by partiality. The moral point of view (as it is defined within the narrow conception) is a combination of both impartiality and benevolence. I will not attempt to answer the important question about how we are precisely to describe this combination. In what follows, I will concentrate instead on the content of our altruistic concerns. What are we concerned about when we are concerned about others? About their interests, their happiness, their dignity ... ?

A first point that ought to be mentioned about this concern is its predominantly negative or protective character. When we really care about X, our attention will be centered on the evils against which X must be protected, rather than on the fulfillment of X's deepest desires or ambitions. This is related to a principle that Harry G. Frankfurt has formulated as follows: 'making things better is, from a moral point of view, less important (measure for measure) than keeping them from getting worse' (Frankfurt 1988, 110).

It is revealing in this regard that parental love, which has a paradigmatic role in what we have in mind when we speak about caring about someone else, can be described as a predominantly *protective* attitude. The primary hope of parents is that their children will be spared hardship, sickness, pain, dishonour or untimely death. What they hope for their children is not something great or exceptional, but rather the modest happiness which consists in the absence of serious ills. Children usually see their lives in another way: they dream of adventures or passions, and hope that they will be beautiful, brilliant, or famous. Parents usually do not share that point of view, and do not take the desires of their children very seriously. And when they do hope that the dreams of their sons or daughters will come true, it is usually with this thought in mind: 'I hope that your dreams will be fulfilled, if you can't be happy any other way'. The difference in perspective reveals something about the distinction that concerns us here: it is clear that the protective attitude of parents could be related to the moral point of view as it is defined by the narrow conception, whereas the attitude of the children towards their own life could be connected with a view about the good life.

The question that must be raised is this: why is the protective attitude essential for the altruistic concern? Or to put it another way: what are the general principles in terms of which we can spell out the meaning of our readiness to protect others against evil? The answer seems simple at first glance. It looks *prima facie* obvious that it must have to do with a combination of the following lines of reasoning:

(i) Caring about other people primarily consists in the readiness to do what they desire or, more precisely, to do what is needed such that their desires will be fulfilled. Since there are no stronger desires than of those who are in need and want to be relieved, altruistic concern will be directed primarily at rescuing people in distress or protecting them from threatening situations.

(ii) What is good or bad for X can always be translated in terms of pleasant or unpleasant experiences for X. In combination with (i), this means that people will desire more strongly to be relieved of painful experiences (or be protected against them) than they will desire to have pleasant experiences. Altruistic concern will consequently express itself primarily in a readiness to guard others from painful experiences.

According to the first premiss of argument (i), the moral relevance of the readiness to help or protect others can be derived from the moral relevance of the readiness to take account of their (strongest) desires. This is wrong, because it is mistaken to presuppose that the seriousness of a distressful situation is determined by the intensity of the desire to be rescued from such a situation or to be protected against it. The desires that some people have to be loved, admired or desired can be quite intense, but these desires are not needs. Frankfurt illustrates this point with the extreme example of a man who is seized by the idée fixe that his life will be worthless unless he has a certain sports car. Would we say that this man needs a sports car? (1988, 113). Someone who has an intense, unfulfilled desire is not necessarily in need. And conversely, someone can be in need without having the desire to be helped: an insane person who mutilates himself and refuses anybody's help is still desperately in need of help. It is therefore not true that the moral significance of our willingness to help others in need can be derived from our willingness to take their desires into account.

The line of reasoning in (ii) is also mistaken. Here it is assumed that the intensity of need is determined by the intensity of the painful experience. It is, however, not difficult to think of examples which contradict this presupposition. We feel a greater degree of sympathy for children that are victims of violence (during a war, for example) than for adults that suffer the same fate; the evil seems therefore worse when it happens to children than when it happens to adults. And yet there is of course no reason at all to assume that the intensity of suffering caused by violence is higher in children than in adults. And although there seems to be no reason to think that an old woman who is raped suffers more than a young woman who is a victim of the same crime, the crime still seems more horrible when an old woman is the victim. Moreover, one can also think of examples where an evil is committed against person X and which does not cause X any pain at all. A child who is sexually abused by an adult is undoubtedly a victim of evil, even if the sexual abuse does not cause the child any pain and even if it causes no psychological scars which negatively influence the child's later development. And when a woman is sexually abused while under anesthetic, she is the victim of a harm which is comparable to rape and which would elicit similar feelings of indignation. The horror we feel when we find out that a murder victim's corpse has been brutally mutilated is not fundamentally different from the horror we feel when we think about the pain that the victim has suffered.

These examples show that (1) the evil perpetrated against X is not necessary experienced by X and that (2) it would be mistaken to believe that an evil experienced by X is radically different from an evil which is not experienced by X. It is clear that the latter kind of evil evokes the same feelings of indignation, pity and horror as the former kind of evil. But what is it that connects these two forms of evil? What is the content of a concept of evil that applies as well to violent treatment of dead human bodies as to rape and murder? In the line of thought that follows, I will try to give an answer to this question.

4.3   MORAL TABOOS AND HUMAN DIGNITY

The tendency to believe that (for example) sexual conduct which does not give anyone any unpleasant experiences can still be morally wrong, or that someone can be wronged when his dead body is mutilated, will be automatically associated with so-called 'moral taboos'. One usually uses the term 'moral taboo' in referring to prohibitions which are experienced as extremely binding, but cannot easily receive a rational justification and for this reason appear to be in a certain sense arbitrary, or at least very much relative to a specific culture. The breaking of a taboo can elicit very intense emotional responses, sometimes even in cases where the transgression is unintentional. From the standpoint of enlightened rationality, such intense responses are difficult to accept, especially because they seem to be out of proportion with the evil committed.

Bertrand Russell (who considered moral taboos relics from an uncritical, traditional morality) mentions in his *Human Society in Ethics and Politics* (1954, 30) the example of Moll Flanders in Defoe's novel: when Moll Flanders discovers that the man she has married is also her brother, she can no longer stand him as a husband, although they have lived happily together for years. What Russell wants to show with this example (and what is the object of his criticism of taboo morality) is that the horror provoked by the discovery of the breaking of the incest taboo is out of proportion with the harmful consequences the incestious relation could possibly have here.[2]

---

[2] A few years ago there was a discussion in France about the question of whether a legal marriage could be granted to two people who were related as brother and sister,

Russell would certainly not exclude the possibility that some moral taboos had or have a useful function - but, according to him, we should be prepared to check to see whether they actually are useful or not. This means that Russell does not reject the totality of prohibitions that belong to the sphere of taboos, but that he does reject as irrational the refusal to investigate whether the taboos people tend to obey are well-founded. What is a priori wrong according to him is not the content of any specific taboo, but rather a blind obedience to something whose meaning cannot be derived from the general principles one explicitly assents to. The morality advocated by Russell does not admit of anything which is not fully transparent: it should not contain any elements which are not derivable from the general principles originating from kind or altruistic dispositions.

Russell's view that we should exclude everything that is not derivable from general principles that we consciously adopt, sounds familiar and has become a feature of contemporary common sense. It is, however, clear that this view has consequences that almost no one finds acceptable. Someone who secretly defiled corpses or ate human flesh would not cause anyone harm. But who could say in all honesty that he finds this conduct morally acceptable?

Many philosophers would say, like Russell, that our spontaneous moral reactions and attitudes should be abandoned when they are not in keeping with the general principles that we explicitly endorse: they claim that moral taboos, in as far as they cannot be justified in terms of general principles, ought to be eliminated. However, it seems to me more correct to take another approach and try to see what the point of moral taboos is.

The hypothesis that I want to defend here is that the respect for moral taboos is an essential part of the moral attitude (as it is defined within the narrow conception of morality). In the last section, I formulated the idea that the essence of the moral attitude consists in an altruistic concern which is primarily protective. We can now say that this altruistic concern protects against evils which can be described as degradations or losses of dignity. Cannibalism, necrophilia, rape and torture are violations of human dignity;

---

but were not raised together and only met one another when they were already adults. Arguing that what has no harmful consequences cannot be morally bad, the man and woman at the center of controversy thought that there was no rational basis for forbidding them entering into matrimony.

the degradation they bring about is, I think, the essence of the kind of evil against which we want to protect those for whom we have an altruistic concern.

The thesis that I am defending here implies that the moral significance of the respect for a dead human body is not essentially different from the moral significance of offering help to those who are, say, the victims of torture. Many people will tend to reject this thesis as highly counter-intuitive, and to claim that the evil produced by torture is completely different from the evil produced by the desecration of the dead. This current view is exemplified by J. Feinberg, who claims that the evil inherent in the desecration of the dead is merely symbolic. Feinberg admits that there is nothing wrong with the intense moral feelings which are elicited by the violent and disrespectful treatment of dead bodies. But: 'When we are faced with a choice between symbol and sentiment, on the one side, and the interests of threatened real persons on the other, it could only be moral sentimentality or squeamishness that would lead us to neglect the interests from fear of offending the sentiments' (1985, 95).

The distinction Feinberg makes between real and symbolic evil is much more problematic than it looks at first glance. Let us consider the example of defamation. Defamation is a kind of evil that can occur both when the victim is aware of it as well as when he is not. It would not make much sense to draw a sharp line between the two cases and to say that the evil is real in the former case and merely symbolic in the latter. But if it is possible that someone can be a victim of defamation without being aware of it, why not say that someone who is defamed after his death is also a victim of evil? The distinction between real and symbolic evil also seems artificial when we consider the fear many people have that they might die in public: why should we say that their fear of losing their dignity when dead is completely different from their fear of dying a painful death?

We should go a step further. Instead of claiming that pain is a real evil that should be contrasted with the so-called 'symbolic' evil of, for instance, the desecration of a corpse, we can describe both the latter and the former as forms of degradation. A person in intense pain, who cries and screams with his face distorted by agony, is in a humiliating or degrading situation. He is outside the normal, meaningful interactions; his own pain has turned him into an object, as it were. It is especially against this sort of degradation that we want to protect the people we care about.

4.4 MORAL TABOOS AND THE RELIGIOUS ASPECT OF MORALITY

If it is true that degradation belongs to the essence of the evil that altruistic concern is directed against, then the significance of moral taboos is not as marginal as is commonly thought. Moral taboos (or at least many of them) can be interpreted as protection against degradation arising directly from the essential vulnerability of human existence. Our lives are deeply entangled with a material reality that is in a certain sense alien to us, that never lets itself be integrated in the meaning that we want to give to what we do or are. A newborn child, a person who is badly suffering, or the body of someone who has just died emphatically confront us with this truth. It is also no accident then that moral taboos often concern birth, death and sexuality - realities, in other words, in which the entanglement of the human and the inhuman is manifested most strikingly. By obeying certain moral taboos, we respect the vulnerability that arises from this entanglement.

The thesis that I have tried to defend here implies that the readiness to respect taboos is an important part of the moral attitude (as it is defined within the narrow conception): the degradation against which taboos provide protection, belongs essentially to the kind of harm we want to guard others against, when we are moved by altruistic concerns.

The important role I am ascribing to taboos in morality as a whole is, of course, difficult to reconcile with the widespread opinion that the point of morality is its function. Moral taboos cannot be integrated in the view that we understand the meaning of morality if we know what morality is for. It is in fact characteristic of moral taboos that they do not lend themselves to a reduction to general principles or purposes we explicitly assent to. We cannot explain, for example, which general moral principles would justify our repulsion for cannibalism or incest. The difficulty is twofold. We may perhaps be able to explain what sort of harm is *probably* or *generally* caused by an incestuous relation: we will say, for example, that incestuous relations tend to bring about a certain psychological damage or deformation. But this knowledge would not explain why we tend to condemn incestuous relationships *categorically*. When a father has sexual contact with his little daughter, we *always* think this is bad, even when there are very good reasons to believe that the child did not suffer and was not psychologically damaged.

There is a second difficulty connected with any attempt to justify moral taboos by reference to some function. Even if we were able to ascribe a certain function to taboos, the *motive* or ground for spontaneously obeying these taboos would not arise from our theoretical insight into this function. Imagine that we had knowledge of some anthropological or biological theory concerning the function of the incest taboo. The willingness to take this theoretical insight into consideration is fundamentally different from the spontaneous feelings of disgust evoked in us by the transgression of the incest taboo. A person who lacked this feeling would not have any sense of the sinfulness of incest and would not really understand the traditional interdiction.[3] It may be possible to demonstrate that the traditional sentiments towards dead bodies are in the interests of society; perhaps it could be shown that the weakening or vanishing of these sentiments would be socially harmful. But even if we think that something like this is the case, we still will not be able to experience our readiness to respect dead bodies as a good means of maintaining some socially beneficial dispositions in ourselves. Respect for the dead is not experienced as a means to bring about any beneficial result whatsoever.

One of the implications of the view I am defending about moral taboos is that the moral significance of respecting the dead (by respecting certain taboos) is not fundamentally different from the moral significance of offering help to those who need it. Many people will find this preposterous. What is unacceptable for them is the idea that the futility or uselessness that in a sense characterizes whatever we do for the dead would also apply to the good we try to achieve for living human beings.

It is, however, not at all difficult to see that there is a point of view from which all our moral efforts look just as futile as those we make for the sake of the dead. We know that there are horrifying things now happening in the world, which, if we witnessed them, would give us the feeling that all our moral endeavours and accomplishments are futile. In comparison with the misery of the world, whatever we can achieve will always appear utterly insignificant. Moreover, we know that even the greatest sacrifices we submit ourselves to for the sake of one single individual often turn out to be not sufficient to make that one individual a little less unhappy than before. We also know that even our best intentions can have consequences that perhaps will annul whatever we had hoped to achieve out of noble motives.

---

[3] This line of thought is developed by Roger Scruton in his 'Sexual Morality and the Liberal Consensus' (1990, 261-272).

These truisms should make us wary of representing morality as a kind of collective enterprise and of assuming that the moral value of specific activities consists in their contribution to the realisation of a general goal.

The tendency to identify the point of morality with some useful function is not only widespread; it is also intimately linked with the very idea of a minimal morality (or morality in the narrow sense). The line of reasoning that usually lies at the origin of the distinction between a narrow and broad conception of morality can be formulated as follows: since contemporary Western culture has no widely agreed upon picture of what the good life consists in, there is a need for a minimal morality which determines what is necessary for the good functioning of a pluralistic society. Minimal morality is here introduced as an instrument we need in order to solve a certain problem.

As we have already seen, this instrumentalist approach to morality can only conceive moral taboos as bothersome relics from an irrational, traditional morality. However, we have also seen that (1) the moral attitude, as it is defined within the narrow conception, is to be characterized as a protective, altruistic concern; that (2) what an altruistic concern strives to protect others against can be characterized as 'degradation' and that the point of moral taboos is the protection of human dignity against this degradation.

The upshot of all this is paradoxical. On the one hand, the narrow conception of morality is closely associated with an instrumentalist approach that is fundamentally opposed to moral taboos; on the other hand, it appears that we cannot really understand the meaning of the altruistic concern which is the fundamental moral attitude within the narrow conception, unless we take moral taboos into account.

The question is now this: if morality in a narrow sense cannot be divorced from moral taboos, can it be universal? Or to be more precise: could the protective role I am ascribing here to moral taboos play a part within a rationally construed, universal system of moral values?

I think that the answer to this question is negative. In order to elucidate this, I will start from a concrete example that I have mentioned a number of times already, viz. the respect that we owe to the dead. We would never be able to derive from general, rational principles what the content of our duties towards the dead should be. There is some plausibility in the belief that one can have an insight into what people essentially need as human beings, and that one can derive from such an insight fundamental human rights and the conditions a just society must satisfy. But there is no such plausibility in the belief that we might in a similar vein find out what we owe to the dead. The phrase 'what the dead really need' sounds nonsensical. Since we cannot determine a priori what our duties towards the dead are, our duties will have a contingent, culturally relative character.

It is a striking fact that the awareness of the contingent, local character of these customs can be associated with a sense of their importance. What is known to be culturally dependent can be experienced at the same time as being in a sense morally necessary. The very specific set of external obligations (words, gestures, ceremonial activities) are not just an accidental expression of an inner attitude which could be independently described.

C.S. Lewis has made an interesting remark about this in his *A Grief Observed*, the book in which he describes his reactions to his wife's death. C.S. Lewis writes how shocked he initially was by a man who came to the graveyard to look after the flowers on his mother's grave and who said cheerfully to an acquaintance: 'See you later, I'm just going to visit Mum'. What Lewis found so objectionable was that the respect for the dead degenerated here into a routine, performed without any personal involvement. He realized, however, that what to him initially seemed disgustingly superficial can perhaps also contain a certain wisdom. He writes: 'May this not be in one way better than preserving and caressing an image in one's own meaning? ... the image has the ... disadvantage that it will be whatever you want ... The flower bed on the other hand is an obstinate, resistant, often intractable bit of reality, just as Mum in her lifetime doubtless was' (1954, 19-20).

Our inner attitude towards the dead can only be authentic when it is in a sense marked by its own inadequacy: when thinking about the dead, we should be aware of the inevitable oblivion and betrayal. We have to remember that we forget. And it is precisely for this reason that the fulfillment of external duties is of fundamental importance. By submitting to external rituals and duties, we can come to realize that no thought that we could entertain and no mood that we could conjure up would be an adequate response to the death of someone deeply cherished.

This line of thinking can shed some light on a fact that can be considered a general property of religious ritual. In a ritual context, one normally has to obey very strict obligations concerning the words one has to utter or the acts one has to perform. This strictness can be connected with what I have just said about our obligations towards the dead. It is precisely because in respecting the dead we are concerned with something radically outside our ordinary intentions, projects or achievements, that it also matters that we strictly adhere to external obligations which transcend our subjective attitudes, sentiments or moods. Death is one of those intractable realities that do not fit into the frameworks in virtue of which our ordinary ambitions and projects can have that familiar appearance of importance and solidity. They are, of course, other such realities. Whatever we are and whatever we do is embedded in a reality which is largely beyond our control. One should say, I think, that reality in so far as it exceeds our power of prediction and control and is in a sense even beyond what we can know or conceive, is the defining concern of religion.

Speaking about the contrast between common sense and religion, C.K. Chesterton said: 'All that we call common sense and rationality and practicality and positivism only means that for certain dead levels of our life we forget that we have forgotten. All that we call spirit and art and ecstasy only means that for one awful instant, we remember that we forget' (1959, 54). Religion reminds us of what we tend to forget or exclude; it makes us indirectly aware of the essential, inevitable forgetfulness which is a necessary fact of our existence. This awareness can only be indirect, for the same reason we can only indirectly obey the injunction: 'Think of what you do not think'. It is precisely because we can only indirectly concern ourselves with what our essential forgetfulness tends to exclude that the strict or categorical character of ritual obligation also makes sense: in submitting ourselves to external obligations, we can express the awareness that we want to be related to a reality which radically transcends our inner life. Religion gives us the capacity to experience our essential forgetfulness and powerlessness in a positive manner and to accept or love a radically transcendent reality.

I think that the categorical character which is a feature of moral taboos and which has been attributed by Kant and other philosophers to all moral imperatives, is by no means an expression of universal rationality, but should be understood in the way in which we understand the categorical character of ritual obligations. The results of our moral efforts are limited, transient, and insecure. The good we can achieve is essentially fragile, because it is deeply determined by a reality which transcends our powers. We pay tribute to that fragility by strictly obeying some external obligations; our capacity to recognize the categorical character of certain moral prescriptions or prohibitions can then be seen as an expression of our awareness that it is not within our power to achieve what is most important to us. The willingness to submit oneself to categorical obligations is like a sort of prayer. It is in virtue of this religious or quasi-religious aspect of morality that we can reconcile ourselves with the futility of our moral accomplishments and that we can live with the thought that there is always much more we could and should have done for specific persons and groups or for humanity as a whole. A morality which excluded moral taboos, gets divorced from what makes this reconciliation possible and will, I think, be easily transformed into defeatism or cynicism. For this reason, I am inclined to share a fear expressed by Kolakowski: 'When I try, however, to point out the most dangerous characteristic of modernity, I tend to sum up my fear in one phrase: the disappearance of taboos' (Kolakowski 1990).

Translated by Stuart Rennie

REFERENCES

Chesterton, C.K., *Orthodoxy*, New York 1959.
Feinberg, J., *The Moral Limits of the Criminal Law*. Volume II: Offense to Others, New York 1985.
Frankfurt, H.G., *The Importance of What We Care About: Philosophical Essays*, Cambridge 1988.
Kolakowski, L., *Modernity on Endless Trial*, Chicago 1990.
Lewis, C.S., *A Grief Observed*, London 1954.
Russell, B., *Human Society in Ethics and Politics*, London 1954.
Scruton, R., *The Philosopher on Dover Beach*, Manchester 1990.

Comments

Hans S. Reinders

1 INTRODUCTION

The reconstruction of what Professor Burms is in effect saying about the relationship between religion and morality poses some difficulties to me. He discusses two relationships. Firstly, there is the relation between moral taboos and the narrow conception of morality, which he takes to be problematic. Secondly there is the relation between, on the one hand, a broader conception of morality that is capable of including moral taboos and, on the other hand, religion, which he takes to be necessary. When I understand him correctly, Burms is saying that, because a narrow conception of morality cannot incorporate an adequate account for moral taboos, there is a strong case to be made for what he calls the 'religious aspect of morality'. The categorical nature of moral taboos compels us to acknowledge that what morality demands is beyond our control, including the control of reason. Moral taboos thus reflect a transcendental reality, just like the categorical obligations derived from religious rituals reflect a transcendental reality that is likewise beyond human control. Burms intends to argue, then, that moral taboos cannot be adequately explained as requirements derived from moral reason. This he claims to be a strong indication of the religious dimension of morality. In my view, the argument he uses to establish this claim is defective.

Whether or not moral taboos can be explained as required by moral reason depends, of course, on how the concept of moral reason is understood. Here the first of the two relations that Burms discusses comes into play. It appears from his analysis that moral taboos are incompatible with the instrumentalist account of moral reason that he takes to be characteristic for a narrow conception of morality. According to this conception, people should be willing to control themselves in pursuing their own good and to care about the rights and interests of others who are not included in their projects. The need for protection of the rights and interests of others reveals the primarily negative function of social morality. Social morality contributes to the overall goal of the 'good functioning' of society in which people are engaged in pursuing their own projects.

Given this instrumentalist account, Burms argues, moral taboos are difficult to explain, because the explanation cannot be derived from the overall goal of morality. The reason for is twofold. Firstly, moral taboos do not lose their prohibitive force in cases where transgressing them does not seem to frustrate good social functioning. The categorical prohibition of incest, for example, remains in force even if no one's rights or interests are violated. In cases of other prohibitions, the protection of other people's 'rights' and 'interests' does not provide a sufficient rationale for accepting these prohibitions, as is the case with, for example, the taboos on necrophilia and bestiality. Secondly, the point of a moral taboo is not experienced in terms of its contributing to any morally desirable state of affairs. The 'spontaneous feeling of disgust' that follows from transgressions of a prohibited act occurs independently of rational considerations about the social function of the prohibition.

The conclusion drawn by Burms is that the difficulty of providing rational grounds for moral taboos shows the inadequacy of the narrow conception of morality. It appears to me, however, that there are other interpretations of moral reason possible even in the context of a narrow conception of morality, which do allow for an explanation of both moral taboos and their categorical character. If such an explanation can indeed be given, Burms' argument fails to show that the analogy of the transcendental dimension of both religion and morality is sufficient to indicate a necessary relationship between the two. To explore this possibility, I will draw on a discussion of 'moral abominations' by Jeffrey Stout who, it seems to me, follows essentially the same strategy as Burms, in order to show that the distinction between narrow and wide conceptions of morality is not sufficiently clear. Stout's reasoning does not depend, however, on the curtailment of a narrow conception of morality to an instrumentalist account of moral reason. Nor does the conclusion of his argument lead to a recovery of religion as a necessary background of social morality.

2 MORAL TABOOS AND SOCIAL IDENTITY

In his novel *The Narrative of Arthur Gordon Pym of Nantucket*, Edgar Allan Poe tells the story of a South Sea expedition that is shipwrecked and ends with a most horrible experience by the survivors who are drifting around in open sea, including the narrator Arthur Gordon Pym himself.

On a ship that is nearly turned upside down and surrounded by sharks, without any food and water being left, Pym dreads the prospect of what sooner or later will appear to be the only possible way to survive for him and his shipmates: 'that one of us should die to preserve the existence of the others'. At the moment that it is mentioned by one of his companions, Pym fiercely opposes to any 'cannibal design', the result of which is that he puts himself in an extremely dangerous position by presenting himself as a suitable candidate to be devoured. Eventually he sees no other way than to comply and to accept that straws are drawn in order to determine who will be the one to be killed. Both the lottery and the ensuing execution are carried out quickly. The victim turns out to be the shipmate who first brought up the subject. He does not offer any resistance when being stabbed with a knife in the back.

The narrator is very brief on what happens next:

Such things may be imagined, but words have no power to impress the mind with the exquisite horror of their reality. Let me suffice to say that, having in some measure appeased the raging thirst which consumed us by the blood of the victim, and having by common consent taken off the hands, feet and head, throwing them together with the entrails, into the sea, we devoured the rest of the body, piecemeal, during the four ever memorable days of the 17th, 18th, 19th and 20th of the month.

What is so morally repulsive about an act of cannibalism as narrated in this story? Burms appears to be arguing that within the instrumentalist conception of social morality this question cannot even be raised, because this particular act does not seem to go against the grain of any of its basic concepts or principles. No one's rights are forfeited since all men consent, the lottery is carried out fairly, the execution proceeds immediately and without cruelty. Although taking someone's life is normally not in the victim's interest, in this case it might even be argued that the alternative for the unfortunate shipmate is an extremely torturous death from starvation and thirst. If so, where is the reason to be horrified?

There is a clear reason, however, which is indicated by the narrative, but which has nothing to do with the protection of the rights and interests of the victim. It has to do with the moral identity of perpetrators of cannibalism who are socialized according to the values that are inherent in our culture. Jeffrey Stout tells a similar, though much more artificial story. Two men in the same position as Arthur Gordon Pym have to decide among them who will eat from the corpse of a third, deceased shipmate and who will eat a remaining portion of meat from an albatros (the possibility of this choice is what makes the story artificial). None of them wants to choose, however, and they resolve the problem by disguising the food, so that neither of both men knows who eats what. Afterwards one of them enters a seafood restaurant, orders a piece of albatros, discovers the difference of its taste and shoots himself. The reason is, according to Stout, that becoming a cannibal - at least in our culture - is to be no longer fully human:

Being unambiguously human entails, for us, a kind of dietary restraint. Some objects in the environment count as food, others do not. Ingestion of the wrong objects threatens one's status as human. Eating dirt or feces is degrading in the straightforward sense that it puts you in a different (lower) class. Eating human flesh strays outside the normative diet in another direction, but the effect is the same - to render the diner's status as a human insecure. Nonhuman carnivores make no bones about eating human flesh. To eat human flesh is to become like them, to straddle the line between us and them, to become anomalous (Stout 1988, 151).

Violation of the prohibition on cannibalism can be explained in moral terms of what it means to be human. Of course, what it means to be human depends on a wider context of beliefs regarding what Stout calls 'social structure and cosmology'. Any society that, for one reason or another, does not maintain a sharp boundary of the social order at this point, will presumably show that its members feel little repulsion at the sight of cannibalism (Stout 1988, 152).

3 MORAL TABOOS AND ETHICAL THEORY

It appears to me that Stout is in a better position to account for certain aspects related to moral taboos than Burms, because he does not disconnect moral taboos from moral reason.[4] Burms seems to be left in an intuitionist position where he has to take moral taboos as 'moral primitives', which leaves unclear whether or not moral taboos are and should be susceptible to moral criticism and if so, how. Secondly, in showing that moral taboos cannot be justified sufficiently in terms of their contribution to the good functioning of society, Burms ignores the other possibility, which is that the justification has to do with the agent's self-respect rather than with the good of society.

To elaborate on the first point, let me just mention one of Stout's examples, the taboo of homosexuality, that is missing in Burms. That it is missing need not be surprising: homosexuality may still be a taboo in the United States, as it certainly was some time ago in Western Europe, but equally certain this is no longer the case for many Europeans. The fact of this change in moral attitude indicates that there is no need to treat the taboo of homosexuality as a 'moral primitive', since it can be perfectly explained in terms of the wider context of beliefs regarding 'social structure and cosmology', as Stout puts it. The erosion of sharp divisions between male and female role in contemporary society has allowed for different interpretations of 'natural order' and the nature of sexuality. In significant aspects of sexuality there is no tenable distinction between the morals of heterosexuality and homosexuality, once these changes are reflected upon properly. After a sufficient amount of 'cognitive psychotherapy' [5], it should not be too hard

---

4 At one point I find Burms' text particularly unclear. He questions the adequacy of a narrow conception of morality by asking what we are supposed to take care of with respect to other people. He thereby intends to criticize 'one currently prevailing and prima facie evident answer to this question' (p. 95) - which then turns out be the instrumentalist answer. When coming to his conclusion, however, he seems to generalize his findings from one particular conception of narrow morality to hold for other such conceptions as well: 'On the one hand, the narrow conception of morality is closely associated with an instrumentalist approach that is fundamentally opposed to moral taboos; on the other hand, it appears that we cannot really understand the meaning of the altruistic concern which is the fundamental moral attitude within the narrow conception, unless we take moral taboos into account' (p. 104). Clearly Kantian conceptions of narrow morality would not necessarily fit in Burms' analysis and, arguably, they will allow for explanations of moral taboos by focussing on the moral identity of the agent, thereby providing reasons that instrumentalist explanations restricted to the protection of the rights and interests of others fail to provide (see below).

5 I borrow the phrase from Richard Brandt 1979, 11-12.

to see that homosexuality should not be maintained as a moral taboo, since homosexuals may very well experience their sexlife as the expression of affective relationships, just like heterosexuals do. Thus there is no reason for homosexuals as such to be considered as agents belonging to a distinct category of agents. By taking taboos as 'moral primitives', Burms seems to imply that in transgressing a taboo, we ignore the fact that it reflects our dependency on a transcendental reality that is beyond the critical powers of reason. As Stout's analysis indicates, however, the experience of moral taboos is mediated by particular beliefs about the moral order and the structure of society that are not beyond rational criticism.

With regard to the second point, the unwarranted justification of taboos in terms of 'good functioning', it occurs to me that there is an alternative to Burms' views. While it may be true that revulsion from transgressions of moral taboos is unaffected by theoretical explanations of their social function, this does not at all mean that they cannot be explained in terms of moral reason. Take the example of incest. What would be morally wrong about a sexual relationship between a father and his daughter in case the daughter assents? Given the evidence about the longterm consequences of incestual relationships for the victims, the answer is that such a relationship is against the girl's interests even if she does assent to it. The psychological condition of affective dependency should be taken to imply that children should not be taken as witnesses to their own experience in these cases. Burms suggests that within the narrow conception of morality no other answer can be provided, so the question is: what sort of moral reason for the taboo on incest can be offered beyond the protection of the daughter's rights and interests?

A possible reason may be offered by saying that a sexual relationship with her father is 'degrading' for the girl, even if she does not evaluate this relationship negatively. Burms seems to be indicating this sort of reason, but he does not explain the notion of degradation any further. Presumably he might want to say either that 'degradation' expresses a moral intuition for which no further justification can be given or that 'degradation' is a mere shorthand for 'having one's rights and interests violated'. There is a possible third explanation, however, which provides a different moral reason for the taboo on incest, but it is not of the instrumentalist variety that Burms is attacking. This reason points in the direction of the father rather than of his victim. He should not use the affective dependency of his daughter for the satisfaction of his own sexual lust. Even if it was not experienced negatively by his daughter, he should still recognize that using his child as an object of his sexual desire is not only degrading for his child, but also for himself as a father. These considerations indicate that even if moral taboos as 'moral primitives' cannot be adequately explained by the instrumentalist version of a narrow conception of morality, there still may be room for other sorts of moral reasons. For example the reason that respectable moral agents should never commit certain acts that are degrading to themselves as agents, even if no other person would be harmed. A full justification of this claim, of course, presupposes other social and cultural beliefs that agents hold about themselves. While this may be taken as proof that the distinction between narrow and wide conceptions of morality is invalid, as it is by Stout, it does in no way compell us to acknowledge a religious aspect of morality. Burms may be right in claiming that the project of constructing a rational universal system of morality must fail, therefore, but he does not show why the failure of an instrumentalist conception of morality should lead us towards religion as a necessary dimension of social morality.

REFERENCES

Brandt, R., *A Theory of the Good and the Right*, Oxford 1979.
Stout, J., *Ethics after Babel. The Languages of Morals and their Discontents*, Cambridge Mass. 1988.

5

Radical Transcendence and the Unity of Morality and Conception of Life

Paul J.M. van Tongeren

5.1 INTRODUCTION

In the context of this volume, the question of the importance of faith and conception of life for morality[1] is situated in connection with another one concerning recent developments in morality and ethics, namely that of the relation between what have been called narrow and broad morality. Are we (post-) moderns still capable of moral conviction, or can we no longer make our way forward except on the level of public discussion, where different broad moral convictions and traditions of conceptions of life meet one another? Do we still really hold convictions which can be confronted with those of others, or do we only speak the language of the arbitrator who passes judgment on the confrontation - or better, who fixes the rules to which both (all) parties must relate themselves? (Van Tongeren 1988).

The connection between this question and that of a relation between the conception of life and morality is clear: increasingly, morality is identified with the narrow morality of public discussion and the universal rationality that it claims, while life conceptions and religion are associated with particularity and contingency. The rule of narrow morality would therefore be a victory of reason, but at the price not only of broader morals, but also of the (religious or not) conceptions of life and their function for morality. Hence

---

[1] On this occasion, I will not go into the distinction between faith and the conception of life, nor that between religious and nonreligious conceptions of life. Unless stated otherwise, I refer always to the religious conception of life, and specifically that of Christianity. On the question of to what extent humanism can be called a conception of life, cf., e.g., Van Tongeren 1991a.

is an ethical countercurrent which tries to rehabilitate broad morality, small particular communities and contingent traditions frequently brought into connection with a revitalization of the conception of life and its importance for morality.

Such a connection is dangerous. Not so much because it - as the supporters of the narrow-morality perspective fear - will allow morality to slip into the irrationalism of religion, but rather because it adopts, via the theme of narrow morality, a very specific standpoint with respect to (i.e., above) the plurality of conceptions of life and moral convictions - before we have even explored the reality of convictions themselves through an explanation of the experience in which they have been given to us.

The question of a relationship between conception of life and morality is not identical with that of the universalism of the narrow morality and the particularism of the broad morality; it is the question of whether that which makes the narrow social morality as well as the broad morality into moralities, and of that which makes Christianity or any other religious or non-religious conceptions of life into conceptions of life have, anything to do with one another. When we as philosophers speak of the relation of (religious or not) conception of life and morality, we must take a step back, not only from the concrete form that our own engagement with a conception of life has assumed and from our attachment to a particular religious (or a-religious) tradition, but also from the dominant (understanding of) morality; both in the service of exploring what our conception of life and moral experience can show us.

In an earlier publication I have - also in connection with the question of the relationship of morality and the conception of life - brought out the notion of transcendence as an element of such an explanation of moral experience (Van Tongeren 1992). In this contribution, I will further work out the meaning of this notion for the stated problem. From a short resume of that earlier text I will move toward the questions for which I seek an answer in this new investigation.

My overall answer to the question of a relation between morality and conception of life was at that time as follows: if morality implies transcendence, and if conception of life - at least religious, that is to say, in this case, Christian conception of life - can be called a cultivation of association with transcendence, then religion can for that reason and in that respect be considered a very apt surrounding or school for morality. Most of my attention was then given to describing the idea of morality and especially to the manner in which transcendence is implied in it.

I consider morality - slightly nuancing what was said before - as the whole of convictions and propositions concerning the question of what constitutes a (common) life that can be called good, fine and worthwhile and the practice, ways of activity, customs and attitudes from which these convictions are distilled or in which they are expressed. 'Good', 'fine', and 'worthwhile' stand for a quality which can be recognized as challenging, attractive and appealing (without that appeal going out from something or someone other than that which has the quality), and that can also be known exclusively such that its working is felt simultaneously (that is to say only in practical knowledge or moral experience). Besides that which itself has moral quality it is of course possible for anything to relate to it instrumentally. However, that receives no further consideration here.[2]

Then, I described transcendence as the breaking through of our conscious control and manipulation. Consequently, it is given in the attractive, challenging, demanding working of the moral. By way of references to the history of philosophy, a story from the Judeo-Christian tradition and aspects of an analysis of experience, I have indicated that and how transcendence is necessarily given with the moral: the moral appeal or the moral attraction presents itself to me and I react; the concreteness in which it presents itself (this face, this question) affirms transcendence, that is to say the escape to my own direction and control; moral motivation is the foundation for each choice I make, and is thus not itself chosen by me; the pretension to univer-

---

[2] I realize that this description of morality is problematic. It is a question of whether this gets beyond the tautological: good, beauty and the worthwhile are other words for 'moral', and say something about it, but by far not enough. Even with the added characteristic (the designated quality has a certain form, that is, a certain activity), it is till not sufficiently clear as to what is the content of this quality with that particular activity. There are also other than moral qualities which are attractive, etc. The reference to life as good, beautiful and worthwhile presents a certain limitation, but we would first want to know that out of which that good and beautiful, etc., exist; and secondly, why it is rightfully called so! The first can only happen in a never-completed explanation of the moral experience. Only in an explanation of this experience - that is - for it is only in that that we can know the moral; never fulfilled, because we are part of an ongoing history. With respect to the second point, it seems to me that it is a question of whether there is possible - for us - another justification for the content of morality than that which is sought in the dialogue between different moral traditions and communities to which I will return.

sality that is given with each moral conviction is grounded in this transcendent origin of morality: whomever does not share my convictions does not hear what I hear or else makes me doubt whether I hear what I think I hear.

But this is too crude to leave as it is. The description of morality as well as that of transcendence is still extremely vague, as is the relation between morality and (Christian-religious) conception of life. In fact, this relation remains so external that there is no question of a real one; it is a purely instrumental connection: as culture of intercourse with transcendence, religion is a fitting environment for morality insofar as it always has a moment of transcendence within itself. Even if we had more precise knowledge of what morality, religion and transcendence would mean, this pronouncement on their relation would say little more than that they do not contradict each other. Is this all that can be said about it, or is there a still more fundamental unity joining the two together?

To the extent that such a unity could be demonstrated, there comes another problem. One obviously suspects that religion is not a necessary condition for morality and that morality must thus also be able to stand without religion. How else could it be that nonreligious people can nonetheless be moral? And that they are so seems plainly evident! Or are we to suppose that they are not really a-religious, that anima humana naturaliter religiosa? And does not the so-called narrow morality make it clear that we can (and must) get loose from the particularities given with the (religious) conception of life, precisely in moral terms? Without such a moral universality, is the problem of plurality not unsolvable?

But how is the relation between these two situated in the religious man? The believer will after all always understand the moral claim that he experiences in a religious context. Is it a mistake for him to connect these two? Can that connection occur otherwise than in a heteronomous way? Does the relation between religion and morality threaten the autonomy of morality? Is morality autonomous, then, and if so, in what sense?

In this text, I will try to answer these and other such questions by moving further along the same path taken before. This means that once again - and still more than before - the notion of transcendence is central. What is transcendence? Via a terminological clarification (section 5.2) and a deepening of the notion (section 5.3), I will return to my stated questions (section 5.4).

5.2 TERMINOLOGICAL CLARIFICATION

'Transcendence' and 'transcendent' are ambiguous and therefore misleading terms. The verb 'to transcend' means to exceed, surpass or bypass something. That which is surpassed is then the 'immanent,' that which remains within the boundaries. 'Transcendence' and 'transcendent' must, I think, be applied primarily as participium praesens activum of this verb 'to transcend,' meaning excessive, or perhaps as its independent infinitive form, in the sense of the exceeding.

But 'transcendence' can also be applied as a substantive, acquiring the sense of that toward which there is exceeding, that which lies on the other side of that which is exceeded or surpassed. And, as an adjective, 'transcendent' is in the same way ascribed to that which lies on the other side. For this I propose to reserve the term 'the transcendent' (including, if need be, 'The Transcendent', in the personal sense it sometimes receives) - with or without capital letters. 'The transcendent' is that which (or who) remains on the other side of the limit.

There is an essential difference between 'transcendence' and 'transcendent' in the sense of the action or the way, on one hand, and 'the transcendent' in the sense of the aim or end, on the other - the one being the working and the other the cause, agent or subject of that working. It is, however, important to bear in mind (and this reduces the difference between 'transcendence' and 'the transcendent') that this designation of what exists on the other side as 'transcendent' says nothing other than that it is excessive. Of the transcendent as such, we know only that it is not here.

In the interest of completeness, I add still a third term: 'transcendental' refers to that which as the condition of possibility of the immanent, can only be thematized in relation to it, without itself belonging to or forming a part of it. It is, so to speak, the limit insofar as it can be thought from the inside, from the limited. As limit, it is past the limits, without being elsewhere, i.e. outside the limits. Kant's transcendental philosophy is one in which - as theoretical philosophy - understanding and reason are thought as the condition for the possibility of knowledge and as the horizon of known reality, and - as practical philosophy - freedom is thought as the condition for the possibility of duty and as the horizon of the reality of activity. Transcendental consciousness is that by which we are given a reality that can be experienced; it is the condition for the possibility of knowledge and experience. Transcendental freedom is that by which a task or obligation is assigned to us; it is the condition for the possibility of duty and morality.[3] 'Transcendence' is a relative concept. It refers to and is related to a limit, and therefore also to the space within the limit. Moreover, it is a purely formal concept insofar as it does not refer to a *specific* limit and thus has nothing to say about the nature of the limit or limited to which it is related. The concept can therefore be used in a very general sense. The definition that I gave in my 'Morality, Transcendence, Conception of Life' (1992) also shows that what is defined is in no sense restricted to the moral domain: 'break through of conscious control and manipulation' takes place continuously. We could say that every experience testifies to transcendence. Experience is a breaking through the familiar, normal pattern. In a certain sense, all experience is 'negative experience' - negation of what is normal and expected. Heidegger thus writes:

Mit etwas, sei es ein Ding, ein Mensch, ein Gott, eine Erfahrung machen, dass es uns widerfährt, dass es uns trifft, über uns kommt, uns umwirft und verwandelt (1959, 159).

[To undergo an experience with something - be it a thing, a person or a god - means that this something befalls us, strikes us, overwhelms us and transforms us (1982, 57).]

Still, we will not call every experience transcendent, no more so than we would all 'limit-changing research.' The reason for this can once again be clarified through experience, for the breaking-through of self-evidence is only a single moment of what we call experience, a moment taken up in a movement in which what is foreign or shattering is taken in. The history of the concept of experience since the Enlightenment (i.e., the history running from Kant via Hegel, Husserl and Heidegger to Gadamer and farther; cf. Van Tongeren 1991b, 7-9) allows us to see that experience has always designated a process of joining the foreign to what is already one's own (*eigen*). We become acquainted with the foreign, we reply to a question facing us, we comply with an expectation made known to us. It is therefore the case for moral experience, too, that it testifies only to a passing transcendence. Our response to a moral summons, the manner in which we direct ourselves to

---

[3] Moreover, Kant's philosophy of freedom and of religion form important texts to be explored for the stated problem of this collection. Unfortunately, that can not be done here.

the ideal, all this belongs to the moral experience by which we try to appropriate the foreign and to accommodate it to our own dwelling (*èthos*).

This means not that in experience (whether moral, scientific, aesthetic or religious) there will be no talk of transcendence, but that transcendence is only one moment of experience, and one which passes by not only in fact, but also essentially - in order for there to be any talk of real experience. In the terminology of my earlier contributions, intercourse with transcendence is precisely the manner in which transcendence is *immanentized*.

But then religion becomes problematic, for here there is talk of intercourse with transcendence in which transcendence is not immanentized. Do morality and religion go about entirely different 'business'? Or is the transcendence designated as 'passing by' not (or not entirely) that which we supposed in morality? Is there - in morality, too - talk of a more substantial and more radical transcendence?

5.3 TRANSCENDENCE

We are thus faced with at least two questions: can morality carry on more *radical* talk of transcendence, seeing that in morality it is, after all, a matter of realizing the transcendent claim here and now? and do we not speak of transcendence in so general a sense that there is no talk of a specific tie to *morality* and that there is thus no question of any argument concerning the unity of the (religious) conception of life and morality? Science, too, for example, is a reaction to a challenge that we feel in concrete situations, which brings us into contact with a reality outside of us so that we have objective pretensions to what we say scientifically... But this is no reason to say that religion forms a good context for science!

In order to avoid too easily ascribing to morality something which is not essential to it and on that basis formulating an illusory relation between morality and religion, I will first enter into a short discussion of the possibility of a more radical transcendence in science.

5.3.1 Transcendence, Science and Fiction

In his 'Absolute Truth and Transcendence' (1982), Arnold Burms has shown how behind his fear of relativism and the postulate of an absolute truth (which we approach in the sciences), the scientist conceals a legitimate desire for something which transcends science. With Einstein, Burms states that:

> *the content of the paraphraseable, cumulative, literally neutral speech of science (is) ultimately oriented towards something else which is radically nonscientific* (118).

> *Science brings us into contact with the transcendent, with a deeper meaning, when it calls us to a sense of something that falls wholly outside of the cumulative scientific process - outside in the radical sense: it does not belong to the cumulative process itself of science, but nor does it lie in the extension thereof, it is neither its conclusion nor its endpoint* (119).

Burms makes it clear that - when that other, transcendent itself is brought into science, it is itself made into scientific truth - there emerges a scientific fundamentalism. This objectionable fundamentalism is the consequence of a denial of the radicality of the transcendence which is at issue here.

But radicality means in this case that this transcendence is also wholly not of the order of science. The term 'absolute truth' wrongly suggests that it lies in the extension of scientific truth. However, it does concern the (ultimate) meaning of science that is itself not scientific. It is not clear of what nature this is for Burms. He uses aesthetic and moral as well as religious categories.

This refers us to our problem: is this meaning also radically transcendent to *aesthetic*, *moral* and *religious* intercourse with it, or is it (rightly and 'nonfundamentalistically') 'immanentized' therein? Is there talk of a transcendence so radical as to withdraw from every human assimilation, formalization or actualization - even those of art, morality and religion?

I wish to take up this question in the first instance by way of another manner in which Burms has made his excursus on science.

On the one hand, Burms gives a place to transcendence in connection with science, but, on the other hand, he does so in such a way as to suggest that, without the reference to transcendence, science could still remain possible - namely, as a purely immanent activity. He would probably not esteem this the best sort of science and would grant more respect to someone such as Einstein, who connected his scientific activity with a sensitivity to mystery. But he would not deny that without this reference to absolute truth or what that term conceals, successful scientific practice is still possible.

That raises the question of whether the same can be said of morality. One could say that whoever claims to have captured the absolute goodness or ultimate meaning of morality (its transcendent aim) itself, is a moral fundamentalist: in other words, someone who thinks that moral truth can be realized here. Can the analogy be extended? Can a genuine moral practice continue after transcendence has been removed from morality?

To answer this question, a third analogy must be made. Art refers to transcendence in the sense of absolute beauty. Whoever thinks that absolute beauty can be concretely realized in art probably does not fail as an artist but does become very unhappy. But is the artist who completely removes from his work any reference to transcendence still an artist? It is remarkable that at the end of his article Arnold Burms returns to the meaning of the notion of 'absolute truth' via this analogy with art. The idea of 'the Book that will make all others superfluous' is a meaningful poetic fiction that fascinates and stimulates poetic creativity. The article closes with: 'This status can also be attributed to the idea of absolute truth: it is then a moving fiction.'

I would like to suggest that art is more intimately allied with its transcendent ideal than is science. In that connection it is significant that the perfect book (or the perfect poem, painting, etc.) is called a fiction, that is to say an artistic creation: it is itself in the same manner as is art, it participates in the art that it creates. This does not take away the fact that in an artistic effort transcendence can still be preserved to the extent that artist recognizes the fictionality of his ideal.

Should we not say something like this of moral 'activity': that it is affected by a moral ideal of which it at the same time recognizes the (reality-transcending) ideality? Just as art creates a moving fiction, so morality forms a tempting and compelling ideal. In both cases there is a deep alliance which does not take away radical distance.

5.3.2 Transcendence, Art and the Lasting Appeal

It is a question of whether the foregoing does justice to the radicality of transcendence. Is not the designation of the absolute ideal as 'fiction' a way of binding the ideal to its origin in the domain that it should transcend? It seems doubtful whether we can continue to believe in an ideal that we have produced ourselves.

But if the artist were to maintain that he has not created that ideal (and I believe he will), then the fiction testifies to something other than its own fictional power. For a first working-out of what is meant here, I return to the concept of experience. We have already seen that experience as a breaking-through of a pattern (of the manner in which our receptivity is folded in) is only a single moment in a process in which that breaking-through is taken up and the foreign is made one's own. We call that process experience. At most, one can speak here of transcendence in only a relative and transitory manner.

In this connection, it is remarkable that Gadamer works out the concept of experience in a discussion with reflexive philosophy, most notably that of Hegel, in an effort which he formulated as follows:

Es geht für uns darum (...) eine Wirklichkeit zu denken, an der sich die Allmacht der Reflexion begrenzt (1975[4], 325).

[We are concerned (...) to conceive a reality which is beyond the omnipotence of reflection (1975, 307.)]

This means that for Gadamer the concept of 'experience' would be precisely a matter of doing justice to our contact with transcendence, on the one hand ('zu denken'), and to the transcendence of that which we think, on the other ('begrenzt'). He can do so by considering experience not in an abstract way, i.e., as an isolated experience in which the breaking-through of a habit forms that habit and is taken up in it, but concretely as that which is made up out of such 'experiences'. And rather than the same appropriation on a larger scale, this is precisely the consciousness that there is no end to the forming (i.e., to the breaking-through of every form):

Vielmehr zeigt sich der Erfahrene im Gegenteil als der radikal Undogmatische, der, weil er so viele Erfahrungen gemacht und aus Erfahrungen gelernt hat, gerade besonders befähigt is, aufs neue Erfahrungen zu machen und aus Erfahrungen zu lernen. Die Dialektik der Erfahrung hat ihre eigene Vollendung nicht in einem abschliessenden Wissen, sondern in jener Offenheit für Erfahrung, die durch die Erfahrung selbst freigespielt wird. (...) Erfahrung is also Erfahrung der menschlichen Endlichkeit. Erfahren im eigentlichen Sinne ist, wer ihrer inne ist, wer weiss, dass er der Zeit und der Zukunft nicht Herr ist (1975[4], 338ff).

[Rather, the experienced person proves to be, on the contrary, someone who is radically undogmatic; who, because of the many experiences he has had and the knowledge he has drawn from them is particularly well

equipped to have new experiences and to learn from them. The dialectic of experience has its own fulfillment not in definitive knowledge, but in the openness to experience that is encouraged by experience itself (...) Experience is experience of human finitude. The truly experienced man is one who is aware of this, who knows that he is master neither of time nor the future (1975, 319ff).]

The artistic fiction of the Book that will make all other books superfluous is the expression of the experience of the artist, in this latest sense of the word experience. The artist is called by very concrete events, things, people and thoughts. Whether he more or less succeeds in his artistic rendering of them, he will always be called anew and set again to painting, writing, etc. This sense of being continuously called upon, a sense of the restrictedness of one's own creativity in relation to that which summons, challenges or attracts him; that sense is expressed in the inverted metaphor of the successful artwork (or, in Plato, in that of Beauty itself, the Idea of beauty). The inversion in the metaphor constitutes the fictive character of the image. But it is not the fiction which moves one, but that which this fiction expresses; the concrete evocation which always comes from elsewhere:

't Is net of zoo'n zee wat van me wil. Daarin is God ook. God roept. 't Is waarachtig geen lolletje, overal is-i. En overal roept-i Bavink. Je wordt mal van je eigen naam als-i zoo dikwijls geroepen wordt. En dan moet Bavink Schilderen. Dan moet God op een brokkie linnen met verf. Dan roept Bavink 'God.' En zoo blijven ze mekaar roepen.
Begrijp jij wat die zon van mij wil? Vier-en-dertig ondergaande zonnen heb ik tegen de muur staan, achter elkaar, omgekeerd. En toch staat-i daar weer iederen avond (Nescio, 58 and 74).
[It is as if such a sea wants something from me. God is also in it. God calls. Truly, it is no joke, he is everywhere. And everywhere he calls Bavink. You become crazy from your own name if it is called so often. And then Bavink must paint. Then God has to appear on a piece of linen with paint. Then Bavink calls 'God.' And so they keep calling each other. Do you understand what that sun expects from me? Thirty-four setting suns I have standing against the wall, reversed. And it nevertheless stands there again every evening.]

5.3.3 Radical Transcendence and the Moral Claim to Attention

There seems to have been a leap from the experience of finitude to a sea, a sunset and the infinite God who calls out. The leap accentuates the difference between two manners in which transcendence can be thought: as exceeding a limit, it can be thought from one side of the limit as much as from the other; from inside and from outside. In the first case, it is thought from immanence; that which is not given in immanence but breaks through it is transcendent, for it comes from outside immanence. In the second case it is thought from transcendence: that which announces itself to immanence is not immanent but transcendent.

It might seem that the two come down to the same thing. Outside remains outside and inside inside. Still, there is probably an important difference. The question is namely whether every account of transcendence from immanence does not necessarily do injustice to the radicality of transcendence. This question is especially urgent when we take into consideration the fact that such immanence refers to the entire domain of our knowing, speaking, writing and creating. But then, are immanentizing descriptions which do injustice to transcendence all that is possible?

When transcendence is thought from immanence it is clear that immanence forms the framework for the manner in which transcendence is thought; even when transcendence/the transcendent is thought as the other of immanence/the immanent, the former is worked out from the latter: even in this negative manner, transcendence is still thought according to immanence.

When transcendence is thought first, something else seems to happen. I write 'seems' because in reality it is still the same thing that happens. Transcendence is that which is thought at the other side of the limit. The other side - viewed from the one who thinks, experiences, speaks. The other side is precisely as such not given. Even when I think it as the first, I do so from this side, and thus inevitably in the manner of transcendence.

This is what happens when we speak of a transcendent God. However close God is to us, as transcendent He is there where we are not. When we took Him as cause (and/or as aim) of our immanence, we gave Him primacy. But in that expression, an oversight also becomes clear: that which gives something or someone primacy has already placed itself first. From there comes the inevitable anthropomorphism of our speaking about God. Perhaps this is the impulse behind negative theology which, on the one hand, escapes mastery by the immanent by speaking of God only in terms that deny immanence, but, on the other hand, precisely by that negation shows itself to be tied to the negated.

Is there then no escape from immanence? (other than in terms of the revelation of God himself, now distinguished from the (= our) terms in which we understand it).

Perhaps a reference to Heidegger can help us here. We generally move in immanent reality, the reality in which we reside and always will remain. But sometimes the that of reality can light up as something which withdraws itself from immanence. With that, we come to what Heidegger designated as the fundamental question of metaphysics: 'Warum ist überhaupt Seiendes und nicht viel mehr Nichts?' (1978^2, 121). [Why are there beings at all and not rather nothing? (1978, 112).] The fact that there is reality is itself not a part of what reality there is, and therefore withdraws itself from immanence.

Moreover, this formulation from Heidegger's thinking of Being is still problematic. Heidegger is concerned not so much with the 'that' of 'reality' as with the 'Being' of beings, that is to say with the way in which beings come into existence at all, a manner which, it is true, takes place in man, in Dasein's understanding of Being, but which, rather than under man's command is arranged by Being itself. This occurring of Being, this going over from Being to the Being of beings, Heidegger calls 'transcendens': 'Sein ist das transcendens schlechthin' [Being is the transcendens pure and simple] (1972, 38; 1962, 62). Man is ek-sistence, that is: not closed into his own Being, but the place where the being - also the being that he himself is - first appears in its Being; as such, as the place where the emerging of Being, transcendence par excellence takes place, man himself is transcendence: 'Ek-sistenz ist Transcendenz' (1968, 24ff, 35 ff; 1978, 216 ff, 229 ff.)[4]

When in the line of Heidegger the accomplishment of Being, that is to say the event in which beings are concealed and revealed, when that (the 'that' of immanence) is understood as transcendence par excellence, and when, further, human being is understood as being-there (Dasein) by which that 'there' is where the event of transcendence takes place, and when in that line man can be called the 'shepherd of Being' (1968, 19; 1978, 210), then the next step is clear: to characterize man by the moral duty to make this

---

[4] Moreover, there is on this point in Heidegger's work a shift from man as transcending to Being itself as transcending, even though, the latter is already formulated in *Sein und Zeit*. On this, cf. De Schutter 1988, 472.

take place. Which means for me: the duty to attention as the first moral duty.[5]

Man is essentially the place where Being lights up, where beings appear as... This means that the essence of man lies in the happening that can be called 'transcendence' ('dass der Mensch nur in seinem Wesen west, in dem er vom Sein angesprochen wird' (1968, 13) [man essentially occurs only in his essence, where he is claimed by Being] (1978, 204), but also that the happening of transcendence can occur only in man. Without or outside man, nothing happens. Man is the place where the greatest wonder takes place, namely that there is something and not rather nothing. Heidegger himself refused to translate this into an ethics, but what he says implies an important 'relativizing' of every moral problem.

All moral questions always relate to beings (humans, embryo's, conclusions, procedures, etc.). Beings are always in one manner or another understood in their Being. The understanding of Being is the way in which Being (beings in their Being) lights up. The way in which beings in their Being are understood specifies the way in which we perceive and solve our problems. When we do not think back to this happening in which beings appear, we remain enclosed in a misunderstanding, an understanding of Being absorbed into forgetfulness of Being. Heidegger concretizes this conclusion in terms of technology. The 'essence' of technology is the reign of the technical understanding of Being, that is to say of the understanding of the Being of beings as made and being-makeable. If we do not reflect on the reign of technology we will be mastered by it, even in the way we think about the problem of technology. In this manner, every moral problem (every problem, every form of speaking) is related to an underlying understanding of Being, as are beings understood in their Being.

This reference back is not the replacement of one problem with another, more fundamental one. A problem is also a being, for instance. As well, reflection on the happening in which beings light up is not a way to bring us to a point in which we can decide for another way to understand. Being happens in a specific way in the understanding of the Being of that being which we ourselves are. But we are not the masters of that event of Being. The only thing that we can do is pay attention to what happens. 'Being is the transcendens pure and simple.'

---

5 I am indebted to Drs. C. Bremmers for this thought.

5.3.4 Transcendence, Alterity, Ethics

Beginning from the expectation that transcendence is essential for the connection between the (religious) conception of life and morality, I have tried to further work that notion out. Via Burms' consideration of science, Gadamer's reflection on experience and its connection with art, we came to Heidegger's reflections on the happening of Being and the moral claim that seemed implied there. By means of some contemporary authors we have thus met with the search for radical transcendence as a basic motive of human knowing, doing and making. Orientation to radical transcendence in a certain sense relativizes everything that follows upon it: experience becomes essentially consciousness of finitude; knowledge of beings seems built upon a generally forgetful understanding of Being; first philosophy seems to be passivity. However, in all of the cited authors ethics seems to play at most an implicit role: it is true that Gadamer used the moral wisdom of Aristotle (phronèsis) as his model for knowledge of experience, but he concentrated on art and knowledge rather than on ethics; Heidegger refused to speak of ethics, but nevertheless described the essence of man in clearly normative terms. The (rather more designated than followed) course then must certainly be completed with Levinas, in whose work an entirely different radicalization of transcendence is brought to order, and which does expressly translate it into ethics. The problem of philosophy that we earlier came up against in the formulation of Gadamer as 'how to think reality without it vanishing in the all-powerful reflection' also has a central place in Levinas:

*Le savoir est une relation du Même avec l'Autre où l'**Autre** se réduit au Même et se dépouille de son étrangeté, où la pensée se rapporte à l'autre mais où l'autre n'est plus autre en tant que tel où il est déjà le propre, déjà **mien** (1984, 12ff.).*
*[Knowledge is a relation of the Same with the Other where the **Other** is reduced to the Same and is stripped of its strangeness, where thought is related to the other but where the other is no longer the other such that it is already the proper, already **mine**.]*

Against this, Levinas seeks a different thinking, one different than that of an appropriating consciousness, a thinking 'qui ne ramènerait tout transcendence à l'immanence et ne compromettrait la transcendence en la comprenant.' (ibid., 21ff.) [which would not return all transcendence to immanence and would not compromise transcendence in comprehending it.]

Levinas finds that thinking in the idea of Infinity, which is at the same time religious revelation and an ethical command:

> *la révélation religeuse (...) est 'connaissance' d'un Dieu qui, s'offrant dans cette 'ouverture', demeurerait aussi absolument autre ou transcendent* (ibid., 22).
> *[religious revelation (...) is knowledge of a God who, offering himself in this 'opening', would also remain absolutely other or transcendent.]*

This idea of Infinity makes it such that the finite is affected by the infinite without the one being a negation or neutralization of the other; an affection that becomes desire for goodness which exists in responsibility for one's neighbor:

> *Socialité qui, par opposition à tout savoir et à toute immanence - est relation avec l'autre comme tel et non pas avec l'autre, pure partie du monde* (ibid., 27).
> *[Sociality which, as opposed to all knowledge and all immanence - is relation with the other as such and not with the other as pure part of the world.]*

First philosophy, which for Heidegger is thinking of Being, is for Levinas ethics. And yet, on this point neither Levinas nor the other authors mentioned speak of what we generally call ethics; there is no theory on how relationships between people should be regulated, no notion of ethical principles, let alone any pronouncement of the question as to the conditions for how we in some measure could reach a consensus. Still less do we find again in most authors the concrete form of any conception of life or religion. What, then, does all of this have to do with ethics as we know it, and with the background issue of a relation between (religious) conception of life and morality?

5.4 TRANSCENDENCE, CONCEPTION OF LIFE AND MORALITY

If, in its concrete form and in spite of every perversion it incurs, religion contains truth, it will have to do with the deepest ground or core of human being. It will have to exist in openness for such a ground, in recognition of dependence, the realization of not being itself (individually or collectively) at the beginning and the end of human life.

If morality does not coincide with the form which it in fact always takes, if it is something besides a superstructure in the service of changing forces, if in its imperfect forms it is an expression of a fundamental destiny of being-human, then morality and religion will have to be joined with one another at a profound level.

Through closer exploration of the concept of transcendence and of the manner in which it functions in connection with science, art, philosophy, morality and theology, we have indeed discovered that the relation between morality and the conception of life remains much more intensive than the external and instrumental connection that we initially found to be the case. That earlier connection between the conception of life as a culture of (and schooling in the intercourse with) transcendence, on the one hand, and, on the other, the morality which must necessarily embrace a moment of transcendence, proved secondary to what applies prior to the distinction between morality and the conception of life: human life is as such (as human) possible only through a transcendence that requires attention (Heidegger's 'thoughtful thinking') or justice (Levinas). Previous to the compartmentalization of human life into morality, religion, art, science, politics, etc., that life is marked by a 'happening' described as transcendence and which makes it such that an adequate life will have to exist in connection to what withdraws itself from the immanence of that life.

What does this mean for the questions that we set forth in our introduction and for the frame in which was established the question of a connection between morality, the conception of life and faith - that is, the situation of a pluralism of moral convictions and the distinction between narrow and broad morality?

Both morality and the conception of life constitute forms of such a relation of human life to the transcendence by which it is possible for it to exist. In this sense, morals and conceptions of life - however contingent and particular - are expressions of what is essential for human life. That means not only that they (together with many other domains of human existence) are joined on a proto-level, but, above all, that with this is given a test by which they can be evaluated: wherever morality or religion distort that relationship to the transcendent by reducing everything to immanence, they alienate themselves from the transcendence that characterizes human existence and makes it possible, thus becoming irreal or inhuman. There are different ways in which such an immanentization can occur. The fundamentalism that identifies the particular with the universal exhibits one way. A neutral universalism which supposes that every particularity can be surmounted forms another. Neither can pass the test of transcendence.

With that, some distance is taken from the position that (rational) morality supplies the competence to judge the legitimacy of the convictions and practices of a religious conception of life; that is to say, distance from the position which combines the thesis of the logical independence of morality with the idea of a universally valid morality (cf. Musschenga's introduction). Morality is no more qualified to pass judgement on a conception of life than the reverse. Both must be tested on this point: do they honor the transcendence upon which human life rests?

This then makes possible a confrontation with the distinction between narrow and broad morality of which I spoke in my introduction. One is certainly inclined to ask how the very different forms that can be given to attention to transcendence should relate to each other, and whether the answer to this question is not precisely moral in nature, and thus if narrow moral restrictions must not be placed on the concretization of this attention by different conceptions of life and broad moralities. In other words, is there not a most-elementary morality prior even to this proto-moral and conception-of-life attention to transcendence that I have described? And is that not the narrow morality which must withdraw itself from as many particular forms as possible in order to attain a pure rationality acceptable to everyone?

In the first place, this question, at least in this formulation, fails to appreciate that rationality is on the one hand also an expression of attention to the foregoing transcendence (we do not make the laws of reason, but obey them), and on the other that it is given only in particular identifications (MacIntyre's *Which Rationality?*).

But in the second place, the profound transcendence which we discovered must itself serve to answer the question of the rules for the co-existence of the different forms in which it can be held fast. Every religion and every morality (including the narrow) must be submitted to this test: does it maintain transcendence in the manner which cultivates association with it and acceptance of it?

This produces fewer rules than does the so-called narrow morality. But much of narrow morality is no longer able to claim universal validity for all rational beings, instead existing only in the widening of its own circle through an overlapping consensus. The transcendence-test does satisfy this central claim of every narrow morality, that it recognizes the plurality of broad moralities and promotes their peaceful co-existence. It does so by guaranteeing openness through the requirement of the preservation of transcendence in every morality and conception of life, which in principle makes possible other identifications of transcendence and other designations of the relation with it.

And because in this transcendence it is a matter of the condition for the possibility of human existence, that is to say because it is that of which the importance for us can not be surpassed, the possibility of other identifications of it and real confrontation with them must necessarily be of interest to us. Interaction with other convictions must have the form of a dialogue which forms the concretization of the condition in which we find ourselves: to be dependent on an event that we can not master. We are unavoidably interested in the assurance of our ground for existence and thus engaged with our position in the dialogue. But equally unavoidably, we are interested in every other position that can present itself as an adequate representation of that ground.

To conclude: if morality and conception of life are so closely related to each other, what does that mean for the question of the relevance of the concrete conception of life such as we know it for morality?

It will be clear that the understanding of and attention to transcendence is the first requirement for everything that human life can embrace, and thus also - certainly - for morality. To the extent that this attention to transcendence can be called conception of life and even religion, it does indeed hold that anima humana naturaliter religiosa. That does not conflict with the fact that many people are not religious. In the first place, what is involved here is a religiosity that does not recognize itself because religiosity for us always has particular forms: it is almost impossible for one to be religious without also being Jewish, Christian or some other believer. Here, it is a matter of a level of religiosity which comes before all else. In the second place, this openness is fundamental for human existence, but nevertheless generally not given. We mostly do not live truly humanly, we generally do not really live, but just let things happen as they will. By reading a poem, meeting another person, or whatever else, we are reminded of the supporting ground of our existence and we experience the need to pay attention to it. Without this attention, there is no question of humanitas.

Even though - as we saw - with this need to pay attention, there are limits to the possible forms which this attention can take, that attention itself can not determine the choice between different possibilities. It makes a demand on every form, but does not determine their (logical, religious, moral, empirical or practical) order. From this it becomes clear that the question of their relation as formulated in the introduction to this book always suggests a certain hierarchy: the 'dependency thesis' has morality follow religion, the 'independence thesis' subjects religion to morality. Instead of indicating such a sequence, I have suggested that every religion and every morality is subject to something upon which they all make a claim, but which can not be completely encompassed by any of them.

Aside from this attention to primordial transcendence, (this or that) conception of life is thus not a necessary condition for morality. The different conceptions of life and religions are concretizations and cultivations of this original attention. This is not a relativizing of their meaning, because the concretization is not a superfluous addition but the form in which something exists. Nothing can exist without concrete form. Our openness for transcendence does not exist otherwise than in the form of specific foldings. And in that concretizing, the conceptions of life and the morality of a human person (such as his science, politics and art, etc.) must fit together since they all come out of and form an answer to the aforementioned transcendence. Hence it is not strange that a Christian does not express and explain his moral convictions apart from his Christian faith. No more is it strange when such a Christian is less than satisfied with my story about religiosity, and, moreover, contests it. Religiosity for him is not such a feeling of dependency, is not such a feeling of receptivity, is not such a willingness to be a 'place' where Being can find its place, etc., but commitment to God who has revealed himself in His Son, answer to the Word of God. This concretization which the conception of life takes in Christianity is not an external form that could be severed from the 'general religiosity' which I have described. It is the manner in which this general religiosity exists. This means that my description of religiosity is an abstraction which, however, exists in reality for those who have taken leave of concrete forms, but do not want to completely lose what is thereby given up. It exists as residues probably as the seed from which new forms can emerge.

It will be clear that the described connection between morality and (religious) conception of life does not imply a heteronomy for morality. No more does it mean that others who are not Christian or not even believers - as opposed to religious people - would hold an autonomous morality. Complete autonomy is not given to people. The heteronomy of which all our autonomous legislation is an expression can, however, be understood in a variety of ways and be expressed in different conceptions of life. Those differences refer to an engaged dialogue in which the different identifications scrutinize each other and themselves by means of each other.

Translated by Jeffrey D. Bloechl

REFERENCES

Burms, A., Absolute waarheid en transcendentie [= Absolute Truth and Transcendence], *Tijdschrift voor Filosofie* 44(1982), 104-123.

Gadamer, H.-G., *Wahrheit und Methode. Grundzüge einer philosophischen Hermeneutik*, Tübingen 1975[4] (1=1960). [English translation: *Truth and Method*, edited from the second edition (1965) by Garret Barten and John Cumming, London 1975.]

Heidegger, M., *Unterwegs zur Sprache*, Pfullingen 1959. [English translation: *On the Way to Language*, translated by Peter D. Hertz, New York 1982.]

Heidegger, M., Was ist Metaphysik? [1929]. In: idem, *Wegmarken*, 1978[2] (1=1967), 103-121. [English translation: What is Metaphysics?, translated by D.F. Krell. In: *The Basic Writings of Martin Heidegger*, edited by D.F. Krell, London 1978.]

Heidegger, M., *Über den Humanismus*, Frankfurt 1968. [English translation: *Letter on Humanism*, translated by Frank A. Capuzzi with J. Glenn Gray and D.F. Krell. In: *The Basic Writings of Martin Heidegger*, London 1978.]

Heidegger, M., *Sein und Zeit*, Tübingen 1972[12] (1=1927). [English translation: *Being and Time*, translated by John Macquarrie and Edward Robinson, London 1962.]

Levinas, E., *Transcendence et Intelligibilité*, Genève 1984.

Nescio, *De Uitvreter*, etc. Den Haag/Rotterdam (no year given).[12] (1=1933).

Schutter, D. De, Heideggers filosofie van de transcendentie, [= Heidegger's Philosophy of Transcendence], *Tijdschrift voor Filosofie* 50(1988), 453-491.

Tongeren, P. van, De smalle moraal: pluralisme of uniformiteit? [= The Narrow Morality: Pluralism or Uniformity?], *Algemeen Nederlands Tijdschrift voor Wijsbegeerte* 80(1988), 92-102.

Tongeren, P. van, Humanisme, levensbeschouwing en filosofie [= Humanism, Conception of Life and Philosophy], *Rekenschap* 38(1991a), 100-103.

Tongeren, P. van, *Moraal, Recht, Ervaring* [= Morality, Law, Experience], Nijmegen 1991b.

Tongeren, P. van, Morality, Transcendence, Conception of Life. In: A.W. Musschenga, B. Voorzanger & A. Soeteman (eds.), *Morality, Worldview, and Law*, Assen 1992, 39-52.

Comments

Gerrit Manenschijn

Van Tongeren transfers the question of the relationship between conception of life and morality to the fundamental level of human existence. For this purpose he uses the concept of radical transcendence. He realizes that the unity of conception of life and morality is not to be found in all kinds of contingent relationships between concrete conception of lifes and moralities. He wants to go beyond a merely instrumental and external relationship between conception of life and morality. To do this, it is necessary to transgress from the immanent into the transcendent. This transgression requires that existing forms of conception of life and morality are 'emptied'; to reach his aim, Van Tongeren needs more or less abstract, almost empty shells of morality and conception of life, since with concrete forms we don't find an necessary connection between the two, and sometimes no connection at all. If we remain within the boundaries of what can be determined empirically (the immanent), we cannot reach the fundamental level of the necessary connection, we cannot even imagine it. Whoever wants to reach that fundamental level, must let himself be enticed into crossing the boundary; he must look for the transcendental foundation of both conception of life and morality, to find there the unity between both.

Van Tongeren made an attempt to do this in an article he refers to, but in his own opinion he did not get further than halfway his goal that time. He now thinks the relationship he outlined in that article was too rough and too undefined. The relationship between morality and religion (a term which gradually replaces the term 'conception of life' in the course of the article; I will come back to that in my appraising remarks) was defined too instrumentally, namely merely as the idea that religion, as a culture of contact with the transcendent, offers a suitable context for morality, insofar as morality always contains a moment of transcendence. The aim is now to deepen this notion of transcendence.

For this purpose, Van Tongeren refers to the views of Burms, Gadamer, Heidegger and Levinas. Burms demonstrates that science ultimately aims at something radically nonscientific, namely the transcendent. From Gadamer, Van Tongeren takes a conception of experience that surpasses the empirical, and crosses the border to the alien, which, subsequently, will be made familiar. This implies a double movement: to experience means to make contact with transcendence, but transcendence is also experienced in what we think. Thus, experience becomes the experience of human finitude.

Transcendence can be conceived as transgression from within: transcendence is what breaks through the immanent; but it can also be understood as transgression from without: what presents itself irresistably, though not within the immanence, is itself not immanent but transcendent. But also in the latter case (the revelation model), our point of view is inevitably the immanence, because this is the domain of human knowledge, speech, writing and creation. When we speak of God as a transcendent God, we imply that He is not where we are. But we can only speak about a transcendent God if He is near to us. We say that God is transcendent, but by saying so we imply that our point of view is the immanent.

According to Van Tongeren, Heidegger pointedly presented this paradox in his famous statement: 'Ek-sistenz ist Transzendenz'. Van Tongeren paraphrases this statement as follows: 'Man is ek-sistence, that is: not closed into his own Being, but the place where the being - also the being that he himself is - first appears in its Being; as such, as the place where the emerging of Being, transcendence par excellence takes place, man himself is transcendence ...' (p. 127). I interpret this paraphrase as transcendence being no longer only that which goes beyond all immanence, but also that which presents itself as transcendence within the immanence. To be a human being means to experience this, to experience the transition of Being into the being of beings. It is man's moral task to let this actually happen. Van Tongeren calls this the duty to be attentive. The problem is, however, that Heidegger does not relate this to a concrete ethics. What does this duty to be attentive exactly mean?

According to Van Tongeren, we can find out more on this point in Levinas, because his radicalization of transcendence does allow for a translation into ethical terms. In Levinas' view, the Infinite is both a religious revelation and an ethical demand. The ethical demand means radical responsibility for one's neighbour. But still, Levinas does not offer much of a concrete ethics either. Can we, in spite of that, be more specific than this?

Van Tongeren thinks so. If it is true that morality and religion, although they appear only in imperfect forms, are the expressions of a fundamental destination of human existence, they must be linked on a fundamental level. There is more than just an external and instrumental connection. Human life as such (as human life) is only possible through a transcendence which compels attentiveness (Heidegger) and justice (Levinas). Morality and religion are both manifestations of this relationship between human life and the transcendence through which it can exist.

This view implies, however, that the 'thesis of dependence' (morality is dependent on religion) as well as the 'thesis of independence' (morality is autonomous with regard to religion) must be considered as superficial descriptions of the relationship between morality and religion. Insofar as morality and religion are the expressions of a fundamental destination of human existence, they form a unity. But this unity is fundamental indeed, so it cannot be reduced or analyzed any further, since it consists in a radical transcendence that precedes any morality and religion.

As I said above, to uphold this view Van Tongeren needs almost empty shells of morality and religion. This is clearly shown in his approach of religion, which he conceives as general religiosity, formulated in abstract terms. He adds to this, however: 'This means that my description of religiosity is an abstraction which, however, exists in reality for those who have taken leave of concrete forms, but do not want to completely lose what is thereby given up.' To me, this seems to be the most significant and revealing phrase in the whole essay. It says that philosophy of Being like Heidegger's or Levinas' has something to offer especially to those who have become alienated from the concrete forms of religion they grew up with (Catholicism, Protestantism), but who have not lost, and don't want to lose, a sense of religiosity. This brings me to my appraising remarks.

1 It seems to me that Van Tongeren has succeeded in showing the inadequacy of conceptions which interpret the relationship between religion and morality merely empirically and instrumentally. With his hermeneutical method, he brings to light fundamental links between religion and morality, which remain hidden if we limit our thinking to conceptions such as the theses of dependence and independence, since these basically

refer to just an external and instrumental connection. Van Tongeren's appeal to transcendence as transgressive experience in religion and morality has convinced me as being correct and effective.

2 However, I have my doubts about the 'empty shells' of morality and religion Van Tongeren uses, following the example of Heidegger and Levinas. If it is correct that on the level of true human existence there is a connection between all forms of morality and religion on the one hand, and radical transcendence on the other, I would have liked this connection explicated. If such an explication is possible at all within Van Tongeren's hermeneutics. In other words: to what extent does he get further than Heidegger and Levinas?

3 Van Tongeren uses the terms religion, faith and conception of life indiscriminately. In note 1 he says, however, that he does not want to discuss the distinction between faith and conception of life, which implies he acknowledges that there is a difference. I regard it as a shortcoming he does not go into it; 'conception of life' can be regarded as a general concept, and 'religion' as one of its sub-categories, or they can be considered as equivalent sub-categories of an even more general concept, whatever this may be. It can also be defended that religion is something different from conception of life, particularly if one takes into account the contents of existing religions and conceptions of life. I myself find the last view the most plausible. Someone who does not believe in God anymore may very well have a conception of life. I think that the conception of life employed by Van Tongeren serves as a substitute for concrete forms of religion, in which the general religiosity that is characteristic of all religions, is still present. The passage about the people who have abandoned existing forms of religion, but have retained a certain sense of religiosity, is quite clear. Someone who does not feel comfortable anymore with traditional forms of religion, has not necessarily lost his sense of the transcendent; he may still be ready to meet new forms of spirituality.

4 I have serious doubts about the almost empty shell of ethics, without which Van Tongeren cannot maintain his appeal to transcendence. Assuming that there is a transcendent moment in morality and religion, surely this 'shell' cannot be filled with just anything? Heidegger speaks

of the 'duty of attentiveness', but to whom, in what, and to what extent do we have this duty? Levinas speaks of 'responsibility for one's neighbour', but what does he actually mean by that?

To start with Heidegger, did his thinking of Being in any way resist the immorality of National Socialism? As far as he personally was concerned certainly not, but wasn't that also a fault of his philosophy? Did the man Heidegger (who was a coward and betrayed his Jewish colleagues) not at all contaminate his philosophy? In my opinion he did.

Levinas' philosophy, on the other hand, principally rules out racism, ethnocentrism and sexism. The other appears to us in his absolute right to justice. That is the ethical advantage Levinas has over Heidegger. But what does justice mean? Can we, in our complicated world, manage without a 'Theory of Justice' (Rawls)? Is the very right to justice enough to set us in motion? Van Tongeren might answer that he didn't want to bring up this question, but the essential unity of morality and religion, which inevitably involves a great degree of abstraction. I acknowledge that. But if it is true that the transcending moment in religion and morality points to the deepest foundations of our being, this must somehow be apparent in the concrete contents of religion and morality. In other words: Van Tongeren's view opens up the way from imperfect religion and morality to transcendence, but the question is: is there also a way from transcendence to less perfect religion and morality?

A good tree cannot bring forth evil fruit. (Matthew 7, 18). I would like to know the tree of radical transcendence by its moral fruit.

Translated by Birgit Kooijman

6

The Meaning of Sanctification
Stanley Hauerwas on Christian Identity and Moral Judgment

Hans S. Reinders

6.1 INTRODUCTION

Suppose someone told you that he was brought up by certain convictions about the world and our existence within it; that he learned to appreciate these convictions as giving his life a sense of direction, but that all this does not make much of a difference for what he thinks good and right to do. Would this not strike you as a rather peculiar, if not implausible attitude? How could a particular way of understanding oneself and the world be independent of what one thinks one ought to do? Yet this independence is what Christians and other religious people are supposed to accept about the relation between their religious and their moral beliefs, at least according to some moral philosophers. These philosophers argue that morality is independent of religion and that, consequently, there cannot be such thing as 'religious' or 'Christian' ethics. Surely Christians and other believers are entitled to their own convictions, but whether these convictions are morally justifiable is not for religion or theology to decide. The justifiability of moral convictions is to be tested against 'independent' moral principle and reason.

In this essay I will examine the rejection of this philosophical thesis on religion and morality by a theologian who in recent times has become one of the major voices in the field of Christian ethics in the United States of America, namely Stanley Hauerwas. Hauerwas not so much defends the possibility of a religious ethics; he rather attacks the moral theory underlying the 'independence thesis'. The claim that moral convictions are to be tested against moral principle and reason is characteristic of what Hauerwas calls 'the standard account of moral rationality' (Burrell & Hauerwas 1976). Crucial for his critique of 'the standard account' is the relation between

Christian identity and moral judgment. It is on this relationship that I will direct my analysis of his thought in this essay.

My exposition of Hauerwas' views on this subject will be analysed through three key notions. The first is that Christian convictions shape the way in with Christians describe the world and that this description entails a 'morality'. The independence thesis assumes that religious sentences are descriptive statements of (metaphysical) fact, while moral sentences are not concerned with description, but with evaluation. According to Hauerwas' account of the matter this assumption is false, because the 'gap' between the two modalities - description and evaluation - does not exist (section 2).

The second notion regards the importance of character in Hauerwas' thought. As he explains, Christian ethics should not be considered as reflection on moral actions to be performed by Christians, but as the description of a way of being. The notion of character is central to this description. Christians have their character formed according to the story of God's reconciliation with the world. Consequently, Christian identity governs the moral judgments by Christians, mediated not by moral principle but by character (section 3).

The third notion regards the issue of how their belief in God actually shapes the Christians' self. As Hauerwas explains, a mental transformation has to occur through the confession of sinfulness. Only then it is possible to shape one's life according to the conviction that the God of Jesus Christ is a forgiving God. Christian character is formed by learning to accept God's forgiveness and act accordingly. Thus, there is a strong connection between 'truth' and 'truthfulness' in Hauerwas' theory. The transformation of the self that is characteristic of Christian existence is a precondition of knowing Christian convictions to be true. As my analysis will show, Hauerwas' conception of Christian ethics is strongly dependent on this epistemological thesis. It forms the basis of his claim of 'the unity of belief and conduct', which indicates, in theological terms, the importance of the notion of 'sanctification' in his theory (section 4).

Hauerwas' conception of Christian ethics cannot but create a sharp opposition between the Church and secular society. In this connection, he develops a strong moral criticism of the notion of individual freedom as it is understood in contemporary society. Thus, the practical content of his views is in conflict with what is the received moral opinion even among many of his fellow Christians (section 5).

The main aim in this essay is to offer a systematic presentation of Hauerwas' views, which have drawn less attention in Europe than they have in the United States. Hauerwas has repeatedly challenged his interpretors by claiming as a characteristic of his conception of Christian ethics that it defies such a systematic account. To refute this claim I will quite extensively describe and analyse his views in order to show that the notion of sanctification lies at the heart of his thought (cf. Milbank 1987; Hütter 1993). After having presented his views, I will take issue with Hauerwas at one particular point and offer some reflections that I think adequate to indicate a major epistemological weakness in his line of reasoning (section 6).

6.2 THE INTERPRETATIVE FRAMEWORK OF CHRISTIAN MORAL IDENTITY

When Hauerwas claims that Christian theologians do not have a theory of moral rationality, since they have a Bible and a Church (1988, 67), this is not supposed to mean that the Bible or the Church serve as a replacement for ethical theory. They do not answer the same sort of questions that philosophers seek to answer. Theories of moral rationality are constructed to answer philosophical questions about the logical features of moral reasoning and judgment, e.g. the question whether concrete moral judgments are deductively derived from certain fundamental principles. According to Hauerwas, such questions are inappropriate to account for the nature of Christian ethics. The reason is that Christian ethics is not just another ethical theory.

If it were such, the question to ask would be whether belief in God does or can make a difference for moral judgments and their justification. To answer this question positively would be to show that Christians derive their moral judgments as conclusions from arguments in which their interpretation of the will of God serves as the major premise. Since Hauerwas dismisses such an account of moral reasoning as inadequate, Christian ethics must be fundamentally different. It does not follow the same canons of reasoning as secular ethics. Christian ethics, as Hauerwas understands it, is not concerned with justification of moral judgment, unlike, for example, Divine Command theory. The task for Christian ethics is to develop a positive account of the narrative contexts within which Christians understand themselves as people with particular commitments and vocations. These contexts are furnished by the Christian tradition that is embedded in the community of the Church. Only within such contexts one can intelligibly account for the particular practices of moral reasoning by Christians. This does not mean, however, that the narrative understanding of moral reasoning only applies to the Christian community, for this is not what Hauerwas claims. On the contrary:

> *It is my contention that there is not nor can there be any tradition-free account of practical reason. There are certainly different traditions whose material content will make a difference for the kind of questions discussed, but each tradition in its own way will reflect the community that makes the activity of moral reflection intelligible* (Hauerwas 1988, 71).

Within this tradition-oriented view, practical reason can neither be criticized nor does it operate on the basis of an abstract understanding of what morality is. Nor can it be understood on the basis of abstract principles. The framework within which human action is to be morally assessed is best conceived of in terms of a narrative, not only because Christian convictions take this form, but because 'all significant moral claims are historically derived and require narrative display' (1981a, 99).

6.2.1 Describing the World from a Christian Point of View

Hauerwas' narrativist methodology of Christian ethics implies the rejection of the distinction between description and evaluation that has dominated much of recent moral philosophy. This distinction is rejected because it assumes moral reason to reflect on a given state of affairs that is described independently of the reflective process itself. According to Hauerwas this is a false assumption. To put it somewhat crudely: there are no 'given' states of affairs. When I choose to act in a certain way, this is because I identify with one out of many possible descriptions of this particular act. In the process of identifying myself with some descriptions rather than others, my moral agency is shaped.

Accordingly, Christians have their moral agency shaped 'by the description of the world that claims it has been redeemed by the work of Christ' (1975, 203). They have learned to accept that they are a people who live from God's forgiveness and this self-understanding enters into their intentions and actions. In this sense, Christian moral identity is shaped by truthfulness to God as the true Lord of the world. This is what, according to Hauerwas, makes the difference:

The Christian understood in this way is one who, because of his character, is committed to reshaping [of] the world and, in the process, himself according to the dictates of God's Kingdom. This is the central aspect of the Christian's moral experience, for the essential moral quality of a man's existence is not simply that he acts rightly or wrongly in accordance with certain external norms of justice or law but in the general orientation of his life, because of the way he insists on understanding and describing the world (Hauerwas 1975, 204).

In this connection, Hauerwas has always maintained that the Christian way of describing the world is at once descriptive and normative. In his earlier work, he frequently refers to a not widely known philosophical treatise on the logic of moral language, called *Moral Notions*, written by an analytical philosopher by the name of Julius Kovesi. This treatise has influenced Hauerwas' thinking on the relation between description and evaluation to a considerable extent (Hütter 1993, 116-123). For this reason I will briefly summarize Kovesi's theory.

The theory departs from the observation that analytical moral philosophy assumes moral concepts to be characterized by a 'logical gap' between description and evaluation. According to Kovesi, this gap does not exist because there is a relation of dependence between the two. In characterizing a given act as an act of murder - which is Kovesi's example - the description of this act is based on a particular evaluative point of view (see also Reinders 1988, 46-50). Certain elements in acts of killing are considered to be morally relevant and therefore enter into the description of these acts as 'murder'. It is not the case that we have first 'hardboiled facts' which are subsequently submitted to moral evaluation, for without a particular evaluative point of view we would not know which facts to select, that is, which descriptions to accept as relevant to our judgment. Since there is room for disagreement on the issue of what constitutes a case of murder - e.g. whether or not it must be an act and if so, whether or not this act must be intentional - there is also room for different conceptions of murder embedded in different evaluative frameworks that determine different standards of a correct use of 'murder'. 'Moral notions', as Kovesi puts this point succinctly, 'do not evaluate the world of descriptions, but describe the world of evaluations' (Kovesi 1976, 65).

Since evaluative frameworks are no free-floating entities, but belong to particular communities and cultures, the rules for the correct use of moral notions are conventionally determined. By describing a given act as 'murder', one does not merely express one's feelings towards this act, nor does one state one's private opinion about it, but one asserts the resemblance of the act in relevant respects to accepted descriptions of former cases of murder within a given tradition. This does not only imply that moral notions are always embedded in larger conceptual schemes and interpretational frameworks. It also implies that they describe intentionally: they are meant to make a practical difference, which they can by virtue of their being recommending or approving or rejecting and so on. Given this explanation of moral notions, to learn the rules of their correct use is to learn something that is at once descriptive and normative. It exhibits a conventional way of seeing things as well as a way of judging them. This is the reason why Hauerwas says that correct moral judgment is much more about perception than about decision (cf. Hütter 1993, 121). Perceptions and ways of seeing things are constituted by interpretional frameworks that in their turn are embedded in traditional convictions and beliefs. Hence the hyperbolic claim that in the end there is no watershed between the categories of 'action' and 'belief':

The task of Christian ethics is to help us see how our convictions are in themselves a morality. We do not first believe certain things about God, Jesus, and the church, and subsequently derive ethical implications from these beliefs. Rather our convictions embody our morality; our beliefs are our actions. We Christians ought not to search for the 'behavioral implications' of our beliefs. Our moral life is not comprised of beliefs plus decisions; our moral life is the process in which our convictions form our character to be truthful (Hauerwas 1983, 16).

From a theological point of view, then, ethics is not concerned with the formulation and justification of moral principles against which actions can be tested, but with the analysis of how Christian convictions enter into the formation of character. In contrast: much of modern philosophical ethics assumes that the necessary coherence in moral life comes from underlying universal principles.

Hauerwas rejects this assumption. The so-called universal principles of morality are but theoretical extrapolations of particular moral views and experiences. Since the attempt to derive universal principles from contingent facts must fail, these principles cannot provide the coherence that is looked for. Coherence does not come from a universal conception of moral reason, but from the ability of living a moral life. This ability requires character, not principles (cf. 1985a, 133-134).

6.3   THE EXPLANATION OF 'CHRISTIAN CHARACTER'

The main conceptual tools for this view are developed in Hauerwas' doctoral dissertation, published in 1975 as *Character and the Christian Life*. In this book he discusses the notion of character within the context of 'action theory'. In the 'Introduction' to a second edition of this book, Hauerwas has criticized this approach, because it falsely assumes that 'action' is a basic category of analysis (1985b, xx). Following MacIntyre, Hauerwas now takes the concept of an 'intelligible action' to be more fundamental; through this concept he also explains why in recent times narrativity came to dominate his methodology. Actions can only be understood as 'intelligible' within the context of narrative histories. The self-criticism considering the original approach taken in the book is not meant to deny, however, that his analysis of the notion of character is still valid. The point of the analysis remains to show that 'character' provides us with an appropriate description of someone's agency in concrete terms (1985b, xxii). Character is the embodiment of the self as moral agent:

Nothing about my being is more 'me' than my character. Character is the basic aspect of our existence. It is the mode of the formation of our 'I', for it is character that provides the content of that 'I'. If we are to be changed in any fundamental sense, then it must be a change of character (Hauerwas 1985b, 203).

Underlying this notion of character is Hauerwas' analysis of human agency in terms of self-determination. Our capacity for self-determination is grounded in the fact that we can move ourselves to act in discriminating ways by ordering our actions through our reasons and beliefs (1985b, 202). These reasons and beliefs do not 'cause' nor just 'explain' our acts, but they 'enter into the formation of these acts', in that we choose to live by certain beliefs and intentions rather than others (1985b, 114). The 'self' as a moral agent is shaped by its being engaged in the world and setting a course among the multitudes of possibilities that confront it. This determination of 'self-agency' is what we call character (1985b, 115). Hauerwas recognizes, however, that if our character is shaped through the actions and projects in which we engage ourselves, it must have a sense of direction. Our character is not merely the result of our choices, it also shapes our intentions and actions. Thus, our character shows a certain flexibility and changeability, while at the same time this allows for the possibility that not all our choices are equally important and that they not all equally stem from and affect our character (1985b, 118). This problem is resolved by making a distinction between descriptive and normative aspects of our character (ibid.). There are many aspects of our character that do not fit into a 'singleness of purpose' model. One reason is that in many situations we are not sure as to what our basic intentions and beliefs are. Another reason is that, given the ever changing circumstances of our life, 'singleness of purpose' might degenerate into 'narrowness' or fanaticism. Our character therefore requires 'the continuing qualification of our agency'. There are many aspects of life that we cannot avoid confronting, even if we would rather choose to do so, but that have be to be integrated in our character. Thus to account for the coherence of our character we have to move on to the normative dimension.

This, I take it, is what Hauerwas means when he argues that although we can act without a sense of direction to a considerable extent, we cannot do so unlimitedly without losing the possibility of self-determination. Consequently, character is best understood as a direction or orientation:

The fact that our character is of a certain kind or denotes a certain kind of orientation does not mean that all we shall do in the future is necessarily programmed into what we are now. Our character gives us direction; but as such it does not have to determine all that we shall be in all that we do (...) Character is directing, but it is not compelling in the sense that it represents an external force over which we have no control. Character, however, may be thought of as compelling in the sense that it may direct our life in a rather definite and limited fashion (Hauerwas 1985b, 123).

If we retain the possibility to develop and change, despite our character, does this not imply that there is yet another 'authority' above or behind our character, something like a transcendental subject? Hauerwas explicitly denies this. In fact it is one of the major aims of his book to replace both Kantian dualism and behavioristic determinism as far as the interpretation of moral agency is concerned (1985b, 22-26). By focussing on character as the embodiment of our agency, Hauerwas intends to overcome the misconception common to both these views, which is the assumption that actions can only be understood in terms of external causes. The dualist assumes a transcendental self in order to preserve human freedom, the determinist rejects the idea of an 'inner cause' and explains the agent's actions as caused by external, situational factors (see also 1985b, 202). What both conceptions of agency fail to see is that 'there is no need to posit a "cause" of man's actions' (1985b, 26). The self is its actions and experiences and in that sense the self and our agency are identical. The concrete embodiment of this self-determining agency is our character. Thus the question still remains as to how the possibility of development and change of character can be accounted for if at the same time character is the determinant of our agency.

6.3.1 Character and Continuity rather than Action and Decision

In raising this question we arrive at one of Hauerwas' most central concerns in moral theory, which is to save the notion of the self from abandonment to either occasionalism or decisionism. What is considered most defective in modern philosophical ethics, is the absence of a notion of the moral life as a coherent whole (1985b, xxx-xxxi). In this respect Hauerwas appears to be strongly committed to MacIntyre's 'fragmentation hypothesis'. Because the conception of coherent moral life is lacking, many of our contemporaries experience moral judgments as arbitrary, i.e. depending on circumstance and private opinion. This experience is reflected in the concentration on individual actions and decisions, particularly in the field of applied ethics. By taking the resolution of moral conflicts and dilemma's as its central task, ethicists have turned morality into a problem solving device, thereby making applied ethics a branch of decision theory. In order to tackle 'hard cases' they proceed by subsuming incidental decisions under the rule of a single moral principle. Underlying this approach is the assumption that moral problems are recognized independently of particular sets of convictions that people happen to have. This assumption is based on the ideal of ethical objectivity requiring that the agent's subjective beliefs and convictions are ruled out. Accordingly, the 'logic' of moral decisions is explained in terms of lawlike operations of moral reason, regardless of the particular identity of the agent. As already indicated, this approach issues in a distortion of our moral life, for without having a clear sense of their identity as moral agents, people would not know what moral problems to confront.

Morality is not primarily concerned with quandaries or hard decisions, nor is the moral self simply the collection of such decisions. As persons of character we do not confront situations as mud puddles in which we have to step; rather the kind of 'situations' we confront and how we understand them are a function of the kind of people we are (Hauerwas 1981a, 114-115).

Theologically speaking, Hauerwas sees the concentration on action and decision reflected in the metaphor of command that has largely dominated protestant ethics (1985b, 2-5). This metaphor is appropriate only if one assumes theologically that God's ways of dealing with man are most adequately represented in lawlike requirements. The logic of divine commands, however, is 'the logic of imperatives directed to specific cases and practices' (1985b, 8). The problem with this logic is that it does not and cannot concretely account for the content of a Christian life, because it ignores the relation between the person and his actions:

We are more than the sum total of our individual actions and responses to particular situations whether the moral significance of such a response is determined by the situation itself or by its correspondence to a principle. The language of character cannot be avoided in Christian ethics if we are to do justice to the significance of the continuing determination of the self necessary for moral growth; for our actions are also acts of self-determination whereby we not only reaffirm what we have been, but what we will be in the future (Hauerwas 1985b, 8).

By invoking the notion of character, then, Hauerwas is combatting what he sees as the distortion and fragmentation of our moral existence, that prevents us from acquiring the virtue of constancy (1985b, xxx). Through our character we achieve an orientation in our lives by ordering our desires, affections, and actions according to certain reasons rather than others. It provides an orientation and continuity to our existence' (1985b, 203).

6.3.2 Christian Character

The notion of character thus interpreted has to be qualified from a theological point of view in order to arrive at a notion of 'Christian character'. To have one's character formed as a Christian is not different from having one's character formed as a nonbeliever.

The explanation of Christian character requires a narrativist account of the Church as a community that lives from 'the story of God', for it is in becoming part of this story that Christians acquire their particular intentions and beliefs:

The difference is not in how one's character is formed, but rather in the actual orientation the Christian's character assumes because of the particular content of that which qualifies his agency. To be a Christian is to have one's character determined in accordance with God's action in Jesus Christ. This determination gives one's life an orientation which otherwise it would not have (Hauerwas 1985b, 227).

Consequently, it is through the particularity of the Christian story of God's action in Christ as it is told and lived by the Church, that Christians come to understand the particular commitments and vocations in which they participate. In Hauerwas' understanding of this story the notions of forgiveness and nonviolence play a crucial role (1983, xvii). To characterize the Church as a community that has learned to live from God's forgiveness is to say that nonviolence is the vocation of Christians in the world. Through this commitment they bear testimony to their belief that God rather than earthly power rules the world. To become part of the community of the Church, then, is to become part of a process of learning to embody forgiveness and peace in our moral lives.

The concrete features of the Christian life, as Hauerwas understands it, will be spelled out further in the section on Church and society (see below), but before that there are some important theoretical implications in his views that deserve to be made explicit. If the 'particular content' of Christian beliefs is determined by 'God's action in Christ', the question arises of how this belief in God's action affects the agency of the believer. This is a crucial question for Hauerwas, given his claim of the unity of belief and conduct (1985b, 182-183). At this point he affirms what 'the standard account of moral rationality' denies, namely that different convictions and beliefs imply different contents of morality.

6.4 SANCTIFICATION AS THE FORMATION OF CHRISTIAN CHARACTER

Theological accounts of how God's salvific work affects the believer tend to be disappointingly obscure according to Hauerwas, because they fear to offer a psychological explanation of the mystery of God's grace for man. In his view, however, the true mystery is not how the believers' selves are formed by the grace of God, 'but that the God who is our creator wills to love even the disobedient men we are' (1985b, 194). He claims that his ethics of character enables him to make 'intelligible' the transformation that Christian convictions work in the believer (see also 1985b, 179).

The traditional locus to discuss this transformation is the notion of sanctification. Although Hauerwas has uttered second thoughts on the importance of the notion of sanctification (1985b, xxviii), it nevertheless provides an important key to his moral theory. As we will see, it brings together many of the different strings in his analysis. The notion of sanctification raises many of the troublesome issues that have been extensively discussed in the history of protestant theology, most prominently the relation between God's action towards the believer and the believer's response. In order to present Hauerwas' account of these issues, it is appropriate to expand a little on some aspects of the theological debate.

The orthodox position in the debate has always been that the relation between the action of God and the action of man is to be explained as a movement from the first to the second, and never the other way around. Since the human will is tempted by sin, man is not free in choosing to be good, but has to be empowered by God. Religious people do not become virtuous by their own achievement, but only through God's salvific action, which is the redemption from sin.

This explanation raised the further question of how God's action affects the believer. Does it bring about a change in his life and if so, how? Confronted with this question, many orthodox theologians saw themselves faced with the following dilemma: if no change occurs, it appears that God's action is powerless and man is able to resist His divine will. On the other hand, if a change does occur in the life of the believer, how can this not be genuinely his own response to God's grace? Although the former possibility was not acceptable because of the sovereignty of the divine will, the latter always raised suspicion, for in concentrating on virtue and character, it seemed to open the possibility 'that the moral life is not continually in need of grace' (Meilaender 1984, 36).

According to Hauerwas, this dilemma originated from the fact that protestant orthodoxy had adopted the conceptual scheme of theological voluntarism (1985b, 1-10, see also xxvi-xxvii). To escape an 'ethic of achievement', it stressed the 'forensic' nature of the believer's moral response. But in doing so, it got stuck with the metaphor of command and obedience. Since the will of God is the one and only good will in the universe, moral action is impossible but through obedience to His commands. Consequently, Christian ethics within the protestant tradition became, on the whole, voluntaristic in that it was mainly occupied with the 'external' grounds of moral action, i.c. God's will.

In order to overcome voluntarism and the subsequent occasionalist and decisionist distortions of the moral life, Hauerwas raises the issue of how the believer's moral self is determined in Christ. Voluntarism presupposes a conception of morality as a lawlike device, which turns the moral life into following external demands or attempting to be good. This does not only pertain to principle-based, but also to virtue-based ethics. In Hauerwas' view, Christian moral life is distorted when it is taken as 'a pattern of rules to follow' or 'a set of virtues to be achieved', rather than as 'a mode of being to be lived out' (1985b, 182). Sanctification operates on a deeper level, which he tries to show by referring to the doctrine of the 'Fathers' of calvinist and methodist theology (Calvin, Wesley and Edwards). Despite the differences in their understanding, they were united in one central theme:

This theme is their stress on the importance of the change of the 'person' as the essential element in man's sanctification. This idea of the change of the 'person' has close parallels to the importance of character for ethical behavior. This emphasis on the 'person' is a recognition that sanctification is not accomplished simply by doing prescribed acts; how we act is equally important, for it is in the 'how' that our character is formed as well as the act itself (Hauerwas 1985b, 196).

Central to this understanding of the transformation that is worked in the believer through the grace of God is the confession of sinfulness. The conviction that God is a forgiving God implies that the believer sees himself as someone who has to be forgiven. Therefore the conviction of God's forgiveness cannot be held without directly affecting the self. One cannot accept being a sinner without having one's heart and mind changed. The confession that one is a sinner as such already presupposes that the self is in the process of being transformed through this confession. Christians cannot enter into this confession without intending themselves to be changed and to become a forgiving people.

Talk of sin, therefore, is a claim about the way we are, but our very ability to know we are that way requires that we have already begun a new way of life. That is why the Christian doctrine of sanctification is central for assessing the epistemological status of Christian convictions (Hauerwas 1988, 10).

On this account, the transformation of the Christian self is not to be taken as an unanalyzable event in which God changes the person, but as a process in which character is formed, thus bringing constancy, integrity and growth into the believer's life. Character is the determination of the empirical self, beyond which there is no 'I' or 'me' that can be affected or changed by God's activity without changing that self. Being 'sanctified', therefore, involves a determination of the person as a whole that brings about a general orientation, rather than providing a particular set of moral acts or dispositions. This general orientation is to be taken as a 'horizon' or a 'boundary' that is derived from one's basic commitments and beliefs about God. To be qualified by the language of faith is to become a different person (1985b, 203). It means that Christians are obliged to act in a certain 'way' that is shaped by the actual determination of their character. Thus explained, there is no need to regard sanctification as a mysterious process 'that occurs behind or apart from our actual behavior' (1985b, 207). Instead, it occurs in and through the unity of action and belief that shapes the self of the believer as agent.

6.4.1 Indicative and Imperative

When I understand Hauerwas correctly, with this account of the transformation of Christian character he wants to show the irrelevance of a distinction that has greatly dominated modern moral philosophy, namely the distinction between 'is' and 'ought'. This distinction is used to back up the argument that no normative moral conclusions follow from a given description of the world. Hauerwas' conception of Christian ethics is intended to attack this argument.

In theological language, the distinction between 'is' and 'ought' is parallelled by the distinction between the 'indicative' and the 'imperative'. Following nineteenth-century liberal theology, many protestant theologians hold that the 'indicative' - in Hauerwas' terms: the story of God's redemption of human sinfulness - implies that man is free to take responsibility for shaping the world according to the tasks he sees himself confronted with. In their view, the 'freedom in Christ' implies that there is no such thing as a specific Christian ethic. Christians share their moral responsibility with other people, they are confronted by the same demands and do not have a particular access to moral truth that other people do not have. In the liberal theologian's view, therefore, a gap exists between the 'indicative' and the 'imperative'. The gospel does not entail a particular kind of 'ethic'.

Undoubtedly, at this point liberal theology is strongly influenced by Enlightenment philosophy, which developed its own equivalent of the same distinction: the distinction between 'isness' and 'oughtness'. Notwithstanding the fact that this distinction has permeated modern moral philosophy, Hauerwas considers it to be a rather artificial one, because - as we saw - the descriptive and normative aspects of Christian life cannot be separately accounted for (cf. 1981b, 69-70). The above account of the transformation of the self and the formation of Christian character reveals the interplay between his views on these matters. Learning to see the world and one's existence within it in the light of a different story, is to have one's agency determined by it, which in turn is how one's character is shaped. To be Christian is:

> *to have a particular way of illuminating the world, but in so doing the Christian forms himself in accordance with the image of the very thing he illumines, for Christian belief must be understood not as mere adherence to a set of propositions, but as an adherence that dictates that he try through his actions to conform the world to the truth of those propositions* (Hauerwas 1985b, 206).

The truth of Christian convictions is, at least in part, established by the fact that they do give direction and unity to the life of the believer. What Christians do cannot be separated from what they are, and what they are bears intimate connections with their character 'as formed in sanctification' (1985b, 206). Through the formation of character, then, the self of Christians acquires the integrity and continuity to remain faithful to the reasons and beliefs that they hold true about the world. Consequently, Hauerwas can say that

> *There is a kind of 'isness' to the 'oughtness' in that the ought is what in fact we are. In this sense Christian character can be understood as a pattern of expectation that at once involves statements about what we are and what we can be expected to do. The very idea of expectations combines the descriptive and the normative in the sense that what we ought to do is in fact what we are* (Hauerwas 1985b, 205).

Hence the claim that sanctification mediates between 'indicative' and 'imperative', between 'being' and 'doing' and between 'isness' and 'oughtness'. The importance of this point is in what Hauerwas says about the truth and truthfulness of Christian convictions. In his view, the truth of a given claim must correspond to the nature of what is claimed. The truth of Christian convictions cannot appropriately be established by isolating them as propositions, but only within the context of the story of God. The point of this story is to get involved in a way of being. Thus

> *story is a way to remind us of the inherently practical character of theological convictions. For Christian convictions are not meant to picture the world. They do not give a primitive metaphysics about how the world is constituted. Rather the gospel is a story that gives you a way of being in the world. Stories, at least the stories that I am interested in, are not told to explain as a theory explains, but to involve the agent in a way of life* (Hauerwas 1977, 73).

The 'inherently practical' nature of Christian convictions implies a indissoluble connection between 'truth' and 'truthfulness', which for Hauerwas are almost synonymous. On the one hand, the truth of Christian convictions appears in the fact that they do change the believer and determine his agency accordingly. On the other hand, the truthfulness of the believer in living the Christian life attests to the truth of his convictions (cf. Hütter 1993, 130). As far as the truth of Christian convictions is concerned, then, there is no way of establishing this truth 'independently' of the context of Christian life itself. This means that learning to live 'the story of God' is a precondition of understanding it, rather than vice versa.

> *Christian convictions transform the self to true faith by creating a community that lives faithful to the one true God of the universe. When self and nature are thus put in right relation we perceive the truth of our existence. But because truth is unattainable without a corresponding transformation of self, 'ethics', as the investigation of that transformation, does not follow after a prior systematic presentation of the Christian faith, but is at the beginning of Christian theological reflection* (Hauerwas 1983, 16).

The Christian faith, as Hauerwas understands it, is no alternative worldview that can be presented in the form of a 'primitive metaphysics', because the truth of its convictions cannot be established by reference to propositions, but only by reference to lifes. In this sense, Hauerwas maintains, assessing the truth of these convictions cannot be separated from the truthfulness of the people who make those claims (1988, 10).

6.5 THE CHURCH AS THE PEACEABLE KINGDOM

In this section I will attend more explicitly to the practical content of Hauerwas' views. To be able to defend his position on the relationship between Christian convictions and moral judgment, it appears, he sees no other way than redirecting the methodology of doing Christian ethics. Just as the distinction between 'indicative' and 'imperative' is impossible, there is neither a distinction between 'form' and 'content'. This cannot but have far-reaching consequences for the way in which Christians understand their existence in secular society.

To explain why, let me return once more to the rejection of Christian ethics as an account of particular ideals. Take for example the notion of the Kingdom of God. Just like other theologians, Hauerwas takes this notion to be crucial for Christian ethics, though not in terms of an ethical ideal. The moral significance of the Kingdom of God cannot be grasped unless God is actually accepted as the true Lord of the world. This is shown by Jesus' Sermon on the Mount. Among God's people the poor and oppressed are privileged, not because of their poverty and oppression, but because of their reception of God's forgiveness. In doing so, they witness to know who the true Lord of the world is:

They have learned that their King is a gracious King ready to forgive those who are able to be forgiven. By being able to be forgiven by God we learn how to forgive each other. That such a forgiven and forgiving community is possible is but an indication that God's rule is no utopian ideal, but a present reality we are required to live out (Hauerwas 1985a, 116).

Consequently, Hauerwas' interpretation of the Kingdom focusses on reconciliation and nonviolence. This should not be taken to mean, however, that Christians have nonviolence as their fundamental moral principle. Nonviolence is the mode of being that characterizes the life in the community that has learned to live from God's reconciliation with man of the Church. The Church, however, does not have an ethics in the sense of a ruling moral principle. As Hauerwas puts this: 'the church does not have a social ethic but rather is a social ethic' (1988, 101).

In the same vein he explains the notion of peace, which cannot be isolated from the context of the story of God in Christ either. Peace is not the prime moral value of a programme of Christian political morality, but a way of imitating Christ both for the individual believer and the Church. To be 'in Christ', as Hauerwas explains, is to follow Christ on the way He went 'for us':

> *It is not that we have a prior definition of peace and then think of Christ as the great exemplar of that peace. Rather what Jesus has done enables us to know and embody God's peace in our lives by finding peace with God, with ourselves, and with one another*' (Hauerwas 1983, 93).

When seen in this light, the Kingdom of God is a reality that the Christian community is called to present to the world as a contrast model for secular kingdoms. In this connection, the notions of reconciliation and nonviolence acquire a strong political meaning. To the Church, nonviolence is the reflection of its raison d'être as a sign of hope for the world. Nowhere could the Christian community be at greater distance from the dominant political institution in secular society, which is the nation-state. The nation-state necessarily relies on the use of force to secure its own existence, which - by contrast - is what the Church refuses to do (1981a, 84). The reason is that from its very beginning the Church is based upon trust. The Christian narrative about the life and death of Jesus and his resurrection as Christ has made the Church understand that God reigns his Kingdom through forgiveness and love. Only in the resurrection of Christ man is able to find peace with himself and others. Christians trust this story as the truth about their lives that empowers them to reject violence and war. Theirs is the conviction that war cannot be consistent with the Kingdom of God. Hence the 'nonresistant character' of the Christian community which, though often absent, is nevertheless a hallmark of the power of its story (1981a, 101). Once this is understood, according to Hauerwas, the situation in which we are at the mercy of others is no longer a threat:

> *To be forgiven means that I must face the fact that my life actually lies in the hands of others. I must learn to trust them as I have learned to trust God. (...) We cannot live to insure our ultimate security, but must learn to live on a day-to-day basis. (...) For, ironically, when we try to exclude surprise from our life, we are only more subject to the demonic.*

We become subject to those 'necessities' that we are anxious about because without them, we fear we lack the power to control our lives (Hauerwas 1983, 89).

Nonviolence, then, reflects the possibility of a community to forgive sin, as it is based on trust in the primacy of God's act. It is not a moral principle, meant to teach to nation-states how to conduct their political conflicts. It is neither a political ethic. Nothing is more alien to Hauerwas's thought than the idea of the Church providing the state with morally superior strategies to ameliorate its shortcomings or remedy its excesses (1981a, 3, 83).

This does not mean that Hauerwas wants to deny the political relevance of the Church with regard to the nation-state. His point is rather that it cannot be accounted for in secular, nonreligious categories, because the notion of being a forgiven people is what separates the Christian community from the world: 'The world, under the illusion that power and violence rule history, assumes that it has no need to be forgiven' (1981a, 69). The witness of the Church is that the world is world, that it cannot therefore be based upon trust and truthfulness, but only on distrust and coercion. Though the world can understand this as the truth about itself, it has no alternative. For to see an alternative, it would have to know of sinfulness and redemption, which presupposes the message of the Saviour, both of which the world as such does not know anything about. Consequently, the Church can in no way better serve the world than by remaining true to itself:

Put starkly, the way the church must always respond to the challenge of our polity is to be herself. This does not involve a rejection of the world, or a withdrawal from the world; rather it is a reminder that the church must serve the world on her own terms. We must be faithful in our own way, even if the world understands such faithfulness as disloyalty. But the first task of the church is not to supply theories of governmental legitimacy or even to suggest strategies for social betterment. The first task of the church is to exhibit in our common life the kind of community possible when trust, and not fear, rules our lives (Hauerwas 1981a, 85).

6.5.1 The Illusion of Control

Given this explanation, there is one other frequent theme in Hauerwas which he invokes to mark the distinction between the Church and secular morality, which is 'the illusion of self-control'. Since the Christian community is shaped by the intention of seeing the world as governed by the grace of God, the aim of 'self-control' - which is the driving force in most areas of secular society - does not make much sense for Christians. What Christians need most is to abandon the sense of self-control as a precondition for being free to organize their lives according to their own plans. By way of contrast, Hauerwas interpretes Christian freedom as the courage to accept the truth about man - which is that we are not free to live at peace with ourselves and with the world unless we learn to be forgiven by God - and live by it (1983, 43).

When transposed to the level of institutions, the 'deception of self-control' is particularly manifest in the modern nation-state. Since the nation-state is built on the deception of order and control, Christians cannot support - without betraying both their Lord and themselves - the survival of political order and stability that the state seeks for itself. At the same time, however, Hauerwas acknowledges that the non-violent peace prayed for by Christians cannot 'but create instability in a world based on the assumption that violence is the ultimate weapon against disorder' (1983, 144).

Hauerwas is well aware of the fact that this position, from the point of view of state and society, inevitably seems a way of 'doing nothing' against the violence and abuse of power that dominates political life. The peace that governs God's Kingdom is dangerously innocent vis-à-vis the forces that threaten social and political order and stability. Since they have no alternative to offer, as Hauerwas admits, Christians will be acutely aware of a tragic dimension in their existence. The tragedy is not that the existing order only allows limited moral ends to be obtained with imperfect means. It is rather that the peace of the Kingdom, when conceived of as a political ethic, would make the world an even more dangerous place than it already is (1983, 145). Consequently, the moral life of Christians will distinguish itself by the virtue of patience, since there can be no compromise with violence to maintain stability in the world. Therefore, the proper domain for the Christian life to be lived in peace is the community of the Church. Not only in the sense that this is where the story of God is told and one can learn what it means to live by it, but also in the sense that this is the single space in this world where the Christian life is possible at all.

6.6 IDENTITY, UNITY AND MORAL JUDGMENT

Having analyzed Hauerwas' views on the relation between Christian character and moral epistemology in some detail, I will raise two critical issues that are closely connected. The first is related to the claim that Christian character provides a general orientation to the Christian moral life, which accounts for the unity or 'singleness' of this life. As Hauerwas himself has recognized, this singleness should not be taken too strictly, because we confront different aspects of our lives that are not equally attached to our character, and moreover, the ever changing circumstances of our lives are not always equally compatible with our character. Both observations lead to the same conclusion: the formation of a person's character may be exposed to a variety of influences other than his convictions. This raises the issue of whether the proclaimed 'singleness' of our character is not properly understood in terms of 'ideal identity', despite Hauerwas' claims of the contrary. The second issue is related to the notion of tragedy. If it is true that 'tragedy' occurs in case we cannot avoid a conflict between our convictions and certain circumstances we are confronted with, this opens the possibility of moral insight that is not exclusively determined by these convictions. Tragedy cannot occur without the presence of irreconcilably conflicting moral 'truths'. Irreconcilably conflicting moral truths exclude the possibility of a unified and coherent moral view.

6.6.1 Christian Character and 'Ideal Identity'

In a critical essay on Hauerwas' views on sanctification, Patricia Jung has argued that his account of the formation of character is 'intellectualistic', in that he does pay little or no attention to 'involuntary' aspects of character-formation that occur in circumstances and determinations which are not subject to choice (1983, 78-79; cf. also Bondi 1984, 202). Hauerwas recognizes this when in his conceptual analysis of character he makes the distinction between 'character traits' and 'having character', whereby the former is meant to indicate those characteristics that may account for the more contingent aspects of someone's behaviour, while the latter denotes 'a more basic moral determination of the self' (1985b, 16). Clearly, 'having character' is the stronger notion which he presupposes throughout his analysis. In order to explain the difference between the two, he makes a distinction between 'descriptive' and 'normative' aspects, as we already saw. People see themselves confronted by certain aspects of their behaviour that do not 'fit' their character but are nevertheless part of their behaviour. In that case one can say that such 'unfitting' aspects are descriptively, but not necessarily normatively to be seen as part of their character. Character in the strong sense in which Hauerwas uses it, is always connected with projects (1985b, 120).

It appears therefore that because of its normative status, Hauerwas' understanding of 'having character' is equivalent to 'ideal identity'. The notion of 'Ideal identity' - as developed for example by Rorty and Wong (1990, 23) - implies the possibility that a conception of the ideal self can guide the formation of actions. If my reading of Hauerwas is correct, he is saying that the Christian believer has his character shaped by certain convictions (e.g. the belief that God will forgive) which, in turn, form his motivations and intentions. The assumption underlying this claim must be that the reasons and beliefs inherent in these convictions are determining all other aspects of the character. In the light of how they have come to understand themselves, people have their motivations and their intentions formed. This assumption is questionable, however, because the psychological force of the beliefs people have about themselves is not necessarily coincidental with the moral authority attributed to it. As Rorty and Wong have pointed out:

Because the ideal self defines a set of general ends and values, it affects the details of practical deliberation and the directions of choice, often by determining what is salient. But it is frequently difficult to integrate the habits required to actualize an ideal identity with the rest of a person's central traits (...) The psychological force of an ideal is distinguishable from the normative or moral authority accorded to it (Rorty & Wong 1990, 24).

What and who I am may include a lot more than the ideal identity that is inferred from my convictions, not only objectively, but also in the sense that I acknowledge these other aspects to be part of 'me'. Apart from convictions, there is temperament, for example, making someone into a self-assured, irritable or friendly person. There are traits related to social roles: being the responsible elder sister, being the younger colleague or the well-known writer. Or group-related traits such as being black, being middle-class or being an elderly person. As the analysis of Rorty and Wong indicates, these various elements of identity cannot only have relative centrality in various ways, they also may be dominating at different times and in different circumstances (1990, 25 ff.). Even if I consider my motivations and intentions to be informed by the reasons and beliefs inherent in my convictions, I cannot deny my agency to be determined, at least sometimes, by other, 'self-contradictory' and, in that sense, 'involuntary' motivations and intentions.

The problem I see for Hauerwas in this connection regards his claim about the transformation of Christian character: there is no distinction between what Christians believe and what they ought to do, because, given the content of their convictions, Christians are what they ought to be. This is true if (and only if) 'having Christian character' means that the motivations following from these convictions acquire priority over the motivations stemming from other, contingent aspects of one's character. But obviously the distinction between 'character traits' and 'having Christian character' does only make sense because people do not always assign priority among their various motivations in this way. Consequently, the contingent 'involuntary' elements that actually determine the conduct of Christians may not have normative force, although they have psychological force, and reversely: even when the convictions that constitute 'having Christian character' will have normative force, they may not always have psychological force.

If true, this means that Hauerwas' claim about Christian character as constituting the moral reasoning of Christians loses its explanatory force. To say that what Christians ought to do is what in fact they are, is to say that what Christians ought to do is what in fact they are according to the normative beliefs they have about themselves, which is obviously a circular argument. Although this does not rule out the normative claims that accompany Christian convictions (cf. Flanagan 1990, 43), it does undermine Hauerwas' thesis that these normative claims are not to be represented in terms of an ethical ideal. As a matter of fact, the acclaimed 'unity of belief and conduct' - which I take to be central to Hauerwas' conception of Christian ethics - may itself be part of the ideal identity of Christians, rather than being the premise of their practice of moral judgment. What has characterized the experience and self-understanding of many Christians until the present day, it appears to me, is rather the fact that they are not what they understand that God wants them to be. That is why protestant theology has emphasized the simual justus ac peccator, which implies the ongoing need of being forgiven.

6.6.2 Tragedy and Unity

If this criticism holds, it cannot remain without further consequences regarding Hauerwas' anti-dualistic conception of Christian ethics. Particularly his notion of the tragic aspect of Christian moral life points to a serious difficulty for his claim of 'the unity of belief and conduct'. To elucidate this issue, I will return to the notion of nonviolence and its significance for the Christian moral life. There would be no reason to talk of a tragical dimension in this connection, as Hauerwas does, unless there is moral force in the claim that Christian nonviolence may be a dangerous thing to practice. If the world were an even more insecure place than it is at the present time, this consideration might count as a moral reason against Christian nonviolence. The tragedy does not stem, however, from the fact that Christians find the world opposing their nonviolence when applied to the realm of politics. The tragedy - in Hauerwas' view - stems from the fact that Christians have to face the moral consequence of this opposition. The fact that nation-states and other political bodies cannot but understand themselves as based upon distrust and dominance has to be taken into account in the moral stance of Christians with regard to the realm of politics. Christians have to acknowledge that, given the world as it is, the nation-state cannot always live up to the dictates of reconciliation and peace without harmful consequences. Undoubtedly there are moral reasons why Christians (and other people) ought to oppose when the nation-state goes to war or uses violence against its citizens. Undoubtedly there are reasons why Christians (and other people) should refuse to participate and withhold support, but clearly there are also moral reasons why it may be wrong to do so. There may be victims of violence and aggression who ought to be protected (Reinders 1988).

It seems to me, therefore, that since Christians have other stations in life besides being part of the community of the Church, the reasons and beliefs informing their agency may well be in conflict with one another, even to the point where they become 'self-contradictory'. In 1939, a well-known Dutch theologian - K.H. Miskotte - came to acknowledge that the bellicose nature of the Hitler regime 'has alienated us from our pacifism'. Even in perceiving the world from the point of view of their religious convictions, Christians may nevertheless find themselves in situations where they cannot help but identify with contradictory moral descriptions. As Hauerwas claims, the central aspect of the Christian's moral experience is being committed to reshaping the world and himself according to the dictates of the Kingdom.

But it seems to me that the awareness of tragedy cannot but imply that this is not the whole truth about Christian moral experience.

More importantly, however, it also implies that there are other 'stories' of which religious people may find themselves part than 'the story of God'. Whence the experience that all of us frequently have, namely that we perceive that some action is required morally, even if we rather would avoid it if we could? It appears to me that the answer lies in the fact of our institutional relationships with other people for whom we feel morally responsible. Hauerwas is aware of that when he concedes that character has not only a 'private', but also a 'public' dimension, which implies that 'society and its stock of public descriptions can be understood as in a sense forming a large part of the passive aspects of our existence' (1985b, 116). While it may remain an open question to what extent Christians will or should identify themselves with these passive aspects, the question as such already indicates that there are other stories, supplying them with morally relevant descriptions of themselves that do not necessarily fit their convictions.

In my view, these observations warrant the conclusion that Hauerwas' account of sanctification as the epistemological premise of Christian ethics is inconsistent. For precisely at the point where the singleness or unity that 'having Christian character' is supposed to confer upon the moral life of the believer is to be made concrete, Hauerwas resorts to ambiguity:

Sanctification as the formation of character implies that there is a kind of singleness that dominates our lives, but it is not clear in itself in what such singleness consists for the concrete specification of our character. Such singleness, for example, does not mean that the Christian is a person narrowly determined, for the breadth of the Christian life would depend on how the will of God, or the nature of discipleship, etc. is understood. I suspect that the ambiguity surrounding this question is not just conceptual, but arises from the fact that in our everyday living there simply seems to be more that we are called upon to do than can be directly related to our orientation as Christians (Hauerwas 1985b, 214).

I fail to see how this concession could not imply that also for Christians there must be other sources to draw their moral insights from than only the Christian story of God. If so, Hauerwas' attempt to explain the epistemological basis of Christian ethics strictly in terms of that story seems to fall short of giving an adequate account of the variety of moral experiences that religious and nonreligious people share with one another. Having entered the life of redemption and having accepted to live from God's forgiveness, one does not stop being a parent, or a teacher, or a citizen or a tax-payer. Neither does one stop being female, black, middle-class or aging. To assess the moral experiences that go together with these other elements of one's moral life, it seems to me, Hauerwas' account of sanctification as the heart of Christian moral epistemology is insufficient. Undoubtedly, Christian convictions may govern the practice of moral judgment of Christians by suggesting some descriptions of their actions as more appropriate than others, but the explanation of this claim does not have to be as strictly confined to the 'sanctified self' as it is in Hauerwas' account.

Man is in need of redemption, but he is also created in the image of God. By assigning the notion of creation a more central role in moral epistemology, the scope of Christian ethics becomes much wider than Hauerwas' account allows it to be. It opens the possibility of assessing moral experiences that are common to Christians and other people who do not belong to the community of the Church. That does not necessarily mean to betray Christian convictions, but it does open the possibility of being more communicative in assessing Christian ethics. This, I take it, no one will deny to be a virtue in its own right.

REFERENCES

Bondi, R., The Elements of Character, *Journal of Religious Ethics* 12(1984), 201-218.
Burrell, D. & S. Hauerwas, From System to Story: An Alternative Pattern for Rationality in Ethics. In: D. Callahan & H. Tristam Engelhardt, Jr. (eds.), *The Roots of Ethics. Science, Religion, and Values*, New York/London 1976, 75-116.
Flanagan, O. & A.O. Rorty, *Identity, Character, and Morality - Essays in Moral Psychology*, Cambridge, Mass./London 1990.
Flanagan, O., Identity and Strong and Weak Evaluation. In: Flanagan & Rorty, 37-65.
Gustafson, J., The Sectarian Temptation: Reflections on Theology, the Church, and the University, *Proceedings of the Catholic Theological Society* 40(1985), 83-94.
Hauerwas, S.M., *Truthfulness and Tragedy. Further Investigations into Christian Ethics*, Notre Dame 1977.
Hauerwas, S.M., *A Community of Character - Towards a Constructive Christian Social Ethic*, Notre Dame/London 1981a.
Hauerwas, S.M., *Vision and Virtue. Essays in Christian Ethical Reflection*, Notre Dame/London 1981b.

Hauerwas, S.M., *The Peaceable Kingdom: A Primer in Christian Ethics*, Notre Dame/London 1983.

Hauerwas, S.M., *Against the Nations - War and Survival in a Liberal Society*, Minneapolis/Chicago/New York 1985a.

Hauerwas, S.M., *Character and the Christian Life: A Study in Theological Ethics.* With A New Introduction by the Author, San Antonio 1985b.

Hauerwas, S.M., *Suffering Presence*, Notre Dame/London 1986.

Hauerwas, S.M., Reconciling the Practice of Reason - Casuistry in a Christian Context. In: *Christian Existence Today*, Durham, North Carolina 1988, 67-87.

Hauerwas, S.M., *Naming the Silences - God, Medicine, and the Problem of Suffering*, Grand Rapids 1990.

Hauerwas, S.M., The Politics of Salvation - Why there is no Salvation outside the Church. In: *After Christendom*, Nashville 1991, 23-44.

Hütter, R., *Evangelische Ethik als kirchliches Zeugnis. Interpretationen zu Schlüsselfragen theologischer Ethik in der Gegenwart*, Neukirchen-Vluyn 1993.

Jung, P.B., Sanctification: an Interpretation in the Light of Embodiment, *Journal of Religious Ethics* 11(1983), 75-95.

Lammers, S.E., On Stanley Hauerwas. Theology, Medical Ethics, and the Church. In: A. Verhey & S.E. Lammers (eds.), *Theological Voices in Medical Ethics*, Grand Rapids 1993, 57-77.

Meilaender, G., *The Theory and Practice of Virtue*, Notre Dame 1984.

Milbank, J., Critical Study: S.M. Hauerwas, Character and the Christian Life. A Study in Christian Ethics; S.M. Hauerwas, Against the Nations. War and Survival in Liberal Society, *Modern Theology* 4(1987), 211-216.

Reinders, J.S., Violence, Victims and Rights. *A Reappraisal of the Argument from Structural Violence with Special Reference to Latin American Liberation Theology*, Amsterdam 1988.

Rorty, A.O. & D. Wong, Aspects of Identity and Agency. In: Flanagan & Rorty, 19-36.

Comments

Antonie van den Beld

1 INTRODUCTION

My comments on Reinders' contribution about Hauerwas is limited to two points. The first concerns the thesis that morality is logically independent of religion. Secondly, I suggest a different interpretation of the unity of Christian beliefs and Christian conduct as advocated by Hauerwas, one that is less liable to criticism than Reinders' interpretation.

2 IS MORALITY LOGICALLY INDEPENDENT OF RELIGION?

As a Christian ethicist, Hauerwas assumes the so-called independence thesis to be untrue. Morality is not logically independent of religion. This point of departure I share with Reinders. We do not get much farther with this agreement, however, as long as it remains unclear what exactly is meant by the thesis. Surely, it can be interpreted in more than one way. If the thesis refers to the idea that a systematic, consistent morality need not necessarily be based upon religious or theological beliefs, I do not object to it. To me, it seems not only arrogant but also false to say that a coherent morality on a secular basis does not exist or could not be developed. If, on the other hand, the thesis meant that a coherent morality can only exist on a secular basis and that religious or theological arguments as such can never form part of the explication or justification of a moral position, I consider it to be untenable. Note that one can hold the opinion that religion's and theology's claims to truth are extremely doubtful and that therefore it is sensible to exclude them from the ethical discussion. One could also prefer to leave them aside on mere pragmatical grounds: after all, to reach a moral consensus is already difficult enough without religious and theological issues being involved. Both views, however, are compatible with the rejection of the thesis - in the second sense - that morality is logically independent of religion.

Frankena's classic essay in favour of the thesis was in fact mainly directed against the idea - current in Christian-theological circles at the time - that morality cannot stand on its own (Frankena 1973). By now, this is not an issue anymore. Today, it is important to emphasize that morality and religion are intimately connected for people with a religious view of life and the world. A nonreligious person's moral convictions are not separate from his outlook on life and the world either. It cannot be denied that morality and religion (or worldview) are basically bound up with each other. Thus, I sympathize with Hauerwas when he rejects the thesis of independence, on condition that he has in mind the second interpretation of it, which seems to be confirmed by Reinders' article about him. However, I fully endorse the first interpretation of the thesis. This does not mean, though, that I consider a secular, naturalistic morality to be adequate.[1]

3 HAUERWAS AND THE UNITY OF FAITH AND CONDUCT

When reading Hauerwas - either at first hand or in quotation, as in Reinders' article - one might be struck by the rhetorical nature of his writing. More often than not, his rhetorical qualities appear to exceed by far the power of his arguments. As an example, I will cite two claims which are of crucial importance for his view on the relationship between morality and Christian faith.

The first (1) is: 'Rather, our convictions embody our morality; our beliefs are our actions' and the second: 'There is a kind of "isness" to the "oughtness" in that the ought is what in fact we are'.[2] Of course, I do not want to claim that rhetorical figures of speech such as hyperbole and paradox do not belong in a philosophical or theological essay, but if they are used, they

---

[1] Elsewhere, I have tried to argue that an adequate morality coheres better with a theistic than with a naturalistic worldview, see Van den Beld (1992, 22).
[2] Quoted by Reinders, on p. 146 and p. 155 respectively.

should not blur the clarity of the argument. This, however, is often what happens in Hauerwas. One is then left with statements which can be interpreted in diverse ways. Indeed, charity cannot be denied to Reinders in his treatment of Hauerwas' texts. Both (1) and (2) allow for an interpretation which he passes over in silence. Statement (1) could be interpreted as: the moral convictions of Christians can be deduced from their behaviour. If you want to know what a Christian believes, you just have to look at what he does (or does not do). A similar interpretation might go for (2): if you want to know the character of a Christian, watch his behaviour. Reinders has good reasons to ignore this interpretation, for it would not do justice to Hauerwas' intentions. Reinders' interpretation of (1) and (2) is essentially as follows. If you want to know what you can expect from a Christian concerning his behaviour and his character, try to find out what he believes. After all, Christian faith is not only normative but also descriptive - that is to say, it not only prescribes but at the same time describes the practice of Christian everyday life.

According to Reinders, this unity of faith and conduct, so dear to Hauerwas, cannot be maintained. What may be expected of a faithful Christian - in terms of actions and character - does not necessarily coincide with what he actually does or is. What a Christian believes is (part of) his ideal identity. Ideal and reality do not correspond completely. Christians' experience of life demonstrates that their real identity falls short of their ideal identity.

It appears to me, however, that a more plausible interpretation of Hauerwas' intentions can be given. In order to substantiate this claim, I have to follow Flanagan and distinguish between someone's real (practical) identity and the identity represented by the person in question himself. The first is constituted by the 'dynamic integrated system of past and present identifications, desires, commitments, aspirations, beliefs, dispositions, temperament, roles, acts, and actional patterns, as well as by whatever self-understandings (even incorrect ones) each person brings to his or her life'. It is the identity of an individual considered from an objective angle: 'It is the identity which, according to a useful fiction, we come to see on Judgement Day' (Flanagan 1991, 135). Self-represented identity, on the other hand, is someone's more or less conscious self-image. One of the purposes it is designed for, insofar as it has been designed consciously, is to mirror the real identity. What is essential, however, is that the real identity is not only mirrored, but also shaped by the self-represented identity. Thus, the represented self can have 'motivational bearing and behavioral effects' on the real self (Flanagan 1991, 137, 138).

I think that Hauerwas' emphasis on the unity of Christian beliefs and Christian conduct can be clarified through the two concepts of personal identity as explained above. Considering yourself as a believer does not mean that you adhere to an ethical ideal which is realizable in principle, but the actual realisation of which is doubtful. It does not mean either that next to your real identity you have an ideal identity, which includes your being a christian. Considering yourself a believer is rather a form of self-representation that claims to mirror part of the identity of your real self, including your behavioral dispositions. Moreover, such a self-representation can influence your real identity and the conduct that results from it. Flanagan is fully aware of the possible discrepancy of real and represented identity. This discrepancy might take on the characters of insincerity, self-deception, shame or guilt. I assume that these and similar concepts can be included in Hauerwas' system as well. Finally, as to the interpretation that I have given of Hauerwas' ideas about the unity of faith (Christian beliefs) and conduct, I do not know for sure whether it corresponds with his intentions. I can only hope that I have presented a reasonable interpretation that could contribute to the discussion on the relationship between morality and religion.

Translated by Birgit Kooijman

REFERENCES

Beld, A. van den, Does an Adequate Morality Need a Theistic Context? In: G. van den Brink a.o. (eds.), *Christian Faith and Philosophical Theology. Essays in Honour of Vincent Brümmer*, Kampen 1992, 22-38.

Flanagan, O., *Varieties of Moral Personality. Ethics and Psychological Realism*, Cambridge, Mass. 1991.

Frankena, W.K., Is Morality Logically Dependent on Religion? In: G. Outka, J.P. Reeder (eds.), *Religion and Morality. A Collection of Essays*, Garden City 1973, 295-317.

7

Narrative Theology and Narrative Ethics

Albert W. Musschenga

7.1 INTRODUCTION

The thesis that Christian morality is a unique and uniform whole has been undermined from different sides during the last decades, first of all from the side of biblical studies. The idea that there was such a thing as the Old Testament ethics or the New Testament ethics was more and more abandoned. Of course, it had been known since much longer that both in the Old and the New Testament a great diversity of moral views could be found. But gradually the search for unity and common rationales behind that diversity was given up altogether. The diverse, and sometimes even contradicting views on all sorts of matters came to be seen as an undeniable fact which did not need to be smoothed by way of forced harmonizations. More and more, the Bible was regarded as a genuinely human and historical book, in which people's experiences with God through the ages were recorded, rather than a book containing the accounts of true stories and giving precepts which might still be directly applicable today. In short, the insight had grown that the ethics of the various authors of the Bible were far from uniform and highly determined by socio-historical factors. Once this multiformity and the historical distance were recognized, it became very difficult to use the Scripture for the justification of one's own moral standpoints.

The argumentative use of the Bible had been criticised from other quarters too, namely from the side of analytical ethics. Analytical ethicists had convincingly demonstrated that no specific morality could be deduced from the Christian doctrine because morality is logically independent from religious belief (Frankena 1973). It is impossible to deduce 'ought-sentences' from the 'is-sentences' in the Christian doctrine without being guilty of the naturalistic fallacy. Of course, serving God means acting according to His will. But for a Christian, the reason to call the power he has met in his life 'God', is that he knows by experience this power wants the good. This implies that he must already have a conception of the moral good, on account of which he can recognize that power as being morally good, i.e. as God (Nielsen 1990[2], ch. 2). A Christian cannot give an adequate justification of his moral judgements by simply referring to his religious convictions. Moral judgements must be justified with moral arguments. Morality is universal and independent of religion (Kuitert 1988). But how did one account for the fact that at least some groups of Christians are clearly different from non-Christians as far as their morality is concerned? Two explanations have been given for this. The first one departs from the difference between 'content' and 'packing'. Morality is not available as a separate good, it always appears in a packing which is characteristic for a particular cultural context. The second explanation is based on the difference between critical, rational morality on the one hand, and conventional, traditional and group-related morality on the other. The morality Christians adhere to is not automatically good. A morality is good only if it can stand the test of universal, rational principles. A Christian group may distinguish itself from other groups by a particular morality, but that does not imply that it is good, nor that it is typically Christian. A good morality is good, and a bad morality is bad, no matter who adheres to it and practices it. And a typically Christian morality does not exist. However, Christians owe it to their status (their faith) to practise a good morality.

For many Christians it meant a liberation when in moral discussions instead of referring to the Scriptures, they could put forward 'simply' rational arguments, and when it could no longer be demanded from them to conform to a historically determined ecclesiastical group morality that was supposed to be the Christian morality. But other Christians - including those who where basically happy about the end of moral paternalism - did not welcome the total secularisation of morality. They felt faith and morality to be essentially connected, like warp and woof of a fabric. Theories which did not do justice to that feeling of essential connectedness could not be right. Such was the case with the 'foundationalist' theories: 'foundationalist' theological theories which reduced faith to a cognitive set of universal and contextless is-sentences, and 'foundationalist' ethical theories which reduced morality to a set of universal, rational principles. The criticism on the separation of faith and morality is therefore closely linked with the criticism on 'foundationalism' in theology and ethics.

Among theologians, the hermeneutical views of Gadamer are gaining ground (Gadamer 1975). In this hermeneutics the emphasis shifts from the author of the texts and his intentions to the interaction between the text, the reader and the community in which the texts are read. A reader can read a text only within the context of his own culture and tradition. He does something with the text and the text does something to him. The result is what Gadamer calls 'a fusion of horizons': that of the tradition reflected in the text on the one hand, and that of the reader on the other. The understanding of texts is no longer an individual search for the true intention of the author; understanding is only possible within the framework of a tradition and a community. For the believer, the Christian community becomes an indispensable interpretation community.

Within ethics, the thesis of the universality and autonomy of morality is more and more criticized. Especially under the influence of Wittgenstein, the idea of a universal, rational morality as a critical authority which is raised above all traditional moralities, is questioned. There is not just one morality, but a multiplicity of particular, sometimes incommensurable traditions, which are inseparably connected with their cultural context. This may be the context of a Christian culture and a Christian conception of life. And for this reason, there might be certain moral traditions which can indeed be called 'Christian'.

In both developments described above, one finds a renewed attention for context, tradition and community. Also the attempts to reconnect Christian belief/theology and morality/ethics by means of the concept of narrativity should be seen against the background of these developments in theology and ethics. After all, stories are pre-eminently local and determined by the context of a community and its traditions. The assumption is, that narrative theology and narrative ethics can do justice to the interrelatedness of faith and morality.

The narrative approaches in theology and ethics should be seen in connection with the growing attention for the story in other fields, particularly in history and other social sciences. Therefore my discussion of narrative theology and narrative ethics will be preceded by a short outline of the narrative approach in history and social psychology. Next, I will deal with narrative theology, and finally with narrative ethics.

I distinguish between a weak and a strong version of both narrative theology and narrative ethics. In the weak version, narrative theology claims that theology has to be narrative because faith has a narrative structure. Weak narrative ethics claims that ethics should be narrative because moral experience and moral communication have a narrative structure. Nussbaum, for example, in her book about the relationship between literature and ethics, says that some novels are works of moral philosophy: the novel may be a paradigm of moral activity (Nussbaum 1990, 148). So for Nussbaum - who does not use the term 'narrative ethics' herself - good ethics is a narrative. The weak version can also be found in Mieth. He regards narrative ethics purely as a correction of normative systems (Mieth 1976).

The strong versions of narrative theology and narrative ethics are related. They claim to offer an alternative for certain dominant trends in theology and ethics. Proponents of the strong version of narrative theology reject what they call 'academic theology'. Adherents of the strong version of narrative ethics argue that moral rationality is narrative and that the justifications of moral decisions are narrative in their structure. For them, the central ethical question people should ask themselves when taking decisions is not whether a particular decision is right, but whether it fits into their life story. Moral rationality, understood narratively, is always local and contextual. Within this view there is room again for Christian ethics. In a narrative Christian ethics, the central question is whether a particular decision corresponds with the image of the person one wants to be as a member of the Christian community. Speaking of the strong version of narrative ethics, I particularly have in mind the narrative ethics of Burrell & Hauerwas (1976). My criticism on their strong version of narrative ethics concerns especially the idea of the narrative structure of moral justification. In my opinion, this idea is inadequate. In line with this criticism, I will contend that a narrative Christian ethics in the strong version is both too pretentious and too meagre. I will include the weak version of narrative ethics in the discussion again at the end of my article. When I speak of narrativism in ethics without further qualification, I refer to the strong version of narrative ethics.

7.2 NARRATIVISM IN HISTORY AND SOCIAL PSYCHOLOGY

I will not try to define the word 'story'. It is used in different ways in various sciences. Within narrativism, it is used differently in various branches of learning. Historians, for example, employ a different definition than social psychologists. A common basic feature of narrativism, however, is its opposition against positivism, scientific rationalism and formalism. First, I will make a few observations on the various narrativist approaches in history.

Opinions differ about the function of the story in historiography. According to the radical narrativist trend, the historian cannot explain events according to the scientific, deductive-nomological covering-law model. Historical explanations are of a different nature. The historian has explained an event when he has been able to demonstrate its inevitability (Gallie 1968). The question why Jesus Christ had to die is answered in the form of a story. It is a successful story if the listeners are carried away by it in such a way that afterwards they say: 'Indeed, it was inevitable, Christ had to die on the cross'. But the crucifixion has nothing to do with the laws of nature. Consequently, a historical explanation can never be indisputable, logically compelling evidence, although it does lay claim to truth. The view that the historical narrative is an alternative explanation model starts from the tacit and, according to Mink problematic, assumption that history is an untold story, and that it is the historian's task to uncover it. The historian does not create a story, he finds it behind the facts (Mink 1987, 188). According to this view, the form, i.e. the story, does not add anything new to the content of what it represents. It is 'rather a simulacrum of the structure and the process of real events. And insofar as this representation resembles the events of which it is a representation, it can be taken as a true account'. Once the historian has revealed the true story, he can also represent it in a non-narrative way (White 1984, 3). Other historians, such as Mink, question whether historical narratives can claim truth. Mink emphasises the cognitive function of the narrative form of stories. This does not only consist in 'relating a succession of events but to body forth an ensemble of interrelationships of many different kinds as a single whole' (Mink 1987, 198). One and the same event can be told in many different ways and may, in one form of the other, be part of different stories. Of course, its meaning varies accordingly. The 'evidence' itself does not dictate which story is constructed, and neither which of the stories is to be preferred. The narrative form in history is, just as in fiction, an artifice, the product of individual imagination. '(...) as historical it claims to represent, through its form, part of the real complexity of the past, but as narrative it is a product of imaginative construction, which cannot defend its claim to truth by any accepted procedure of argument or authentication' (1987, 199). Mink's conclusion is that narrative history and narrative fiction are more related than can be accepted by common sense (1987, 293).

Does it affect the value of historical narratives when their claim to truth is thus questioned? According to White the point is not whether a story gives better or more complete explanations than a chronicle, i.e. a chronological list of events, for a story is not an alternative explanation model. Following Ricoeur, White says that the function of the story is a different one, namely to put a meaning on the events; in other words, it has an allegorical function (1984, 22 ff). History, Ricoeur says, is about people's actions in the past. And for 'reading' actions, the same hermeneutic principles apply as for reading a text (Ricoeur 1979). A historical narrative should make clear the point of a certain course of events. An event can be called historical only if it is more than a single occurrence, something unique. It has significance inasmuch as it adds something to the development of a 'plot'. The historical narrative does not impose a meaning on events that are in themselves meaningless, as it is an interpretation of meaningful human experiences and actions, for human experience as such has a narrative structure.

This view forms a link between narrativism as it appears in history and narrativism in other social sciences. Stories are told everywhere, in every culture. That is not mere chance, Stephen Crites would say. In his influential article 'The Narrative Quality of Experience' he states that the narrative form is primitive in human experience. Only the narrative form can comprehend the tensions, surprises, disappointments, reversals and accomplishments of actual, temporal experience (1971, 306). Crites distinguishes between sacred stories, i.e. stories which are hidden in the depths of human consciousness, creating people's sense of themselves and the world, and mundane stories, the stories that are actually told and are situated in a - real or imaginary - reality (295, 6). Sacred stories are not necessarily religious, though they may be. They are reflected in mundane stories, but the latter should not be seen as a direct articulation of the first.

The statement that human experience is primarily narrative in its nature, leads to the view that our sense of self, our personal identity, has a narrative structure. This is in fact a central idea in all narrative theology and narrative ethics. In the narrative movement within social psychology, the idea of the narrative structure of the self has been developed in particular by Gergen & Gergen. They introduced the term 'self-narrative' as a substitute for the traditional 'self-concept'. In developing a self-narrative the individual attempts to establish coherent connections among life events. The distinction between self-narrative and related concepts as rule, role prescription, interaction ritual and script is that self-narrative does not possess inherent directive capabilities. The individual does not consult the narrative for information. Self-narratives function much more as histories within the society more generally. They are symbolic systems used for social purposes as justification, criticism, and social solidification (Gergen & Gergen 1983, 255,6).

Although self-narratives are always personal interpretations of a life story, they are at the same time social, in a double sense. Firstly, because the author uses symbols, concepts and categories which are stored in the language of his community and its traditions, in order to interpret what has happened to him, and what he has done and experienced. The influence of Mead's theory on the social origin of the self makes itself clearly felt here (Mead 1974[19], ch. III). Secondly, the aim of the self-narrative is to enable the author to make himself understood by others. It is a means by which someone may inform others about his aims, his life history and the relation between them, and about his possible future. Stories are the best way to express one's identity, not only for individuals but also for groups, nations etc.

Similar arguments are put forward by many other authors. The self-narrative, or to put it differently, the personal identity, is a hermeneutic concept. It is an attempt to understand the whole of a life history from the limited perspective of a particular moment, and vice versa: to understand the meaning of the moment through the whole of the life story. What Gadamer has said about understanding in general and what he calls 'the hermeneutic circle', applies also to self-understanding, namely that understanding moves constantly from the whole to the parts and back again. It is also Gadamer who has pointed out that understanding should not be conceived as an act of subjectivity, but as placing oneself in a process of tradition in which past and present are continually merging. The tradition within which we interpret our personal life story and our own world, represents the social and communal dimension of our personal identity (Gadamer 1975, 245 ff; Stroup 1981, 109).

7.3 NARRATIVE THEOLOGY

Theology is a conglomerate of disciplines. It is not surprising, then, that narrative approaches taking root in other social sciences may also be found in what presents itself as narrative theology. Narrative approaches may be found in biblical studies as well as in systematic theology and practical theology. I will concentrate, however, on biblical studies and systematic theology. The narrative approach in theology mainly focuses on two themes, namely *the relation between faith and experience*, and that between *faith and historical reality*. The first theme is particularly relevant in systematic theology, the second in biblical studies. First I will deal with the relation between *faith and experience*.

Religious faith is closely linked with the personal identity of the believer. If personal identity has a narrative structure, as the narrativists say, then conversely, the narrative will be the primary form of expression of personal faith. In this view, personal faith is not primarily the endorsement of is-sentences about God and his relationship to man and the world, but a story in which a believer expresses his experiences with God. The reign of intellectualism is often seen as one of the causes of the present crisis of faith, because no room is left for human experience. The intellectualistic conception of faith corresponds with a systematic theology that conceives its task as articulating and testing the is-sentences of the religion and making them into a coherent whole. A rejection of the intellectualistic conception of faith calls for a different conception of systematic theology.

Some authors go as far as setting 'narrative theology' against or even above 'discursive, argumentative theology', which strives for clarification and critical analysis of the Christian doctrine, and attempts to enhance its coherence. I call this approach the *strong version of narrative theology*. One can sense such a contradistinction of narrative and academic theology in an article by Cone. In his opinion, black theology, having developed within the context of the struggle for freedom, is narrative, whereas white theologians construct logical systems (Cone 1975, 145). A similar contradistinction, but worked out differently, is to be found in Metz. Metz, whose name is inextricably linked with narrative theology, places narrative theology in the field of tension between the human experiences of suffering and the salvation promised by God. A conceptional-argumentative reconciliation of universal salvation and the suffering of man is impossible. A theology of salvation which does not interpret the salvation as being conditional or suspended, and neither ignores the non-identity of the passion, cannot be explicated in a purely argumentative way, but always needs to be explicated narratively as well; it is a fundamentally memorative-narrative theology (Metz 1973, 68).

What power do stories have that scholarly discourses have not? Biblical themes such as the creation, the new-born man, the resurrection etc., exceed the limits of discursive reasoning and they cannot be dealt with by completely dissolving or translating their narrative form (68). An argumentation is a closed sequence of statements, closed in itself. A story has an open end, it points to something beyond itself. Therefore, the story is an appropriate medium to deal with system-transcendent matters.

But not only narrative theologians have drawn attention to the connection between faith and experience. Especially in the seventies, it was a much-discussed theme, for example in the works of Schillebeeckx. He says: 'After all, language, including language of faith, becomes "meaningless" (in a "linguistic-analytical" sense) when it does not contain any recognizable reference whatsoever to the real experiences of man in his world' (Schillebeeckx 1973, 37). People pass on experiences - including religious experiences - by telling each other stories; stories that make things move and show others new life styles. Experiential competence has a narrative structure. 'Story' and 'tradition' are not opposite. Tradition consists of the whole of authoritative stories of a community of faith making history. But tradition is more than a static depositum fidei. Tradition makes experience possible - its positive function - and it directs and selects this experience - its negative function. Critical assimilation of tradition is necessary to develop experiential competence. And it is this competence which enables people to sift the wheat from the chaff in new experiences (Schillebeeckx 1977, 32). Pannenberg speaks in similar terms about the treasure of experience of a living tradition which again and again becomes the point of departure for new, onward leading discoveries. When people place themselves in a certain tradition, they discover a rich variety of life styles. When new generations consciously adopt and cherish a certain tradition, this tradition will change (Pannenberg 1972^4, 88). This emphasis on the importance of tradition corresponds with what Mead says about the social origin and the social character of the self. Mead's ideas are in fact present in Pannenberg's anthropological works (Pannenberg 1983, Part III).

One cannot discuss tradition without explicitly including the Christian community. This is done mainly by American authors in outlines of narrative theology, such as Stroup's. Following Gergen & Gergen, he connects the story with the social, communal basis of personal identity. The stories of the community's identity precede the personal story and the personal identity of the believer. A Christian community uses the symbols and stories from the

Bible as building blocks for the construction of its own story, the story of its identity. Not only stories from the Bible are used as material, however, those from the tradition as well (Stroup 1981, 164).

The second main theme in narrative theology is *the relation between faith and historical reality*. In the narrative approach in biblical studies the Bible is called a collection of stories. This characterization is meant to distinguish the Bible from an 'ordinary' history book. As Weinrich says, there are all sorts of texts in the Old and New Testament which are not narrative, such as legal texts, moral and hygienic prescriptions, admonishing letters, hymns of praise, thanksgivings etc., but from a religious point of view, the stories are the most relevant ones (Weinrich 1973, 50). Stroup also says that the core of the Bible consists of a set of stories (Stroup 1981, 136). After all, we meet Jesus of Nazareth primarily as a narrated figure, often also as a narrated narrator, and the disciples are presented to us as listeners, who, in their turn, orally or in writing, pass on and retell the tales they heard (Weinrich 1973, 50). And in those stories it is not historical truth but relevance which matters (51). Theology has too much conformed to modern historical studies; historians do concern themselves with the story, but only with the true story (54). Authors such as Weinrich mainly have in mind the story as a literary genre. In the words of Mink: narrative fiction rather than narrative history. Their view is opposed to narrative approaches that are only concerned with the true story.

It is undeniably true that the Bible contains all sorts of material which can be called narrative prose, such as the parables. It is pointless to query the historical truth of parables. The Bible does not only contain many narratives, many Books of the Bible show a narrative structure as well, e.g. the stories about the Patriarchs, the Judges, and Jesus. These are no chronicles, i.e. lists of historical facts, but interpretations of events and experiences which had been orally passed down to the authors - experiences and events that in their eyes could not be understood without referring to God.

Some religious experiences had been passed on as stories, and were recorded as such by the authors of the Bible. Thus, the authors of the Bible did not just record stories, they also wrote their own narrative about the history between God and man, based on the - oral and written - material they had at their disposal. In that respect they may be compared with the historian. The historian selects, interprets, and searches for a 'plot'. He wants to reveal the meaning of the events he writes about. A story is more than the sum of the facts it mentions. Ricoeur's idea of the allegorical function of historical narratives also applies to the interpretation of Bible stories.

Although a historical narrative can never be called 'true' according to authors such as White, a historian does want to know whether the facts he weaves into his narrative are true. How is that with the authors of the Bible? It would be going too far to say that those who recorded the seemingly historical tales were in fact writing literary fiction in which historical elements were completely subordinate to the message they wanted to convey. It is true they were not interested in historical truth as such, they did not even think about this. That does not mean, however, that it did not matter whether the stories were based on facts or not; they were not concerned with the events as such, but with their importance as references to God's loyalty and the reliability of his promises. Bible stories are the reflection and interpretation of people's experiences with God at a particular time and a particular place. As such they are not timeless but determined by context. The Bible authors themselves did not distinguish between poetical story and public history (Noorda 1990, 125). To make this distinction afterwards, when interpreting the stories, would mean to ignore their real character.

It may be clear by now that the use of the concept 'story' in theology is fairly diverse. One may find historical, anthropological, as well as literary conceptions of it. Sometimes its meaning overlaps with that of other concepts. Hauerwas, for example, says that we need stories for things we can only describe analogically. That, however, is the function of metaphors. A metaphor may be a story but a story is not by any means always a metaphor (Hauerwas 1977, 78). Because the term 'story' is sometimes used in such a loose manner, it is impossible to sketch a coherent picture of narrative theology.

Authors such as Ritschl and Stroup consider the term 'narrative theology' to be a failure. In their opinion, the aim cannot be to set narrative theology against 'discursive, argumentative theology', which strives for clarification and critical analysis of the Christian doctrine, and attempts to enhance its coherence (Ritschl 1975, 36-40; Stroup 1981, 84-89). Ritschl says that stories are not the mode of expression, but the 'raw material' of theology. Therefore Ritschl and Stroup dismiss what I have called the strong version of narrative theology, although they do acknowledge the importance of stories for theology, not only the stories in the Bible and the Bible Books that are understood as such, but also religious autobiographies such as Augustine's

Confessions, a work that is frequently referred to in narrativist theological literature. The weak version of narrative theology is a theology which acknowledges the narrative structure of human (religious) experience, as well as the narrative structure of its reflection in the Bible. From this perspective, theology may be narrative without carrying that label.

7.4 NARRATIVE THEOLOGY AND NARRATIVE ETHICS

Narrative ethics is not a clearly defined school. However, narrative ethics is always a form of ethics of virtue. A programme for a narrative ethics may be found in an article by Burrell & Hauerwas, 'From System to Story'. They have developed their narrative ethics on the basis of a criticism on what they call the 'standard account of moral rationality' (SA); They have formulated this criticism in three points (Burrell & Hauerwas 1976).

The SA distorts the nature of the moral life:

1 *by placing an unwarranted emphasis on particular decisions or quandaries;*

According to the SA, the function of ethics is to search for rational solutions to problems of choice. Whoever thinks that moral problems can always be solved entirely, overlooks the reality of moral tragedies where a choice has to be made between two evils. Besides, the SA takes it for granted that rationality is the most important competence of moral subjects. Hauerwas & Burrell on the other hand, state that the kind of decisions we face, and also the way we describe them, is a function of our character. And character, moral self, is not formed by taking decisions, but by the convictions and dispositions that we have acquired. Our moral self is formed by - contingent - narratives; it has a narrative structure. When we make a statement in the first person, when we say 'I', then that 'I' is not a solitary 'I', but the narrative of that 'I'. It is exactly the category of narrative that helps us to see that we are not forced to choose between some universal standpoint and the subjectivistic appeals to our own experience. For our experiences always come in the form of narratives that can be checked against themselves as well as others' experiences' (83). We recognize the train of thought that we found in Crites and Gergen & Gergen.

2 *by failing to account for the significance of moral notions and how they work to provide us the skills of perception;*

The exponents of the SA look for universal, contextless, rational basic principles, which all other principles and actions may be justified by and deduced from. According to Burrell & Hauerwas the essence of morality is not made up of such universal, rational basic principles, but of 'thick', 'rich', descriptive-evaluative moral notions such as 'abortion', 'murder', 'adultery' etc. Although they refer to Kovesi, the same ideas may be found in the works of descriptivists such as Foot (1958) and Murdoch (1966) - who aim their criticism especially at the prescriptivist Hare - and those of the social-conventionalists, who were influenced by Wittgenstein, such as Beardsmore (1969), and Phillips & Mounce (1969). Moral notions never stand on their own. They are, according to Murdoch, embedded in 'vision' (Murdoch 1966). The followers of Wittgenstein prefer to speak of local, contingent stories. The moral notions acquired through education enable us to discover what is relevant among all the impressions we receive. Perception and judgement of facts and events are not separated from each other.

3 *by separating the agent from his interest.*

The SA demands from the moral subject to take its decisions from an impartial, universal point of view. This demand implies that a subject looks at his own interests and his own life as an external observer. When making moral trade-offs, my own desires, ideals, special relationships etc. should carry exactly the same weight as those of any other person. The SA demands from moral subjects to alienate themselves from their self for the sake of impartiality. But the field of morality is much wider than that of impersonal, anonymous relationships. With this criticism, Burrell & Hauerwas support Williams (Williams 1974). Furthermore, the picture that the SA gives of disinterest is also incorrect. People who act disinterestedly manage to do so not because they have succeeded in freeing themselves from everything that makes up their self. Disinterest '(...) depends on our self being formed by narrative that provides the conditions for developing the disinterest required for moral behaviour' (Burrell & Hauerwas, 88).

Many themes which are dealt with in the article by Burrell & Hauerwas, were worked out by MacIntyre in *After Virtue*, a few years later (MacIntyre 1981). MacIntyre is the moral philosopher with whom Hauerwas feels most closely related. He is the one who articulates best what might be called the programme of narrative ethics.

MacIntyre says that I can answer the question 'What am I to do?' only when I can answer the preceding question 'Of what story or stories do I find myself a part?' (1981, 201). A moral human is continually searching for the good, which attracts him like a telos. But what is good cannot be determined concretely in advance. Of course, he has an idea of what it is, but that is only limited and provisional. Searching for the final telos, he meets all sorts of things which are good and valuable, but again and again he transcends the existing views on it (204). A human life is a wholeness when a human is able to place everything that happens to him and everything he does within the story of his personal quest for the good. And although a person's life story is always embedded in the stories of the communities from which he derives his identity, this does not imply that he has to accept the moral limitations of these communities (205). So we see that for MacIntyre the ultimate frame of reference is not the community, but the personal story of someone's own life, conceived as a quest for the final telos.

The article by Burrell & Hauerwas dates from 1976. The criticism on the 'Standard Account of Moral Rationality' may also be found in Hauerwas' later works. Similar criticism on the claim to universality and the deductivistic argumentation model of the Kantian and utilitarian ethics has been expressed by many other authors, especially from the side of ethics of virtue. However, for Burrell & Hauerwas, narrative ethics is not just a plea for an ethics of virtue. They share the views of the so-called anti-theorists concerning the primacy of praxis and of the concrete judgement of general principles. In this respect they are related to Nussbaum who recently wrote a book about the relationship between literature and ethics. She says that some novels are works of moral philosophy. According to her, the novel may be a paradigm of moral activity (Nussbaum 1990, 148). So for Nussbaum - who does not use the term 'narrative ethics' herself - good ethics is a narrative.

Speaking of *the strong version of narrative ethics*, I particularly have in mind the narrative ethics of Burrell & Hauerwas. The *weak version* may be found in Mieth. He regards narrative ethics purely as a correction of normative systems (Mieth 1976, 3, 7).

There are obvious similarities between the proponents of narrative ethics and those of narrative theology, regarding their motives and intentions, and the content of their programme. As a matter of fact, it is often the theological ethicists who plead for a narrative ethics. As I said before, narrative theology calls attention to the relation between belief and experience. Language of belief should connect with people's everyday, contextual experiences, as they are stored in stories. Also, wherever people have religious experiences, these are expressed in the form of stories. The Bible stories, too, are the reflection of people's experiences with God. Narrative ethics also calls attention to experience, as reflected in 'thick', descriptive-evaluative moral notions. Here lies a first similarity. Narrative ethics means to be a hermeneutics of moral experience, and stories are an important means to express and convey moral experience.

As we saw, the formation of personal identity is an important theme in narrative theology. Faith should tie in with the question who one is. Personal identity is a central theme in narrative ethics, too. That is the second similarity. This is why narrative ethicists prefer an ethics of virtue in which the actor's character, his motives and intentions is the central issue, rather than an ethics of rules or principles which deals mainly with the rightness of actions. In narrative ethics, the question who I am and who I want to be precedes the question of what I have to do in a given situation. As I have shown, some narrative theologians regard narrative theology as an alternative for the abstract, academic theology, which has no connection with human experience and claims to be scientific. Narrative ethicists such as Burrell & Hauerwas regard narrative ethics also as a criticism on and an alternative for an ethics which leans towards the ideal of universal, impartial, objective, scientific rationality. That is a third instance of similarity with the opposition of narrative theologians against a too academic, scientific theology.

I agree with many of Burrell & Hauerwas' criticisms on the Standard Account of Moral Rationality. They rightly demand attention to the social genesis of the (moral) self. Attempts to derive universal basic principles from some concept of rationality cannot but fail. And, it is true that 'thick', moral principles are of central importance to moral perception. I also agree with their view that it is wrong to equate the moral point of view with the impartial point of view. My criticism on the strong version of narrative ethics is mainly focused on the idea of the narrative structure of moral justifications. According to this idea, the crucial ethical question that must be asked when taking decisions, is: Who am I or who do I want to be? and the answer cannot be anything but a story. My objection against the narrative conception of justification is that justification is reduced to an explanation of someone's decisions within the limited framework of his personal life story. In this conception of justification, it is the personal point of view that dominates, while no room is left for criticism from a suprapersonal point of view.

7.5 PERSONAL IDENTITY

Narrative justification is a person's explanation of a decision within the framework of his own life story. This implies narrative explanation is justification from a personal point of view. A narrative explanation of moral decisions is always interesting, because it shows us how the actor himself perceives his decision and what his purpose was. I will demonstrate, however, that a narrative explanation from the personal point of view of a life story is often insufficient as a justification. First I will show that a narrative explanation of a decision is essential in cases of a particular kind of problems of choice, namely choices between incommensurable options. In this context I will speak about justification or explanation by means of identity referring reasons. What I wish to demonstrate is that even in cases where a justification by means of identity referring reasons is essential, this justification is not necessarily acceptable.

7.5.1 Personal Identity and Problems of Choice

Often when people take decisions that affect their personal life, they have to choose between alternatives. Such choices may differ in complexity as well as in importance. They may be complex but at the same time trivial, or simple but at the same time important, because of the interests and values at stake.

In most cases it is possible to find good reasons for choosing one of the alternatives. If my mother is dying and wants to see me, this is a good reason to cancel an appointment with a friend. For a doctor, an emergency takes priority over a patient who just wants to have his ear syringed. In some situations, however, the choice is not that easy, because the alternatives are incomparable and incommensurable.[1]

---

[1] Two alternatives of action, A and B, are incommensurable if neither is better than the other, and if they are not equally valuable either. It is impossible to determine the relative value of the two alternatives. The test of incommensurability is the absence of transitivity. Two options are incommensurable if 1) one is not better than the other,

There are different kinds of incommensurable options. Sometimes there is a choice between preferences, e.g. relaxed idling on a beach or hiking and enjoying the beauty of the mountains. Sometimes there is a choice between values, such as sports and musical education. But it may also concern choices which have comprehensive and far-reaching implications for the rest of someone's life, like the choice between a life as a monk and a military career. The conviction that incommensurable options of choice exist, is closely linked to the belief that there is not a single highest good but a plurality of values. For Aristotle, a life as a philosopher was the highest good. He valued other walks of life according to the degree in which they approached that highest good.

Moral dilemmas make up a special category. A moral dilemma occurs when two incommensurable moral obligations clash with each other. In case of a choice between two values, it is not reprehensible to avoid the problem by not choosing at all. There is no obligation to do something, then. In case of a moral dilemma, however, not only the choice required by one obligation is forbidden by the other, but next to that neither of the obligations carries more weight than the other, nor do they carry the same weight. That is the difference between moral dilemmas and 'ordinary' moral conflicts, where it is possible to determine which of the clashing obligations counts more heavily than the other. People's interests often clash with those of plants and animals. To solve these conflicts, rules of priority are needed. An example of such a rule is that the central interests of one species should not be sacrificed for the peripheral interests of another. It is not possible to formu-

---

and 2) there is (or might be) an option which is better than one of them but not better than both. A variant of this test is that one option is improved. If it is still not better than the other, we have a case of incommensurability. Suppose I can choose between a relaxed holiday on a sun drenched and almost uninhabited island in the Pacific, and an active hiking holiday in the Pyrenees. Both options are attractive for very different reasons, and therefore they are incomparable. There is a third option: a cultural holiday in Florence. I find this possibility much more attractive than a holiday in the Pacific, but not more attractive than hiking in the mountains. Maybe I could go hiking in the Himalayas instead of in the Pyrenees. I would find that much more attractive. But even then the option of hiking in the mountains is not more attractive than the option of lazing on a beach in the Pacific. On the basis of the test of intransitivity, this would indicate the incommensurability of lazing on the beaches of the Pacific and a hiking holiday in the mountains. The reasons that may be put forward for one option are no better than the reasons for the other.

late such rules of priority for moral dilemmas. Moral dilemmas differ from other choices between incommensurable options in that each choice will leave behind a feeling of remorse. This they have in common with 'ordinary' moral conflicts. A dilemma is a choice between two incomparable evils.

Just like other choices between incommensurable options, moral dilemmas may be more or less weighty. In what follows, I will keep to two kinds of choices between incommensurable options which have radical consequences for the actor, namely dilemmas and choices which affect the way someone is going to give shape to his personal life, or otherwise have far-reaching consequences for it. (I will call these 'comprehensive choices'.)

I said before that it is typical for incommensurable options that there are no general reasons on which a choice can be based. With general reasons I mean both relational and impersonal reasons. My obligations towards my family are relational. They arise from the relationships I have with my wife and daughter in my role of husband and father. Everyone else who has these roles, has similar obligations. They are not unique. My duty to help someone who is drowning, is impersonal. Every other bystander has the same moral duty.

Choices between incommensurable options may also be called rationally underdetermined. This means that there are no relevant and compelling general reasons which tip the balance one way or the other. In other words: it is impossible to determine the relative weight of the options. There is no option that should be chosen. In most cases there is a compulsion to choose: it is impossible not to choose. Does that mean that it is impossible to solve such problems of choice on the basis of good reasons? Is the choice between two incommensurable options inevitably arbitrary and irrational?

Taylor says that choices between incommensurable alternatives - where it is impossible to determine what is the right thing to do - force a person to reflect on who he is/wants to be. Only through such a process of self-interpretation may a person find out what he should do. In that process of self-interpretation the incommensurable becomes commensurable (Taylor 1985, 28). The choice he eventually makes, cannot but bear the stamp of his own personal identity. He cannot produce general (relational or impersonal) reasons for his choice. He can only refer to his identity. I call this identity referring reasons. Identity referring reasons are reasons which refer to the significance of a particular action for the actor himself, against the background of the image he has of who he is/wants to be, rather than to objective qualities of the action or to its consequences.

Suppose both my mother and my best friend are dying. If I decide to be with my friend in his last hours instead of with my mother, I can justify this decision by pointing out the value I attach to friendship in general and this friendship in particular. It is not enough to say that after all he is my friend, because my argumentation should also explain why I did not choose for my mother, although there would have been just as valid reasons to do so. The aim of my argumentation is to explain that, in view of the person I am/want to be, I could not possibly have taken any other decision (which is not the same as: should have taken).

7.5.1.1   Possible Criticisms on Identity Referring Reasons

Choices between incommensurable options are, as I said, rationally underdetermined. That means that there are no compelling general moral reasons to choose one of the options. The question is, whether identity referring reasons, in those cases where they constitute the deciding factor, are always acceptable.

Internal Criticism

Also where a choice between incommensurable options is concerned, we do not take someone's narrative explanation of his decision for granted. We expect the person to give reasons which do not only clarify why he has made the choice, but also why this choice, from the viewpoint of his identity, was an appropriate answer to the situation. Such a justification will not have the character of a deductive argumentation, but will be of an essentially narrative nature. The choice is not the compelling conclusion of an argumentation, but the conclusion of a story to which the narrator has led his listeners. In a deductive argumentation the subsequent stages are linked in a logically compelling way. A story, on the other hand, tries to connect and arrange successive actions and events. Looking back from the end of the story, the listener can accept that the events in the story have led to that conclusion.

Not just any story will do, though, for the acting person should also be able to make clear that it is his story, that the story is consistent with his more comprehensive life story. A life story is more than an account of the things someone has done and the things that have happened to him. It is an attempt to give meaning to this in respect of what someone wants with his life. If I have always treated my friends - or what should pass as friends - like consumer articles that one acquires when one needs them and discards when they have become redundant, it will sound very implausible when I say

I wanted to be with my friend in his last hours instead of with my mother, because that friendship was the most important thing in my life. People would rather tend to think I possibly miss out on an inheritance if I do not meet my friend's wish.

Identity referring reasons may be criticised on other grounds, too. The actor may be fooling himself, he may be insincere, untrue to himself, or superficial, or he may lack the courage to acknowledge the tragical character of a decision. Someone is fooling himself if he is not aware of his true motives. A woman may think that she married her husband out of love, when in reality she was afraid to be 'left on the shelf'. Insincere is someone who does not reveal his true motives, but pretends to act out of motives that are generally considered to be honourable. Such is the case, for example, when someone claims to have joined a resistance movement out of patriotism, when in fact he has done so to be able to kill. Someone is untrue to himself if he makes a decision which contradicts the values and aims he has always advocated and according to which he has always acted, without being able to explain how he reconciles this decision with those values and aims, or why he has deviated from them in this case. A declared pacifist is untrue to himself when he suddenly accepts a job in an arms factory and explains this by saying that in a world where unfortunately wars are being waged - something he is still opposed to - these factories are simply necessary, and that someone has to do the work in them after all. Superficial is someone who insufficiently realises the problematic character of a decision.

External Criticism

Identity referring reasons explain why someone has taken a particular decision. In some cases this is enough. If I ask someone why he married the woman who is his wife, and he says he did so because he loved her, I accept that explanation also as a justification. He is not obliged to marry, or to marry a woman he loves. He is free to marry whoever wants to marry him. But in our culture, love for one's partner belongs to the image we have of a good husband. In many cases, however, a narrative explanation is not sufficient as a justification, not even when a choice between incommensurable options is concerned. Suppose that in a selection procedure for a job vacancy I have to choose between two candidates who are on the whole equally suitable (although they have very divergent qualities). One possibility is to decide by lot. Another possibility is to make a decision based on personal preference. One of them is a woman. Now I happen to prefer women to men, generally speaking, and therefore I choose the woman. Or one of them is a Turk and I choose the other, not because I dislike Turks but because I think that nationals should have preference over immigrants. Or I choose the one who happens to be a good friend. In each case, subjective reasons, based on my own personal preferences and opinions, have been decisive. I just happen to be a womanizer, or someone who puts 'own people' first, and do not mind admitting that.

What, then, is the difference between a case where someone does not get the job because of racist motives of the selection committee, although from an objective point of view she is better qualified, and the example above, where racist motives are decisive in a choice between two equally suitable candidates? The first case concerns an incorrect decision which cannot be justified, whereas in the second case the decision may be justifiable but the reasons are morally objectionable. The term 'decision' - and this applies also to the term 'choice' - may refer to the outcome of a process of decision, as well as to the act of deciding. A decision (as outcome) may be justifiable although the decision (as action) is unjustified. The fact that in a choice between two equally suitable candidates the immigrant is not chosen, is not necessarily problematic. Maybe the choice was made perfectly arbitrarily, for lack of relevant differences. Possibly the staff manager found the man unsympathetic. Another possibility is that he likes to surround himself with young people, and the foreign candidate was the older candidate. Then the choice says something about the staff manager and nothing relevant about the candidate. The choice becomes problematic only if racist motives are into play. Identity referring reasons should not clash with social moral rules. In our society it is generally agreed that discrimination and favouritism are no-go areas. In a case like this, a condemnation of the decision concerns the motives and reasons of the actor. His character is questioned. The immigrant may rightly complain about being discriminated, but he cannot demand that he gets the job after all.

The idea that it should be possible to test identity referring reasons from an external point of view, may also be formulated in different terms. In principle, identity referring reasons should permit universalisation. That means that the actor should not mention reasons containing singular, indexical terms such as proper names. Reasons are based on principles, and principles refer to categories of cases. The actor should be prepared to agree with the statement that in circumstances which are similar in relevant aspects, all people who are similar in relevant aspects should make the same choice. Suppose I were a woman, how would I take it that my boss' fancy for women was the decisive factor for my getting the job? Women with self-respect would take this as an insult to themselves and their sex. But the point is, that justifications based on identity referring reasons usually refer to unique characteristics of the actor. In general, I find that a mother should have priority over a friend when both are in need of care and attention. But the relationship with my friend is so unique and so deep that I cannot but be with my dying friend instead of with my mother. In such cases, the test of universalisation does not work. Although the category of cases to which the principle I have to agree with belongs may theoretically be infinitely large, in reality, for me, it has only one member and that is me.

7.5.2 Personal Identity, Moral Identity, and Community

In the previous sections, I have tried to point out a few things. Firstly, that in certain situations of choice identity referring reasons are the only decisive factor. This is the case in situations where no compelling general moral reasons to choose a particular alternative are available.

Secondly, that identity referring reasons are embedded in a form of communication with the structure of a narrative. Only narrative ethics can do justice to the role of identity referring reasons and pays attention to their narrative structure.

Thirdly, I wanted to demonstrate that a narrative explanation of decisions by means of identity referring reasons is not beyond all criticism.

My objection against narrative ethics is that it only allows for internal criticism and not for external criticism. With internal criticism I mean criticism on the truthfulness, honesty and sincerity of someone's account of his actions, and criticism on the relation between that account and the whole of his life story. With external criticism I mean criticism on someone's actions, grounds and motives from the viewpoint of the social morality of a community, quite apart from his own explanations. This may seem a rather peculiar criticism on a form of ethics which puts so much emphasis on the social character of identity.

Personal identity is one of the main themes in narrativism. In line with Mead's views, attention is demanded to the social genesis and the social embeddedness of the self. Personal identity is a social identity.[2]

According to Burrell & Hauerwas, their view offers an alternative both for solipsistic individualism and contextless universalism. A self is always a social self. The community is included in the self-image. Therefore, moral reasons are always identity referring reasons, in the sense that they refer to a person's identity as a member of his community. Besides this, the community may judge the narratives by means of which a person furnishes himself with a pattern of integrity. The point I wish to make, however, is that according to the narrativists' views, the community can only exert internal criticism on the decisions of its members. This is due to the primacy of self-interpretation in the first place, but also because the final telos is left undefined. The traditional ethics of virtue assumed that there was a human telos which might be described in definite terms. As we saw, MacIntyre, on the other hand, stresses the undeterminedness of the final telos. The good attracts man like a telos, but it cannot be determined concretely in advance. The life of a moral human is a personal quest for the good, and the wholeness of his life consists in his being able to give everything he does and everything that happens to him a place within the story of that quest. Although a person's life story is always embedded in the stories of the communities from which he takes his identity, this does not imply that he has to accept the moral limitations of these communities. As I said, for MacIntyre the ultimate frame of reference is not the community, but someone's per-

---

[2] One may speak of the social character of personal identity in yet another sense. In individualistic conceptions of man, a person is an individual, independent from a social group. Communitarians such as Sandel point out that personal identity may also be defined intersubjectively. Someone who positively calls himself a Jew, shows that his belonging to a social group determines his identity at least partly. His 'I' is partly a 'we' (Sandel 1982, e.g. 62, 63). In itself this need not be more than a factual observation: apparently, some people are able to understand their personality intersubjectively, while others are not. Some people identify with a particular community and others do not. Communitarians, who regard living in a real community and community values as essential elements of the good life, go a step further. To them, someone is good if he defines himself intersubjectively. Thus, the social conception of personal identity becomes a normative thesis. My point is, however, that there is not necessarily a connection between the empirical, socio-psychological thesis about the social genesis of personality and the normative thesis of the communitarians. The normative thesis does presuppose the socio-psychological one, but the socio-psychological one does not necessarily imply the normative one.

sonal life story about the quest for the final telos. I will have to make clear that and how a particular decision fits into the story of my search for the good. No on else can do that, because it is my life story. The community cannot do this either. Here, the primacy of self-interpretation prevails. The crucial question is whether a decision fits into a life story. Decisions ought to be morally sound, according to Burrell & Hauerwas. They say that personal integrity is far more important than a consistency in our actions which is regulated by principles. Stories which provide a pattern of integrity cannot be based on principles. Stories enable us to ascertain whether our conduct fits in with our 'ongoing pattern' (Burrell & Hauerwas, 85). My objection is, however, that moral justification becomes too narrow a concept when it is merely understood as narrative explanation, and when integrity is the only touchstone for someone's decisions. Only for a truly moral human being narrative explanation and justification may, perhaps, coincide. But human beings are not always truly moral.

The painter Paul Gauguin, before setting off to Tahiti, probably weighed the importance of his artistic projects against the interests of his wife and children. He apparently came to the conclusion that, given his special talents, the importance of this artistic project was so great, that he had to sacrifice the interests of his wife and children for it. Even apart from that, he could not have decided differently without violating his selfhood. On what grounds, then, could a narrativist who departs from the primacy of self-interpretation and leaves the final telos undetermined ever condemn Gauguin? Gauguin is authentic, honest, devoted to art as his final telos, and what is more, he can demonstrate that his decision fits in perfectly with his life story.

The argumentation model of the narrative explanation presupposes people whose personal life story is indissolubly connected with that of the community. For ideal moral humans the social morality of the community is not an alien power. They have internalised this morality, and in that sense it has become a part of their identity. Had Gauguin been a more ideal human from the point of view of his community's morality, his obligations towards his wife and children would have weighed more heavily for him, and he would have taken a different decision. Socio-moral reasons, however, can only influence people's decisions if they have become a part of their identity. Let me call to mind what Burrell & Hauerwas say about disinterest. People who act disinterestedly manage to do so not because they have succeeded in freeing themselves from everything that makes up their self. Disinterest '(...)

depends on our self being formed by narrative that provides the conditions for developing the disinterest required for moral behaviour' (Burrell & Hauerwas, 88). I agree with this. Apparently Gauguin's identity was not formed by what his community would regard the right narratives. But my point is, that he was nevertheless able to show that his decision corresponded with the ongoing pattern of his life story. And for this very reason, a narrativist for whom the narrative explanation of decisions is the only argumentation model, has no ground whatsoever to criticize him morally.

It seems, then, that from a moral viewpoint an ongoing pattern in a life story cannot be the end of it. The problem with the theory of Burrell & Hauerwas is that they want to unite two incompatible views, namely Mead's view on the social genesis and the social character of the self, and the idea that a person has a privileged position with regard to describing and explaining his actions. This idea presupposes that a person is more than a product of social forces (Outka 1980, 112).

An ideal moral person, too, experiences tensions between the different values and obligations he has made his own. He is not necessarily an altruist who places himself entirely at the service of others and of suprapersonal interests. A moral human is someone who has managed to find a balance between what Nagel calls 'actor-relative' and 'actor-neutral' values and obligations (Nagel 1986, ch. 9). Someone's self is never of one piece. It is always a more or less successful integration of potentially conflicting parts. This integration is never an unthreatened harmony, but always a temporary state of equilibrium which needs to be established again and again.

So we see that identity is a concept with various meanings. It refers to character, to unity and wholeness of a personality. I will call this identity$_1$. A person without identity$_1$ has no centre of thought and action, he is adrift. The term identity refers also to uniqueness, to that which distinguishes a person from others. I will call this identity$_2$. Most mature persons have an identity$_1$, but need not have an identity$_2$. A person who changes her preferences and ideals every week, and who is not consistent in her behaviour, does not have an identity$_1$. Her changeability and capriciousness, however, do form her identity$_2$. A stable, reliable person out of one piece need not distinguish herself from other person. She may have the same preferences and ideals as everybody in her social environment. In that case, she hardly has an identity$_2$. The identity$_2$ is the core of someone's personality. It may be true that many Kantian and utilitarian theories tend to overlook the highly individual core of a human person, his identity. My point is that this core may be a morally relevant factor, but it does not necessarily possess moral quality. Identity$_2$ need not be a moral identity (= identity$_3$). Someone's ground projects - the term is Williams' - may be worthless or even reprehensible. After all, someone like Hitler had his ground projects, too. People should have the space to give their ground projects priority to those of others. This space is founded on, but also limited by the social morality, for not every ground project is morally acceptable - that depends on its substance. In this context, Nagel speaks of reasonable partiality with regard to personal relationships and life projects (Nagel 1991). There may be moral reasons to demand from people to alienate themselves from their projects anyway. From their personal point of view this is undesirable, but from a suprapersonal point of view it may be inevitable (Flanagan 1991, 91 ff).

7.5.3 Communal Identity and Political Morality

The reservations I have about the primacy of the narrative explanation of decisions come up again when, in the context of a pluralistic society, we look at the relationship between the communal moral traditions of religions or other worldviews on the one hand, and the political morality of a pluralistic democracy on the other.

According to the narrativists, a Christian whose personal identity is determined by his being a Christian, will, when he has to take decisions, first of all ask himself the question: Who am I/do I want to be as a member of the Christian community? I give the example of Mr Van den Heuvel, an employer who is a member of a Dutch pietist and fundamentalist protestant denomination, the Gereformeerde Bond. He is opposed to abortion, homosexuals practising their inclination and married women having paid jobs. Therefore he refuses to employ practising homosexuals and mothers with children. In doing so, the man is not only convinced that he is right, he is also absolutely sincere. As an employer, he does not want to participate, not even indirectly, in practices he considers to be objectionable. The reasons he produces being extracted from the Bible, his fellow-believers accept them as an explanation as well as a justification for his conduct. But these reasons, derived from a communal identity, are not accepted as a justification by the society to which the religious splinter group belongs. They do not correspond with the liberal political morality which is characteristic of a democratic society like the Dutch one. This society may respect the integrity and authenticity of Mr Van den Heuvel, but in the end the only thing that counts is whether his conduct is acceptable in the light of the political morality. It is this political morality that determines whether the narrative granting Mr Van den Heuvel's decisions a pattern of integrity is acceptable. The plurality of particular moral traditions is characteristic of a modern society. In our pluralistic and democratic society, a political morality which determines the limits of comprehensive - religious or nonreligious - moralities is indispensable.

What, then, is the relation between political morality and particular comprehensive moralities? What is the epistemological status of political morality? Does it take priority because it is more rational and therefore more universal than comprehensive moralities? Is political morality a power which is external to comprehensive moralities? I will answer these questions using the ideas of Rawls and MacIntyre.

Rawls gives the following reconstruction of the development of our liberal political morality which originated from the religious conflicts in the 16th and 17th centuries. He distinguishes three phases. In the first phase, the followers of the contesting religions came to accept ideas like tolerance on prudential grounds, as a modus vivendi. A classic example of such a modus vivendi is the formula agreed upon in the Peace of Augsburg (1555): 'cuius regio, eius religio' (translated freely: the prince's religion is also the prevailing religion in his territory). In the second phase, this complex of ideas developed into a moral conception which found support on its own. In the third phase, the broad moralities - at least most of them - adapted themselves to this conception (Rawls 1987, 18, 19).

As far as the first phase is concerned, Rawls is undoubtedly right. But what he says about the second phase is far more difficult to imagine. For he suggests that the modus vivendi developed into a political morality, quite separately from any moral tradition. But these moral values like tolerance did not come out of the blue, did they? There is, after all, an obvious connection between the idea of religious tolerance and the idea - advocated by St Thomas as early as the Middle Ages and reinforced by the Reformation - that faith is only valuable when it is founded on a free, personal consent, and that therefore nobody can or should be forced to believe. But none of the contesting parties - neither Catholics, Lutherans nor Calvinists - advocated complete religious tolerance at that time (Manenschijn 1992). The first ones to do so were humanists like Erasmus, Castellio, Bodin and Coornhert.

In the United States, many white people got rid of their racist ideas about blacks only when the Civil Rights Act had forced them to come into contact with blacks. Their experiences with black people were incompatible with their racist morality, which, as a consequence, they had to abandon. By analogy, one might say that the experience gained during a time of peace between different religions, namely the experience that people with different beliefs can live together peacefully as well as be loyal to the same government, led to insights which were incompatible with the original intolerant or semi-tolerant morality. Such a discrepancy between morality and actual experience leads to what MacIntyre calls an epistemological crisis. That means that within a particular tradition a conflict arises which cannot be solved through the range of thought of that tradition in a way that is satisfactory by the standards of that tradition. This causes the adherents of this tradition either to reinterpret certain ideas, or to adopt new ideas from other traditions (MacIntyre 1977). The latter was done by thinkers such as Locke. In this approach, the overlapping consensus is the fruit of a learning process which, like all learning processes, may be induced by common experiences, but always takes place on an individual level - in this case, the level of the private tradition. The democratic political morality is a historical compromise, albeit a compromise that is upheld nowadays on moral grounds.

I called the liberal political morality a historical compromise and the fruit of a learning process. Thus, I acknowledge that this morality is historically contingent. Epistemologically, it has no privileged status with regard to the comprehensive, religious or nonreligious, traditions. In democratic societies the majority of these - the mainstream of the Christian tradition as well - have embraced the liberal political morality and integrated it into their own body of ideas. For those traditions, the liberal political morality is no longer an external power. (It is, however, for traditions that have not gone through this learning process). I do not mean to say, though, that modern Christians for example never experience any tension between the private viewpoint of their own tradition and the viewpoint of the political morality. They will always have to search for a balance, a compromise between the two.[3]

---

[3] I would do Hauerwas an injustice if I did not point out that he does pay attention to moral demands which go beyond the boundaries of the own moral community. He mentions, for instance, the condition of the universalisability of moral judgements, which, according to him, is a necessary though insufficient condition, because 'it expresses the fundamental commitment to regard all men as constituting a basic moral community' (1974, 85). He even goes as far as to say that each religious ethics which does not conform to this demand, is suspicious (87). Be that as it may, the spirit of

7.6 AGAIN: NARRATIVE ETHICS AND NARRATIVE THEOLOGY

The main task I set myself in this article, was to scrutinize the claims of the strong narrative ethics of Burrell & Hauerwas about the narrative structure of moral rationality. I have shown in what situations a narrative explanation is indispensable, and what its limits are. In a modern pluralistic society no moral tradition has a monopoly. Each moral tradition is just one among many others. An ethics which takes the problems of plurality seriously, cannot confine itself to the question 'Who am I/who do I want to be?' (or: 'Who are we/do we want to be?'). Another ethical question must be added: 'Who am I/do I want to be among/together with others who think and act differently?'. It goes without saying that the willingness to live together with people who think differently should become part of the own identity. And in this sense the theme of identity comes up time and again. All the same, a Christian who lives in a pluralistic society cannot be the same as one who lives in a homogeneously Christian world. The identity of the first is more layered, as he is both a member of the Christian community and a subject of a democratic society. This insight does not follow naturally from any narrative ethics, however. If Christians feel they should also reflect on the problems that arise from living in a pluralistic society, narrative ethics as it is conceived by the advocates of the strong version, does not suffice.

My conclusions certainly do not disqualify the entire project of narrative ethics. I regard the more modest, weak version of narrative ethics as important. At the beginning of this article, I raised the question whether narrative ethics provides a good framework to articulate and analyze the essential connectedness of Christian faith and morality. The answer is positive. In the first place, narrative ethics provides a useful framework because of its emphasis on the importance of stories. Stories are relevant for ethics in all sorts of ways: for the moulding of the moral personality during education, to refine the ability to perceive what is really morally relevant. Stories may shed light on what is unique and unrepeatable in concrete situations. Theories and principles enable an actor to spot the resemblance of a concrete case to previous and future cases, whereas stories can show the uniqueness of the

---

this passage is so contradictory to everything he says about the narrative structure of moral rationality and the contextuality of morality, that it seems impossible to reconcile both arguments.

case in question. The stories from the Christian tradition, too, may have this function. In that respect they are not unique. They are unique because of their content. In the second place, narrative ethics provides a useful framework because it conceives morality as contextual and connected with a particular community. Stories have a formative influence on moral character and moral identity, and direct the moral perception. As stories make up the core of Christian faith, a Christian community distinguishes itself from other communities through the stories by which it has been formed and which still function as a guideline. This idea makes room for the assertion that religious convictions and moral values are so strongly interconnected, that the moral convictions and conduct of Christians must be different from those of non-Christians. And even when the conduct of Christians appears to be identical to that of non-Christians, it remains different because it is explained differently (Robbins 1980, 165). (For this view, see Van den Beld's contribution in this volume).

This view has the advantage that it avoids a too narrow conception of 'Christian': either a set of principles of action - making Christians be different from non-Christians any time and any place - or the mere particularity of their concrete decisions. (In this respect, this view differs from the classical idea of a Christian proprium.) This narrow conception is avoided first of all because to the narrativists principles do not form the essence of morality. And secondly, because morality, including Christian morality, is always conceived as local and contextual. Indeed, the moral profile of Christian communities may vary among themselves. Therefore it is impossible to speak of the relation between Christian faith and moral, or of the proprium of Christian ethics.

Translated by Birgit Kooijman

REFERENCES

Beardsmore, R.W., *Moral Reasoning*, New York 1969.
Burrell, D.B. & S. Hauerwas, From System to Story: An Alternative Pattern for Rationality in Ethics. In: D. Callahan (ed.), *The Roots of Ethics*, New York/London 1976, 75-119. Also in: S. Hauerwas, *Truthfulness and Tragedy*, 15-40.
Cone, J.H., The Story Context of Black Theology, *Theology Today* 32(1975), 144-151
Crites, S., The Narrative Quality of Experience, *The Journal of the American Academy of Religion* 39(1971), 291-312.

Flanagan, O., *Varieties of Moral Personality*, Cambridge, Mass./London 1991.
Frankena, W.K., Is Morality Logically Dependent on Religion? In: G. Outka & J.P. Reeder Jr. (eds.), *Religion and Morality*, New York 1973, 295-318.
Gadamer, H.G., *Truth and Method*, New York 1975. Originally published as: *Wahrheit und Methode*, Tübingen 1960.
Gallie, W.T.B., *Philosophy and Historical Understanding*, London 1968.
Gergen, K.J. & M.M. Gergen, Narratives of the Self. In: T.R. Sarbin & K.E. Scheibe (eds.), *Studies in Social Identity*, New York 1983.
Hauerwas, S., *Vision and Virtue*, Notre Dame 1974.
Hauerwas, S., *Truthfulness and Tragedy*, Notre Dame/London 1977.
Kovesi, J., *Moral Notions*, London 1967.
Kuitert, H.M., Secularisatie en moraal. In: G. Dekker & K.U. Gäbler (eds.), *Secularisatie in theologisch perspectief*, Kampen 1988, 131-149.
MacIntyre, A., *After Virtue*, Notre Dame 1981.
MacIntyre, A., Epistemological Crises, Dramatic Narratives and the Philosophy of Science, *The Monist* 60(1977), 453-472.
Manenschijn, G., Tolerantie in een pluralistische maatschappij. In: A.W. Musschenga & F.C.L.M. Jacobs (eds.), *De liberale moraal en haar grenzen*, Kampen 1992, 127-155.
Mead, G.H., *Mind, Self & Society. From the Standpoint of a Social Behaviourist* [1934]. Edited and with an Introduction by C.W. Morris, Chicago/London 1974[19].
Metz, J.B., Kleine apologie van het verhaal, *Concilium* 9(1973), 58-73.
Mieth, D., *Epik und Ethik. Eine theologisch-ethische Interpretation der Josephromane Thomas Manns*, Tübingen 1976.
Mink, L.O., *Historical Understanding*, ed. by B. Fay, E.O. Golob & R.T. Vann, Ithaca/London 1987.
Murdoch, I., Vision and Choice in Morality. In: I.T. Ramsey (ed.), *Christian Ethics and Contemporary Philosophy*, New York 1966, 195-218.
Nagel, T., *The View from Nowhere*, Oxford etc. 1986.
Nagel, T., *Equality and Partiality*, Oxford 1991.
Nielsen, K., *Ethics without God*, New York 1990[2].
Noorda, S.J., Narratieve theologie. In: F. Ankersmit (ed.), *Op verhaal komen. Over narrativiteit in de mens- en cultuurwetenschappen*, Kampen 1990, 107-130.
Outka, G., *Character, Vision, and Narrative, Religious Studies Review* 6(1980), 110-119.
Nussbaum, M., *Love's Knowledge. Essays on Philosophy and Literature*, Oxford/New York 1990.
Pannenberg, W., *Was ist der Mensch? Die Anthropologie der Gegenwart im Lichte der Theologie*, Göttingen 1972[4].
Pannenberg, W., *Anthropologie in theologischer Perspektive*, Göttingen 1983.
Phillips, D.Z. & H.O. Mounce, *Moral Practices*, London 1969.
Rawls, J., The Idea of an Overlapping Consensus, *Oxford Journal of Legal Studies* 7(1987), 1-26.
Ricoeur, P., The Model of the Text: Meaningful Action Considered as a Text. In: P.

Rabinow & W.M. Sullivan (eds.), *Interpretive Social Science*, Berkeley 1979, 73-103.

Ritschl, D., 'Story' als Rohmaterial der Theologie. In: D. Ritschl & H.O. Jones, *'Story' als Rohmaterial der Theologie*, München 1975.

Robbins, J. Wesley, Narrative, Morality and Religion, *Journal of Religious Ethics* 8(1980), 161-176.

Sandel, M., *Liberalism and the Limits of Justice*, Cambridge 1982.

Schillebeeckx, E., Crisis van de geloofstaal als hermeneutisch probleem, *Concilium* 9(1973), 33-47.

Schillebeeckx, E., *Gerechtigheid en liefde*, Bloemendaal 1977.

Stroup, G.W., *The Promise of Narrative Theology*, Atlanta 1981.

Taylor, C., What is Human Agency? In: *Human Agency and Language, Philosophical Papers* Vol. I, Cambridge etc. 1985, 15-45.

Weinrich, H., Narratieve Theologie, *Concilium* 9(1973), 48-58.

White, H., The Question of Narrative in Contemporary Historical Theory, *History and Theory* 23(1984), 1-33.

Williams, B.A.O., Persons, Character and Morality. In: A.O. Rorty (ed.), *The Identities of Persons*, Berkeley 1974, 197-217.

Comments

Paul J.M. van Tongeren

In his article, Musschenga poses the question whether a narrative ethics offers an adequate framework for articulating and thinking through the - for Christians - essential connectedness of Christian faith and morality. According to him, the connection between the two has become problematic; this is partly due to rationalistic analytical ethics, which considered the gap between 'to be' and 'ought to' as unbridgeable and therefore aimed at clearing morality from every particularity. Musschenga's answer to the above-mentioned question is positive, although he adds that a narrative ethics cannot stand on its own: it is fundamentally impossible to justify normative judgements without a rational argumentation based on principles; this fundamental impossibility is factually confirmed by the demand of pluralism to respect social or political moralities which came into being outside one's own (particular) narrative context.

With this dual answer, Musschenga endorses what he calls the 'weak' version of narrative ethics and opposes the 'strong' version. The most crucial part of his argumentation is in section 7.5, where he demonstrates that a narrative explanation of a decision can be most clarifying without, however, being adequate as a justification. Before coming to this, he presents in more general terms an interesting and learned survey of the narrativist paradigm in the social sciences (especially history and social psychology), in theology and in ethics.

My comments will be directed at Musschenga's representation of narrative ethics. I will try to show that he overlooked an essential element of it, i.e. the hermeneutical element. Although Musschenga mentions that narrative ethics means to be a hermeneutics of moral experience (p. 187) and speaks of explanation of someone's decisions within the limited framework of his personal life story' (p. 188), he does not explain clearly what he means by 'hermeneutics' or 'explanation'.

According to Musschenga, the stories that narrative ethics is supposed to be about, function to express and convey moral experience (p. 187); they are the answers to the question who am I and who do I want to be, and as such they create the conditions and the context for the moral questions (p. 187). They even seem to make this question into the crucial ethical question (p. 188). A narrative explanation, Musschenga states, shows us how the actor himself perceives his decision and what his purpose was (p. 188). He seems to understand the narrative explanation as a personal explanation as well as a declaration; the actor declares his opinion, and explains it by placing it within the framework of his own life story. Therefore, narrative ethics as represented by Musschenga is very much like 'story telling', which is different from philosophy, as Aristotle already observed.

In view of this interpretation of narrative explanation, Musschenga's criticism that identity-referring reasons are not sufficient as a moral justification, is not surprising. It is true that someone can have such reasons for taking a certain decision, but that doesn't mean they are valid (e.g. p. 193). In fact, it is remarkable that Musschenga, in the light of his conception of narrative explanation, is that lenient in his criticism of narrative ethics. If there was really nothing more to narrative explanation than he makes it appear in his article, in my view narrative ethics would deserve a much more radical criticism. I think, however, that Musschenga's presentation is incorrect.

The term *hermeneutics* of moral experience implies that appealing to experience, or referring to someone's personal life story - as Musschenga suggests - is absolutely out of the question. Hermeneutics is the technique of explaining and interpreting, and the theory that tries to formulate what it means that human life is essentially determined by interpretation[4]. The fact that moral experience needs to be explained, means in any case that something in that experience presents itself as receptive to and requiring explanation. That is to say, something in that experience urges itself upon me by its

---

4 I dealt with this concept of a hermeneutical ethics more extensively in my: Moral Philosophy as a Hermeneutics of Moral Experience (1994, 199-214).

pretence of meaningfulness, makes itself known to me as having something to say to me. Besides, it is something that surpasses my comprehension and therefore needs to be mastered and explained. Thus it is clear that it cannot be something that coincides with my own opinions. If my experience coincided with my opinions or convictions, I would know beforehand what it offered me, it would not hold any promise of meaningfulness, and no explanation would be necessary. If we say that experience requires explanation, this signifies that the reception of meaning takes place in the experience.

To me, this is a crucial point because it indicates a moment of transcendence within experience. I draw attention to this moment not only to make a link to my own contribution in this collection, but also because this is the point where Musschenga's criticism of (the strong version of) narrative ethics can be refuted. Experience is not the collected events that form someone's life story, but the (acquired) receptivity to meaning that presents itself. My view of the value of friendship (The example is Musschenga's, p. 191) is of no importance at all, unless it is an indication - however condensed and deformed - of my ability to understand the meaning of friendship. If person A attributes greater value to friendship than person B, this might be explained from their respective life stories, but is of no relevance at all to ethics. What is relevant, however, is to find out the real meaning of friendship; we can try to find this out by explaining our experience of it, i.e. by activating our ability to perceive something of its meaning. Great stories about friendship, stories that provide superior presentations of its meaning, can be of help. This use of literature in ethics accounts for the first meaning of the term 'narrative ethics'. Our receptivity to meaning will also be reinforced every time we try to place a meaning in a larger framework (after all, to understand something is always: to classify it in a larger whole); and because these meanings will always be of a 'practical' nature, the larger framework cannot be but the praxis of life. This accounts for the second meaning of the term 'narrative ethics'.

Musschenga opposes the claim of narrative ethics that people's personal life stories have argumentative power, which is supposed to be even greater than that of 'social moral rules', 'the test of universalisation' (p. 193), or 'compelling moral reasons' (p. 194), whether or not 'from a suprapersonal point of view' (p. 198). I have already pointed out that 'personal life stories' are no arguments or 'data'. They are useful in the search for explanation and understanding of moral meanings that present themselves. In hermeneutical ethics, the aim is to find out what is morally meaningful. [In the life story of Paul Gauguin - the example he adopted from Williams - Musschenga does not look for the things that might carry moral meaning (e.g. the meaning of an artistic vocation, the meaning of a moral dilemma, or - following Williams - the meaning of 'moral luck'), but instead, he is only too ready to judge or even condemn: Gauguin is not an 'ideal human from the point of view of his community's morality' (p. 196), and apparently 'not formed by what his community regards as the right narratives' (p. 197).]

Hermeneutical ethics wants to investigate and explain the stories and events that appeal to us and therefore seem to have something to say to us, in order to come to understand what it is they have to say to us. This means that it is critical of all ethics that parrot the dominant morality and grant it universal validity.

But of course one could raise the question how a hermeneutical ethics can be self-critical as far as the interpretations are concerned of the stories and the meanings they are supposed to carry. How can its explanations ever be verified? How can I know if I understand a moral meaning adequately? How did Gauguin know that (or: whether) it was right to leave his wife and children? How do I know if it is just to attribute such a great value to friendship that it takes priority over the love for my parents? The answer is simple, though difficult to 'realise': I will never know.

As we are dealing here with the understanding of meanings, and as meanings are never given as objective data but only exist within our and other people's understanding of them, we will never know whether our understanding is adequate; and the less we can share our interpretation with others, the less we can be sure of it. This means that everyone who tries to understand, will tend to explain, to 'tell' others what he understands, while other interpretations than his own should be a challenge for him. Thus, our conception of the value of faithfulness to one's wife and children is being challenged by the story of Gauguin. So we enter into a dialogue with the story, like we seek dialogue with others about our interpretations of the story. Although we need a certain consensus to be able to live together, this consensus will necessarily be limited. Just like people will always tell stories, they will always be searching for explanations of the things that present themselves as meaningful.

Translated by Birgit Kooijman

REFERENCE

Tongeren, P.J.M. van, Moral Philosophy as a Hermeneutics of Moral Experience, *International Philosophical Quarterly* 34(1994), 199-214.

Contributors

Antonie van den Beld (1941) studied theology and philosophy in Utrecht, Prague and Harvard. PhD. in theology 1973. He is currently associate professor of moral philosophy at Utrecht University. Among his publications in the English language are: *Humanity. The Political and Social Philosophy of Thómas G. Masaryk* (1975; doct. diss.), and 'The Problem of Akrasia', 'Killing and the Principle of Double Effect', 'On the Inability to Sin in Eternal Life', 'Naturalism and the Possibility of an Adequate Morality'.

Arnold Burms (1946) studied classical philology and philosophy in Louvain, and philosophy in Oxford. PhD. in philosophy in 1978. He is professor of epistemology and philosophy of art at the Catholic University of Louvain. His publications include *Vrijheid, verantwoordelijkheid, menselijke waardigheid en determinisme* (doct. diss 1978) and (with H. de Dijn) *Rationaliteit en haar grenzen* (1981).

Gerrit Manenschijn (1931) studied theology at the Vrije Universiteit in Amsterdam. PhD in Theology (1979). He was a minister in the Dutch Reformed Churches. He is presently professor of ethics at the Theologische Universiteit of the Dutch Reformed Churches in Kampen (The Netherlands). Publications include: *Moraal en eigenbelang in het werk van Thomas Hobbes en Adam Smith* (1979; doct. diss.), *Eigenbelang en christelijke ethiek* (1982), *Geplunderde aarde, getergde hemel: Ontwerp voor een christelijke milieuethiek* (1988); *Mogelijkheid en noodzakelijkheid van een christelijke ethiek* (1989).

Karl-Wilhelm Merks (1939) studied theology in Bonn. PhD. in 1977. He is professor of moral theology at the Theological Faculty in Tilburg. His publications include: *Theologische Grundlegung der sittlichen Autonomie* (doct. diss.), and articles in Dutch and German among which: Freiheit als Grundlage der Moral (1991), Über der Fortschritt in der Moral (1992), Autonomie (1992), Die Rückfrage nach den Grundlagen der Ethik und die Entwicklung der konkreten Ethik aus der Sicht der katholische Moraltheologie und Freiheit statt Beliebigkeit (1992).

Albert W. Musschenga (1950) studied theology at the Vrije Universiteit. PhD. in theology (1979). He works at the Vrije Universiteit as director of the Interdisciplinary Centre for the Study of Science, Society, and Religion ('Bezinningscentrum') and as professor of social ethics. He published on the foundations of morality: *Noodzakelijkheid en mogelijkheid van moraal* (1979; doct. diss.) and on the concept of quality of life: *Kwaliteit van leven. Criterium voor medisch handelen?* (1987). He is the editor of, and a contributor to numerous books on (practical-)ethical questions, among which (with B. Voorzanger and A. Soeteman) *Morality, Worldview, and Law* (1992).

Hans (J.S.) Reinders (1950) studied theology at the Vrije Universiteit in Amsterdam. PhD. in theology (1988). He is presently professor of ethics at the Vrije Universiteit. He published *Violence, Victims and Rights* (1988; doct. diss.), *De bescherming van het ongeboren leven* (1993), and several papers on topics in medical ethics.

Paul J.M. van Tongeren (1950) studied theology in Utrecht and philosophy in Louvain PhD. in philosophy at the Catholic University of Louvain (1984). He is professor of moral philosophy at the Katholieke Universiteit Nijmegen. His publications include: *Die Moral von Nietzsches Moralkritik* (1989); various papers on Nietzsche, Aristotle, the Stoics, on the concept of a hermeneutical moral philosophy, and on several issues in the present debate on ethics.